JOURNAL FOR THE STUDY OF THE OLD TESTAMENT
SUPPLEMENT SERIES
124

Editors
David J.A. Clines
Philip R. Davies

JSOT Press
Sheffield

Law and Ideology in Monarchic Israel

Edited by
Baruch Halpern
and
Deborah W. Hobson

Journal for the Study of the Old Testament
Supplement Series 124

Published by JSOT Press
JSOT Press is an imprint of
Sheffield Academic Press Ltd
The University of Sheffield
343 Fulwood Road
Sheffield S10 3BP
England

Typeset by Sheffield Academic Press
and
Printed on acid-free paper in Great Britain
by Billing & Sons Ltd
Worcester

British Library Cataloguing in Publication Data

Halpern, Baruch
Law and ideology in monarchic Israel.—
(Journal for the study of the Old Testament.
Supplement series. ISSN 0309-0787; 124)
I. Title II. Hobson, Deborah W. III. Series
933

ISBN 1-85075-323-7

CONTENTS

FOREWORD

The three essays in this volume were delivered and submitted in writing in 1986–87 as part of the first annual York University Seminar for Advanced Research. They thus constitute part of the Gerstein Lectures at York University for 1987. The Seminar in which they were delivered, 'Law in its Social Setting in the Ancient Mediterranean World', represented an attempt to promote dialogue among social historians and historically-minded philologians dealing with all aspects of antiquity in the Mediterranean basin.

The other papers presented in the Seminar, or in a small conference held at the end of the Seminar year, appear in a volume entitled *Law, Politics and Society in the Ancient Mediterranean World*, where a fuller description of the Seminar format is provided. That volume reports on the social context of the law in such areas as Old Babylonian Mesopotamia, Biblical Israel, classical Athens, Rome and Roman Greece, Italy and Egypt, Israel under Byzantine rule, and the Middle Ages. One lesson absorbed by the participants in this collocation was the remarkable similarity in social organization and conflict resolution at levels below that of the state in most ancient Mediterranean cultures. All the more, then, is comparison among these cultures valuable for modelling activity and change in any one of them.

The present studies have been divided from the rest of the collection for practical reasons (the economics of publishing) and for thematic ones. All three essays deal with traumatic changes in Israelite culture in the eighth–seventh centuries BCE. All concern the transition from the traditional culture of Israel in Iron IIA (10th–9th centuries) to a new, more widely literate culture in the eighth–seventh centuries. All also examine the impact of this transition on Israelite law and legal theory.

B. Halpern's survey articulates a vision of the transformation of Judah's culture from a traditional to an elite one. It argues that the Near East underwent a Renaissance during the boom of the eighth century BCE. Judahite culture was bombarded with foreign input and internal innovations. This, growing literacy, and the cataclysms of 722 and 701 BCE, paved the way for the socialization of prophetic *Sprachkritik*, and the identification of folk culture as alien to (elite) Israelite tradition and to elite theology. This Reformation, the model for the later Protestant Reformation (and for Pauline theology), led among other things to the definition of a centralized state cult as the only acceptable cult, and to increased individuation and internalization of norms, entailing the breakdown of countryside patrilineages. Revolutionary doctrines of individual moral liability articulated at the end of the period thus reflect both the immediate relationship of each individual to the state and the state god, and the universalization of (written) norms across all segments of society. The birth of the individual in the Western tradition can be traced these developments.

J.B. Peckham's study concerns itself more with the dialogue inside the elite culture proper concerning the status and nature of the covenant with Yhwh, articulated first in the Yahwist (J) source of the Pentateuch. Primarily, Peckham focuses upon the texts of Isaiah and of the Deuteronomistic History (Deuteronomy through Second Kings). Yet each of these, it develops, itself consists of a dialogue between an original canonical text and subsequent interpreters and updaters. The earliest of the texts under study, Isaiah, interpreted contemporary events—Hezekiah's conflict with Assyria—in reaction against J's doctrine of a covenant between Israel and Yhwh, making frequent and explicit reference to particular J texts. Isaiah articulated the view that a covenant is not to be relied upon to the detriment of observation of natural law. To this Isaianic reflection on earlier historiography (mixed with law), the first Deuteronomist responded that Jerusalem's survival in 701 BCE reflected Hezekiah's conformity to covenantal demands, while violation of those demands (i.e. centralization of worship) precipitated Israel's fall to Assyria in 722. The dialogue continued in the exilic or early postexilic period (c. 538 BCE), when Second Isaiah and the second Deuteronomist, as well as the Chronicler, re-evaluated the earlier texts in light of the exile and restoration. Through this dialogue, in a literate, elite tradition, the rationalization of the law in Judahite culture took shape.

P.E. Dion furnishes an in-depth analysis of the central chapter for the enforcement of Deuteronomic norms, Deuteronomy 13, the only biblical law providing against proselytization for gods other than Yhwh. Systematic philological analysis first establishes the text, then indicates its semantic and literary bearings within the Deuteronomic code. This research, combined with close literary–historical analysis and attention to usage, establishes that the chapter is a literary unity, composed by a Deuteronomistic author, that is, sometime after the original compilation of the laws of Deuteronomy itself. Its content, a ban on sedition or treason, and its particular vocabulary both echo Assyrian instruments of statecraft, familiar to Judah in the form of written treaties especially in the seventh century BCE. Both philological and historical evidence thus triangulate on the reign of the Reform king, Josiah (639–609) as origin of the law, which ingeniously applied the requirement of fealty in loyalty oaths and suzerainty treaties—most especially, Esarhaddon's—to the realm of theology. Far from being a utopian notion, thus, as some have held, Deuteronomy 13 reflects the fanaticism of a strong king bent on resculpting both the standing and the character of his nation. Ironically, though couched in terms of loyalty to Yhwh, and thus to Israelite culture, it is precisely a political implement drawn from foreign literary sources, the Judahite equivalent of the Assyrian loyalty oath.

These three studies together throw into relief changes in legal, political and religious culture in Judah in the last 150 years of its independence. Their combined implications for the origins of Western law and civilization, and for the models from which Reformation and Enlightenment political theory were drawn, are substantial. To the history of religion they are perhaps even more material, in its relation to elite and vulgar cultural and political upheaval. How deeply the growing literacy rate of eighth- and seventh-century Judah made it fertile ground for systematic theological ferment is especially evident.

Funding for the Seminar in Advanced Research was provided by the Gerstein Lectures at York University, by the Social Sciences and Humanities Research Council of Canada President's Fund and Conference Programme, and by the York University Faculty of Arts and Senate Committee on Research. Mr David Armstrong served as the executive secretary of the sessions. The Seminar's organizers would like to express their gratification that a joint effort by scholars in a variety of fields met with support from such a diverse range of programmes.

Baruch Halpern and Deborah Whitney Hobson
Toronto, 26 November 1990

JERUSALEM AND THE LINEAGES IN THE SEVENTH CENTURY BCE: KINSHIP AND THE RISE OF INDIVIDUAL MORAL LIABILITY*

Baruch Halpern

I. *Collective or Individual Reward?*

The god of Israel describes himself in one late text as 'visiting the sins of the fathers on the children unto the third and fourth generation of them that hate me' (Exod. 20.5; Deut. 5.9; cf. 7.10). Mediaeval exegetes, in light of Ezekiel and Jeremiah (below), reasoned that Yhwh did so only if the children, too, were evil (cf. Andersen and Freedman 1980: 177-82). However, another logic underlies the text: namely, traitors, those who 'hate' (i.e. reject) Yhwh, were to be uprooted, offspring and all—the fourth generation was the last generation a parent was likely to see (Malamat 1982; Weinfeld 1972: 25). Indeed, when the oracle discloses that Achan has peculated from Yhwh's 'ban', Joshua takes the booty 'and his sons and daughters and ox and ass and sheep and tent'—who did not absquatulate—and burns and stones them by turns (Josh. 7.10-26): the remedy is prescribed in

* This study was stimulated by work supported by the Alexander von Humboldt-Stiftung, in 1984–85, under the sponsorship of Klaus Baltzer and Manfred Weippert. A York University Faculty of Arts research leave, and a National Endowment for the Humanities Summer Stipend brought this draft to completion.

As always, my chief partner in applying historical imagination to the data was Professor Sidney Halpern. I have also shamelessly reaped a rich harvest of insights from A. Baron, Y. Beit-Arieh, K. Baltzer, J. Bradley, M. Broshi, Y. Dagan, Y. Finkelstein, D.N. Freedman, R.E. Friedman, R.S. Hendel, Z. Herzog, D. Hobson, J.S. Holladay, A. Kempinski, A. Mazar, N. Na'aman, S.M. Olyan, W.H. Propp, the late Y. Shiloh, D. Small, L. Stager, and P.R. Swarney. I owe special thanks to S. Gitin, P. Wapnish and B. Hesse, who shared important unpublished data and ideas, and to my students, D. Armstrong, D. Vanderhooft, and G. Pratt, the last of whom contributed the phrase, 'Sennacherib's reform'. A less technical version of this essay will appear in a volume edited by J.A. Hackett.

Deut. 7.25-26. Yhwh, it seems, conducts vendettas.

The principle of collective responsibility, ancestral and contemporary, underlies much of biblical prophecy and historiography. An ancestor shines, and the descendants prosper; a king sins, and the nation suffers. Lawcodes, too, treat Israel collectively, and Yhwh's beneficence toward one's children turns on obedience in the present (as Deut. 4.40; 5.26; 7.13; 10.15; 12.28). Conversely, the threat of national exile, frequent both in Deuteronomy and in the Priestly source in the Pentateuch, presupposes the suffering of innocents.

This view has diverse theological underpinnings. Pollution—moral or cultic—stains the fabric of its environment. Human justice is specific, like a sort of spot-remover; divine wrath is general, fire among the flax. The theology inspires enforcement of the law. It expresses the premise that failure to apply the law is tantamount to abetment.

As an engine of explanation, a perspective on the fate of nations, such a system works efficiently only where individual (male) identity is attenuated. The individual derives his identity from an expanded kinship network—the village or neighbourhood, the town, the nation—which is a horizontal (synchronic) corporation. The line of descent—clan, tribe and nation—transposes the kinship network into a historical dimension: the vertical counterpart of the horizontal corporation, where the upper generations are (or are equivalents of) village, town, tribe, nation. The collective burial of the family and the doctrine of ancestral reward and punishment (Yhwh visits the sins of fathers on children, who are by implication undeserving of punishment) illustrate the point. The Israelite took his identity from a horizontal, or contemporary, and from a vertical, or ancestral, corporation.

In law, this principle was never universal—all Israelite lawcodes stipulate individual punishments for infractions, including capital offences (as Exod. 21.12-14). Collective punishment attached, rather, to particular crimes—those, like that of apostasy in Exod. 20.5 (and Deut. 5.9; cf. Deut. 8.19; 11.6) or Amorite-like cult practice (Deut. 7.25-26; 9.4-5; Lev. 18.24-30; 20.4-5), that could be construed as treasonous, as 'hatred' of Yhwh or, presumably, the state (Yaron 1991; cf. Mettinger 1971: 82). Thus, the Covenant Code invokes the 'ban' for those who 'sacrifice to gods...other than Yhwh alone' (Exod. 22.19), but not for oppressors of widows, aliens and orphans (22.20-23). Deuteronomic law endorses collective punishment (the 'ban') against settlements abetting apostasy (13.13-19; cf. 2 Kgs 10.11).[1]

The forfeit of descendants in such cases reflects the implementation of attainder, routinely applied to civil traitors (1 Sam. 22.19; 2 Kgs 9.26; 10.11) and treaty violators (Judg. 5.23; 21.8-10; 2 Sam. 21.6-9; 2 Kgs 25.7; see Greenberg 1960: 24, and, on vicarious punishment in law, Yaron 1980: 35). This is why King Amaziah's failure to apply attainder against his father's assassins attracts special notice in the Deuteronomistic History (2 Kgs 14.5-6; a Hittite parallel in Kümmel 1981: 464-66; E in Exod. 21.22-23, cited by Yaron 1980: 35 against CH 209-10). It is also why the daughters of Zelophehad, petitioning for the perpetuation of their father's house, are at pains to stipulate, 'he was not among the congregation who congregated against Yhwh in the congregation of Qorah, but died for his [own] sin' (Num. 27.3; see Dearman 1988: 113). Israelite law consistently affirmed the idea of collective punishment in cases of treason.

Nevertheless, around 600, both Jeremiah and Ezekiel repudiated even the attainder of apostates: both assailed the proverb, 'The fathers have eaten sour grapes and the teeth of the children "are set on edge"' (Jer. 31.29; Ezek. 18.1-4). This text does not restrict itself to legal liability for treason, but asserts that the actions and decisions of ancestors result in the economic, political or military misfortunes of the day. The prophets, at least, stick to capital offenses: persons must die for their own sins; the critique misappropriates the implications of the proverb.

The prophets differ. Jeremiah postpones the application of the new principle. First comes Judah's corporate restoration, and only thereafter the era of personal liability (31.27-30): the new regime vouchsafes immortality to Judah as a nation restored, no longer liable to corporate chastisement (31.34-40). Ezekiel claims that the principle of personal liability is already in force (18.2-4, 29-32), and perhaps that it always has been. Further, Jeremiah links the principle to a new covenant (31.31-34), but does not explore it in depth. Ezekiel spells out all the implications and even provides for rehabilitation and backsliding (18.4-28).

The differences are important. By retaining the doctrine of collec-

1. On Lev. 20.4-5, see Greenberg 1960: 28. This text should be read against the background of the related Lev. 18.24-30.

tive retribution in the present, Jeremiah is able to cling to the scapegoating of Jeroboam and Manasseh (as 15.4) for national cataclysm. It is in the future that individual liability precludes a destruction of the re-established collective, unless all its members are evil. And the 'new covenant' repairs the 'evil inclination' of Israel's heart: after the Exile, therefore, Yhwh's promise to Israel of immunity from corporate liquidation improves on the one that he accorded to humanity as a whole after the Flood in J. Jeremiah's 'new covenant' will have the longevity of Noah's, and the guarantee comes in the form of Noah's guarantee: Jer. 31.35-36. uses the terms 'day', 'night', 'seed' and 'they will desist' from Gen. 8.22, adding allusions to creation, and to the turbulence of the sea.

Ezekiel views the old doctrines contemptuously, dismissing the vertical corporate interpretation of guilt as a smokescreen of special pleading against Yhwh's judgments (18.2, 4, 19, 29, 31-32). Each exile, each slave, each cadaver testifies to an individual's sin. This theology resembles P's doctrine of retribution for murder—also after the Flood (Gen. 9.4-6); but P is not systematic. Unlike J, P seems to put limits upon, if not to eliminate, vertical (Num. 26.10 versus Num. 16.31-33; Deut. 11.6) and horizontal corporate identity (as Lev. 4.3, 13); probably, Ezekiel dated individual liability to creation.

The disagreement is predictable. Ezekiel's nationalist party, exiled with Jehoiachin in 597, entertained hopes of eventual restoration. Under their stewardship, the nation had remained intact, the temple standing. Individual punishment reduced the party's culpability, by implying that exile was a function of individuals' sins. Jeremiah's faction—a collaborationist wing of the Josianic coalition led by courtiers descended from Shaphan—was installed in power in 597, and presided over the destruction of Jerusalem. On Ezekiel's reading the Shaphanite crowd must have perverted all of Judah; he says, in fact, that they reversed Josiah's reform (as 8.7-16; probably 11.1-3). Jeremiah's reading permitted an evasion of responsibility—the scapegoating of Manasseh. Only later would the principle of individual responsibility come into play.

But Jeremiah and Ezekiel, the Hillel and Shammai of the sixth century, disagree about everything, starting with the identity of the one true prophet. What is remarkable, therefore, is their concurrence. Other documents of the seventh–sixth century restrict human punishment to individual perpetrators, but allow that divine retribution may exceed this limit (P in Lev. 20.1-5, and in the Decalogue; for Deuteronomy, see above). Yet both Jeremiah and Ezekiel, at the start of the sixth century, accept a doctrine limiting even divine retribution to the individual. The shift has ramifications other than the political ones outlined above. Thus, the concept of a remnant assumes a new nuance: the remnant are by definition righteous, or at least rehabilitated.[1] Moreover, the old system was quite ductile, as its use in Kings illustrates. The new system is rigid. In prescribing a one-to-one mapping of sin and suffering, it alone provokes the agony of Job.

Job (14; 21) dismisses the concept of ancestral reward—the idea of the importance of the vertical corporation after death. Nor do the comforters suggest that Job ransack the family albums or the neighborhood for the causes of his plight (they even hypothesize that Job's children died for their own sins—8.4). Job's dilemma draws its locomotion from the dissonance, then, between rigid reality and the even more rigid theory of individual retribution; he, and he personally, must have sinned. Job, and Ecclesiastes, puncture the theory of individual retribution; against the old, supple idea of corporate responsibility, their lances would splinter harmlessly. The inevitable breakdown of this new theory of divine management—one that Diderot lampooned in *Jacques the Fatalist*—surely helped lever the emphasis of Jewish and later theology from mundane reward to otherworldly.

What facilitated the socialization of the new doctrine? Scholars almost unanimously read it as a denial that Yhwh is so unjust as to visit exile upon the children for their ancestors' sins (see Greenberg 1983: 338-41). The repudiation of corporate guilt by Ezekiel's god

1. Ezek. 14.21-23 speaks of exiles, punished for the sins they exemplify (whose survival in the theology of ch. 18 may imply repentance). 36.19-33 speak of Yhwh's shrieving exiles for restoration for his own sake (cf. Deut. 9.4-5): but these have been 'judged' (i.e. sentenced to exile) already, and are eligible now for rehabilitation. I thank Professor Moshe Greenberg for calling these passages to my attention. It may be added, the restriction of Yhwh's leeway for punishment in Jeremiah and Ezekiel, but not in Deut. or P (esp. Lev. 20.5), indicates that the prophets here innovate over against the law. It is unlikely that the just god of these prophets will have been allowed much to regress to his older habits of familial and corporate, rather than individual, persecution. This is not to say that P must be earlier than Ezekiel (although it seems likely). But P cannot much postdate Ezekiel, on any scheme except an harmonistic reading of Lev. 20.5 (and the Decalogue) to imply that anyone punished is by definition a sinner.

inspires this view. Job's response on the loss of innocents resonates in George Eliot's pronouncement, 'There is no punishment that does not exceed its bounds in pulsations of unmerited pain'. Individual punishment reduced divine retribution to a human scale (as Deut. 24.16). It did away—so the consensus—with the injustice of genetic dental problems (Jer. 31.30). It reflected a desire to 'lie for god' (Job 13.7-8), or to do the duty Tom Paine pronounced 'incumbent on every true Deist, that he vindicate the moral justice of God against the calumnies of the Bible' (1945: 523).

The theological analysis, to some extent, misprises the political implications. Morever, Jeremiah, who embraces the new doctrine in principle, never disparages the justice of corporate retribution. Jeremiah saw the justice in a son suffering for his father's deeds: they were part of the same corporation, literally as well as figuratively, their fates knitted tightly in blood—and economic interests. Does Jeremiah mean to imply, then, that Yhwh is less than just, but will repair his ways in future? Or will Yhwh loose the fate of the individual from the moorings of kinship for entirely different reasons?

In fact, both Jeremiah and Ezekiel espouse what amounts to a statist ideology, one with a long history in Israel (Greenberg 1960: 20-27). Israel was a traditional society, based in local kinship ties, on which a national administration was superimposed. This superstructure occasionally entered into conflict with the clans in the appropriation of resources (Mettinger 1971; Tadmor 1982; Halpern 1981). The state therefore had an interest in limiting the clans' political latitude (Mettinger 1971: 121-22; Halpern 1974). In addition, as observers of the American inner city would expect, kinship units (or gangs with territories) had to be restrained from independently administering extramural discipline: authority is central only so far as the state exercises a monopoly on the legitimate use of force, on coercion. States particularly attempt to contain the vendetta, an expression of kinship solidarity in a state environment, or, from the statist viewpoint, the local usurpation of central authority (see Flannery 1972).

Israel's clan structure incorporated the vendetta—the institution of the 'blood avenger'. But legal limitations were stark. The political context in which Amaziah spared his father's assassins' families (2 Kgs 14.6) is opaque. However, containing the vendetta is said to have been central to David. Confronted with a fratricide, David promises to reflect or investigate (2 Sam. 14.4-9); relieved of possible guilt, he offers temporary immunity (14.10); but only when put in mind of possible vigilantism does he issue an unqualified pardon (14.11-12).

The state, then, shields the weak from the strong, a principle already articulated in the Code of Hammurabi. Similarly, Leviticus (19.16-17), Deuteronomy (19.11-13) and the Covenant Code (Exod. 21.12-14) allow for blood vengeance in cases of premeditated murder (not quite endorsing ongoing vendetta), but allow for sanctuary in cases of accidental or other manslaughter (Deut. 19.1-10). Deuteronomy 24.16 explicitly proscribes the vendetta: 'the fathers will not be killed for the sons, nor the sons for the fathers; each man will die for his own sin'. Legal liability is limited; human justice is specific.

If legal liability is not moral liability, the two go hand in hand. A god who 'visits sins on the children' is logically the god of a society where legal liability is corporate. That legal theory should individualize punishment is predictable, particularly in a state environment. The state therefore promoted ideologies restricting the god, so far as possible, to individual retribution. So, it is no surprise that such theologies should crop up. Here, the line was drawn at treason, when the crown found itself in vendetta. Even so, Amaziah's temperance was no doubt in some measure an attempt to furnish a role model to the lineages, the operating kinship groups in Israelite society.

But what implications had the change for the royal regulation of the countryside lineages? More important, how was the statist ideology valorized so as to permit the repudiation of the obvious causal relationship between the welfare of the ancestors and the circumstances of their descendants? Jeremiah and Ezekiel propose a cosmology in which individual merit corresponds to individual welfare: to each according to his ability. How did Judahite culture travel from the sense that the ancestors' luck determined the circumstances of the descendants to the conviction that Yhwh was responsible, no longer for the fate of the collective, but for the just requital of every individual?

The answers to these questions begin far afield.

II. *Assyria in Judah*

A. *From Field Force to Hedgehog Defence*

In the eighth century BC, the power of Assyrian arms ranged far to the west, taking up permanent station in the region of the Mediterranean littoral. Typically, Assyria faced coalitions of western petty states; and occasionally, those resisting partnership in these combinations petitioned for Assyrian aid to drive off their erstwhile coalition partners (as *KAI* 24.6-8; 215.10-15; 2 Kgs 16.5-9; cf. *KAI* 202A; 1 Kgs 15.17-22).

During the century, western defence strategy underwent a shift. In the ninth century, western coalitions met Assyria in the field. By the mid-eighth century, they were electing the dilatory technique of fortress warfare. This was the only choice for those who sought Assyrian aid against the coalitions—to hold out until relief arrived. For example, Ahaz' response to a Syro-Ephraimite invasion was to hole up in the capital (2 Kgs 16.5-9; Rost 1893: 72.11; Isa. 7; 8.5-8; 10.5-9; 17; Hos. 7.11) waiting for Tiglath-Pileser. But the same pattern soon began to characterize the anti-Assyrian forces. Whether or not the Azriau of Tiglath-Pileser III's annals was Azariah of Judah (Rost 1893: 20.123; 22.131; Tadmor 1961; Na'aman 1974), western strategy from 720 forward was to huddle behind city walls—even the allies at Hamath seem to have taken shelter inside the fortifications (Tadmor 1958: 37-39; Lie 1929: 8.53-57)—and to try to tease a field force out of Egypt (as Hos. 7.11; 8.13; 9.3, 6; Isa. 30.1-5). The 'broken reed' intervened—so the Assyrian stylus—only in defence of Gaza, on its border, in 720 (cf. Reade 1976: 101). Sargon's forces met only token opposition in the region in 716 and 712.

By the last quarter of the century, Assyrian deportations had depleted western manpower—the main deportations were from Hamath, Damascus, Samaria and Ashdod. This was the policy under Tiglath-Pileser, Shalmaneser and Sargon. By introducing foreign populations, these kings undermined the region's capacity for revolt (as Lie 1929: 20–22.120-23; see Oded 1979: 43-54, 63-67).

The results of these measures are gauged in the reduced resistance to Sennacherib in 701: only Sidon, Ashkelon and Judah stood up to be counted (cf. Luckenbill 1924: 30.50-60; 69.19-20). Resettlement had thinned the rebel ranks—as at Ashdod, Damascus, Hamath and

Samaria.[1] No power that had suffered deportations joined the revolt of 701.

The deportations left the allies no choice: they were thrown back on their terrain, their forts, and their storehouses, prospectively supplemented by sea-borne supplies from Egypt (implied in Saggs 1955: 127.25-27; Gadd 1954: 179.42-48; Tadmor 1958: 34; Lie 1929: 20–22.120-25; and see Elat 1977: 131-32). From unified field-force tactics, the allies were driven to conscript-based, static defence. Chronicles hints at increased reliance on the muster starting in the late ninth century (2 Chron. 25.5; 26.12-13; 28.8-15). If so, domestic instability restricted spending even earlier; but this is unsure.

'Hedgehog' defence (the term is B.F. Liddell Hart's)—a pattern of self-contained, fortified nodes—required fewer skilled troops, and less expensive weaponry than field tactics. Its costs were those of fortification, and one political liability, the repercussions of which in Judah the following discussion will explore: it meant abandoning the countryside to the aggressor. In the end, this meant loosing urban royal ideologies from the constraints more traditional modes of thought had earlier imposed—it meant the effective disenfranchisement of the countryside.

B. *Hezekiah and Friends*

2 Kings 16.5-9 suggests that Ahaz first approached Assyria, a distant liege, to avert the loss of southern trade through Eilat. By the time of the fall of Samaria, however, in 722, the new vassal was flirting with rebels. Around 716–715, Sargon styles himself 'subduer of distant Judah' (Winckler 1889: 168: 8) in connection with his campaign of 720 (Tadmor 1958: 38 n. 146); in the absence of evidence that Judah participated in the anti-Assyrian coalition of the time, it is possible that the notice refers to formal submission, or to collaboration in colonizing Philistia and Samaria in 716 (as Lie 1929: 20-22.121-25;

1. Ashdod: Oded 1979: 29,63; Winckler 1889.38.227; ABL 1307; Lie 40.261; *ABL* 158 (supervisory Ru'ua?). Damascus: 2 Kgs 16.9; Amos 1.5; Winckler 1889: 108.57; Lie 1929.12.76-78; *ABL* 158; Streck 1916: 72, 199 (Arabs to Damascus?); Saggs 1955: 138.5-9; Oded, 1979: 64. Hamath: Oded 1979: 29, 64; Luckenbill 1924: 2.183; Winckler 1889: 106.49; 108.55-56; Rost 1893: 22.131-33; Parker 1961: 40. Samaria: Whitaker 1889: 4.11-17; 20.94-97; Tadmor 1958: 33-40; 2 Kgs 17.24 and Cogan 1974: 105-108; Oded 1979: 66, 29; Ezra 4.1-2, 9-10; also, Naveh 1985; esp. Na'aman 1989.

Gadd 1954: 179.37-49). A later text (Winckler 1889: 188) speaks of Egypto-Ashdodite lobbying of Judah in 712. In no case is it sure that Judah suffered military consequences (cf. Tadmor 1958: 80-84; Na'aman 1974; 1986b: 13-14). However, Egypt had sown the seeds of conflict between Sargon and Ahaz's successor, Hezekiah.

Hezekiah revolted irrevocably shortly after Sargon's death, in 705 (note Vogt 1986: 9). The general uprising centred in Babylon. Indeed, 2 Kgs 20.12-13, though displaced because of thematic organization of the regnal account from its place at the outset of the revolt, relate that Babylonian emissaries examined Hezekiah's treasury, a story paralleled in Athens's audit of the Egestaeans before taking them on as 'allies' (Thucydides 6.6; cf. also Luckenbill 1924: 42: 31-37; Begg 1986: 6 on 2 Kgs 20 stemming from a source; the prophecy of his children's exile was fulfilled in 701). One must imagine some similar relationship between the Babylonian Merodach-Baladan and Hezekiah. So strategically central was the Babylonian role in the revolt, in fact, that it was four years before Sargon's successor, Sennacherib, had sufficiently secured his southern front to risk a march to the west. But if Judah's strength figured in Merodach-Baladan's calculations, Hezekiah must have begun plotting revolt sometime shortly after 712—the more so in that his Sidonian allies were in open revolt by 709 (Elayi 1985).

Hezekiah also had backing from Egypt, which had been routed by Sargon in 720 at Raphia, but where the new, 25th Dynasty hoped to recoup its influence in Asia, and perhaps avert invasion. Sidon, too, joined in, in the hope of preserving the advantages in rare earths and other trade that the burst of eighth-century Phoenician colonization in the Mediterranean had once promised (L.E. Stager, in conversation): in Phoenicia, the urge to resist or to satisfy Assyria had in some measure driven colonization; the inflation that probably resulted (cf. Philip II) and contact and competition with Greek traders will have led to an impulse to codify authentic high Phoenician or even West Semitic culture (see below). One suspects that Sidon, Egypt, and Hezekiah together engineered a coup in Ashkelon, on the Philistine coast: a rebel party headed by Sidqa succeeded the government of Sharruludari (or Rukibti) and annexed the forts of accommodationist Ashdod (possibly these had been annexed to Ashkelon after the

Ashdodite uprising of 712).[1] Hezekiah himself installed a puppet government in Eqron, between Judah and Ashdod, deposing the pro-Assyrian king Padi, whom Sargon had perhaps installed in 720 (see Reade 1976: 99-102; Luckenbill 1924: 30.65-31.81).

Notwithstanding this elaborate fabric of alliances, Hezekiah's national defence strategy remained fortress-based. Hezekiah's measures all reflect the expectation of protracted siege operations. They intimate, therefore, a concern that, after the events of 720 at Raphia, relief from Egypt might be neither timely nor effective. Isaiah recites this position regularly (20.3-6; 19.19-25; 30.1-11; 31.1-3), starting in about 712. This was by no means an attack on his liege-lord's policy of revolt. Instead, levering Assyrian propaganda about Egyptian impotence (as 2 Kgs 18.21; 19.9-14; cf. Saggs 1963: 151-54; 1969: 17; cf. Winckler 1889: 188.34; Machinist 1983), Isaiah turns a strategic defect into a decisive justification for Hezekiah's unprecedented mobilization of resources (cf. Deut. 17.16, possibly a reference to sending agents, but more likely to the Amarna practice of selling slaves to Egypt, in this period). Egyptian field-force support, though an asset, was not to be relied on.

C. *At Home with Hezekiah*

Isaiah's analysis proved accurate, and in some quarters among the general staff must have been vigorously urged as an argument against revolt. The nationalists then used it as a rationalization—Hezekiah prepared a static, hedgehog defence; he conceded to the enemy freedom of manoeuvre in the countryside. Pericles laid down the same policy for the Peloponnesian War, in order to wage a sea campaign against the land power, Sparta. Hezekiah's object, however, can only have been to buy time until Babylonian, Elamite or Egyptian intervention, or logistical interruption (or Sidonian coastal raids?), compelled the Assyrians to withdraw. Apparently, like the king of Elam during Sennacherib's seventh campaign (Luckenbill 1924: 40.4.81–

1. Rukibtu came to the throne in Ashkelon (succeeding Mitinti) during Tiglath-Pileser's campaign to the west in 738. Whether Sharruludari succeeded him and was deposed by Sidqa is unsure. The wording of Sennacherib's report ('Sharruludari, son of Rukibtu, their former king') suggest that Sidqa was not of the same dynasty. In any case, the *lmlk* ware in Eqron and Ashdod (Na'aman 1986b: 18 n.11) indicates how far-flung Hezekiah's influence was.

41.5.11), Hezekiah expected outlying fortifications to occupy the besiegers' energy until relief materialized. In this sense, he was no more than recapitulating a strategy that had succeeded for Ahaz during the Syro-Ephraimite War.

Preparing a hedgehog defence involved three mechanical tasks. First, the forts had to be refitted—there is some evidence of this in Jerusalem, where Hezekiah built the Siloam tunnel and probably the first incarnation of the Broad Wall (Avigad 1983: 49-60). Isaiah 22.9-11 preserves a recollection of this activity, including the demolition of suburbs. Like 2 Chron. 32.2-6, Isaiah juxtaposes the fresh fortification to Hezekiah's waterworks (2 Kgs 20.20 mentions the waterworks only), which drained the old pool into a new, lower one inside the new walls; these projects were massive, although their unified physical logic requires further investigation.[1] How intensive the work was south of Jerusalem is unclear (2 Chron. 32.29 mentions city-building). Hezekiah probably refitted bastions not just in the capital, but elsewhere (Tel Batashi, Azekah, Gath, Maresha), including some stockades to protect the Negev caravans (Beersheba II [Aharoni 1974; see below]; Arad X–VIII, Hesi VII, Aroer 4, and Qadesh Barnea, middle fortress). North of Jerusalem, the earliest gate at Tell en-Nasbeh may have been replaced in roughly this period.

Second, Hezekiah had to stock the forts for large numbers both of conscripts and of professional garrison troops, whose job it will have been to prevent popular defection. Provisions made for the conscripts may echo in 2 Chron. 32.28-29, which speaks of Hezekiah's aggregating stores and stables, along with forts, but these topoi are typical of Chronicles, and, one might argue, are the products of the historian's reflection rather than of his sources.

Architectural evidence suggesting a chain of command includes a large four-room house with a courtyard on the city-wall at Tell Beit Mirsim, the so-called West Tower and Gate. The complex was founded in the tenth–ninth century, but reached a fully developed form only in the last phase of stratum A^2 (Albright 1943: 47), just before 701 (Aharoni and Aharoni 1976). At Arad, an earlier fort was refitted with a solid wall (str. X–VIII) in the second half of the eighth

1. See Shiloh 1984: 23, 28-29 for argument that a 5m thick Hezekian wall enclosed the water system of stratum 12 (2 Chron. 32.3, 5, 30), based partly on the expansion of the city to include the western hill.

century (Zimhoni 1985: 84-87; Mazar and Netzer 1986; cf. Herzog, Aharoni, Rainey and Moshkovitz 1984; Herzog 1987). Another substantial four-room house occurs at the city-gate of Tell en-Nasbeh (bldg. 379; McCown 1947: 211-12; note Shiloh 1970: 190), and one dominates the centre of Tel 'Eton (Ayalon 1985: 61). These buildings may reflect the extension of royal oversight to smaller regional centres, from the larger forts, like Megiddo, where governors were stationed from the time of the United Monarchy forward (at Megiddo, buildings 1728 and 338; but see Ussishkin 1989; at Tell el-Far'ah [N], see Chambon 1984 pl. 20, by the gate; for the 'basement house' of Beersheba, see Shiloh 1978: 42 n. 10). The location of the buildings at Tell Beit Mirsim, Tell en-Nasbeh, Megiddo and Tell el-Far'ah at a gate is particularly suggestive, since the gate functioned as a centre of military command and civil administration. That the appointment of royal 'mayors/majors' in the small towns can be dated to Hezekiah's time is, however, unsure, since royal interference in judicial administration may have meant appointments earlier (Dearman 1988: 88-101). Still, that Hezekiah militarized rural Judah or exploited the militarization of immediate predecessors seems an inescapable conclusion. N. Na'aman has even suggested that the list of fortified towns in 2 Chron. 11.6-10, though attributed to Rehoboam, actually reflects Hezekiah's fortification activity.[1]

Ceramic evidence, too, in the form of the *lmlk* ('the king's') store jars, seems to attest the central distribution of food supplies for garrison troops. Scholars have long linked the large *lmlk* pithoi with Hezekiah's preparations for siege (see Na'aman 1979, with references). However, the exiguous numbers of jars and fragments so far recovered suggest rather that their use was restricted to the professional soldiery (note Welten 1969: 141; on distribution, Garfinkel 1984; Na'aman 1986b). Sennacherib's annals make reference to the importation of such troops into Jerusalem (Luckenbill 1924: 33-34.40-41).

As distinct from the landed classes, these mercenary troops had no interest in local fields and orchards the Assyrian army might fire;

1. Na'aman 1986b. Cf. also Fritz 1981, and the antecedent argument by Fritz in *ZDPV* 93 (1977) 30-32 toward a Josianic dating of the list (but this can be reconciled with reflection on the history of Assyrian conquest in the 8th century—Fritz, personal communication); Garfinkel 1988; Na'aman 1988.

even the inducements Assyria offered to defectors—'each man [eating of] his own vine, and each his own fig, and...each the water of his own cistern' until removed to an equally fertile land abroad (2 Kgs 18.31-32) will have seemed generous to the landless and appealed to others going hungry under siege. A modest royal garrison in each fortress—the Amarna materials suggest that 25-100 men would suffice—would have been a small investment to make in protracting the duration of a siege, and was a necessity in any event for directing defensive operations. It is no surprise, then, that the Lachish reliefs sustain just such a distinction (Barnett 1958; cf. Reade 1972; Wäfler 1975). For the professional garrisons, pay and rations had to be provided (as for the *ktym* later at Arad), from the royal paymaster in the capital. This pattern is a mortice into which the *lmlk* jars dovetail.

The *lmlk* store jars were manufactured in a central place, probably in the region of Lachish (Mommsen, Perlman and Yellin 1984). They were produced over a short period of time, as the exiguous number of seals used on them indicates, and stamped with one of four place names and one of two scarab types (Lemaire 1981); some carry private seals (of officials, presumably) as well. The dating of the jars depends largely on that of Lachish level III, which has yielded up something on the order of 350 *lmlk* seal impressions. Not to explore all the issues (see esp. Yadin 1976; Aharoni and Aharoni 1976), the consensus and the current excavator, with good reason, place the destruction of Lachish III in 701. If so, the *lmlk* jars, of both the two-winged and four-winged varieties, were produced just before (Ussishkin 1977: 56; 1985: 142-44; McClellan 1975; Evans 1980: 163; cf. Lance 1971; Holladay 1976: 266-67).

The *lmlk* jars are distributed abundantly, in forts large and small, in the north, on the border between Judah and the Assyrian province of Samaria (see Eshel 1989), and in the west, between the Judahite hills and the Philistine coast. At Tel Batashi, the site of ancient Timnah on the border with Eqron, a public building—probably a barracks attached to an officer's house—served as the local distribution point for stores from the *lmlk* jars. No unrelated ware was found in the building (A. Mazar 1985: 306-308). There was no extensive contemporary destruction elsewhere on the site: the garrison was destroyed by Sennacherib (Luckenbill 1924: 32.6-7), or by local elements traducing Hezekiah. This finally verifies the view that the jars held siege supplies. The concentration of the jars in the public building thus reflects the cleavage posited above between the professional garrison and local denizens: if the townsmen were Philistine (as 2 Chron. 28.18, possibly the Chronicler's reconstruction), the surgical destruction in stratum III would reflect local connivance with Assyria after the restoration of Padi of Eqron (on which note Postgate 1974: 21.1-3 from 699), where there are signs of a small Judahite presence as well (two *lmlk* handles, Dothan and Gitin 1985: 3; note also the one in Ashdod, Na'aman 1986b: 18 n. 11; but some 32 in Gezer—Eshel 1989: 62 n. 12; it is interesting to note the decline in pig-consumption at these Philistine sites: note Hesse 1986; Wapnish and Hesse unpub. a, on Batashi and Miqne).

Few *lmlk* jars have appeared in the Judaean hill country or south (see Welten 1969; Na'aman 1979). The hills have been sparsely excavated, and cannot be discussed with any confidence. But Hezekiah did not, it seems, stockpile southern Judah with the jars (none at Hesi or Malhata, one each at Tel Beersheba [not from the Lachish clay], Ira, Lahav, Khirbet Gharreh and Tell esh-Shuqf, three at Aroer, four at Beit Mirsim, and nine at Arad: Na'aman 1986b: 12; Garfinkel 1988: 70; M. Aharoni 1981).

Arguably, this distribution reflects an expectation that Assyria would ignore the south (hills?). Na'aman (1979: 75; 1986b: 13-14) suggests that Sargon took the Beersheba region when he seized the caravan routes from Arabia. Sargon's interest in the region is indisputable (as Tadmor 1958: 77-78). Still, the loss of southern Judah by Ahaz would have been too juicy for the historian of Kings to pass up (as 2 Kgs 16.5-6). And evidence of Hezekiah's southern expansion (1 Chron. 4.39-43, best located after Wiseman 1951: 23.22) coincides with geopolitical evidence for a presence in the south (the drive to Gaza, in combination with Ashkelon, in 2 Kgs 18.8 = Luckenbill 1924: 33: 31-34), including Edom's supplication to Sennacherib (Luckenbill 1924: 30.56-57).

Moreover, at Tel Beersheba II, a large altar consisting of a number of blocks of stone was dismantled, presumably by Hezekiah. The altar's stones were used in what was apparently the wall of a public stable (Holladay 1986)—a stable being erected only after local sacrifice left off, so as to avoid startling the horses. What this implies for the nature of Hezekiah's cultic policy is not clear-cut (see section V, below). But it is probable that the cultic preparations were conducted, by Hezekiah, with Sennacherib in mind.

The reform at Tel Beersheba weighs against the epigraphic rumour at Arad (Aharoni 1981: 70-74) adduced to suggest a contemporary threat from Edom (Na'aman 1986b: 13; 2 Chron. 28.17 is misappropriated from 2 Kgs 16.6): Judah is the star of Assyrian reports about the region in this era; Edomite and Arab activity was restricted to the far south. Hezekiah left the south unstocked, either because, his resources limited, he anticipated no activity there, or because he counted on Egyptian interest in the Wadi Besor–Beersheba basin. He probably did devote some energy to fortification in the region (above); but desert garrisons relied on local pastoralists for supply, not on *lmlk* jars (2 Chron. 32.29, although central distribution was the rule later at Arad).

Hezekiah's third step was to concentrate the rural population in the forts, to preserve it as an economic resource, so far as possible, against Assyrian depredations. This was the first premise of static defence, as the Athenian and Elamite parallels indicate. Provision, then, had to be made for evacuation, billeting, work details, and sustenance. Immediate implications were two: the rural population had to be set to work updating fortifications, and rehearsed in its removal to the fortresses—it had to be informed that the king planned to abandon the countryside; and, at the fortresses, assuming that rural produce collection was a family chore, temporary quartering had to be arranged. One mark of this stage may survive in the record of Hezekiah's registration of the southern population (1 Chron. 4.41). It stands to reason that universal registration was part of a larger administrative scheme.

Fitting the forts, provisioning the garrisons, and coordinating the population transfer were big jobs. Of them, mobilizing the landowners and other population may have been the most complex; after all, abandoning the countryside meant abandoning the land promised by Yhwh to Israel, abandoning the land of the ancestors. Is it a coincidence, then, that Hezekiah is also the first king who reportedly removed the 'high places' (2 Kgs 18.4), the loci (see further section V, below) of the rural cult? Is it a coincidence that the altar at Beersheba went out of service around this time (Aharoni 1974; cf. Yadin 1976; Aharoni and Aharoni 1976)? Yet how can one reconcile the persistence, in some form, of the Arad sanctuary (level VIII: Herzog, Aharoni, Rainey and Moshkovitz 1984: 19; cf. A. Mazar and E. Netzer 1986; Herzog 1987), and probably that at Lachish

(Mic. 1.13; Aharoni 1975: 30-31) with this programme?

It is unlikely that the reforms were coincidental. They antedated Sennacherib's assaults—at Beersheba, certainly, and, so far as the speech of the Rabshakeh indicates, elsewhere as well (2 Kgs 18.22; for the timing, Evans 1980: 161-63). We may add, early classical prophecy, so full of iconoclasm and assaults on the cult, can have been transmitted in writing only by Hezekian partisanism (Halpern 1987b): the codification and preservation of eighth-century 'classical prophecy' was a Hezekian programme. The policy of centralization, thus, antedates Sennacherib's advent. Traditionally, scholars have linked 'centralization' to theological fanaticism, to economics, and to the realities ensuing on Sennacherib's siege (see Evans 1980: 162). But theological theory in the capital never converged with countryside practice. And the reform regime could anticipate no significant stream of new money, in the form of sacrifices, pouring into the capital; centralization pays off economically only when a regime can seize the lands and other assets of an established church (Philip IV, Henry VIII, Talleyrand; cf. Clayburn 1973). Hezekiah's policy had an ideological matrix in attacks on the cult in classical prophecy. What was its political valence?

The new doctrine was implemented in the context of Hezekiah's centralized urbanization of the rural population. The reform also made political sense as an adjunct to abandoning the countryside. By dismantling the rural cult—but not the state cult housed in temples in the fortresses (Arad, Lachish; no enclosed shrine was found at Beersheba)—centralization desacralized the land sanctified by the 'high places' and by ancestral shrines. It justified ideologically prising the peasantry into the forts, severing the old ancestral and customary ties, and securing the relation of the individual or the family to the central authority, instead of to the land. A rural population favouring appeasement was thus subjected to military discipline to prevent defection—as in the case of the garrison at Tel Batashi. A New Model Army, an army of reform, could be brought to bear against rural conservatism in the matter of the ancestors. The same force could be used to coopt local priesthoods into the state cult. That Pericles faced the same difficulties with less revolutionary measures is clear. The mechanics of Hezekiah's manoeuvres will be the subject of further review below.

III. *Sennacherib's Reforms*

A. *Sennacherib at Large*

The outcome of Hezekiah's policy was predictable. If centralization was a measure for herding the peasantry into forts, Assyrian invasion was the way to herd them out again. Sennacherib claims to have razed 46 forts and countless suburbs, and exiled 201,500 people, along with all the livestock in the country (Luckenbill 1924: 32.18–33.27). These allegations deserve more credence than is usually accorded them, for a number of reasons, some of which should be elaborated.

First, the annals are concessive: they admit that Jerusalem survived; they further stipulate that Hezekiah paid his tribute later, not on the spot, exercising a latitude otherwise unexampled for a defeated vassal. Both elements blemish the victor's achievement (see Roberts 1983: 20; Millard 1985: 70-72; Tadmor 1985). In fact, the rural spoil and deportations, like the depiction of the siege of Lachish in the Lachish Room of Sennacherib's palace, are offered as a second-rate consolation for a partial failure. The conservative course is to take the testimony seriously.

Second, abandoning the countryside invited this kind of devastation, as Pericles, among others, discovered, because devastation is good policy—it taunts the victim to join battle in the field, mobilizes the landed classes to press for submission, and reduces the power of the victim to resist and his resources for resisting aggression. It also demonstrates to potential allies that freedom of manoeuvre lies with the aggressor.[1]

Third, for just these reasons (cf. Saggs 1963: 151-54), it was Assyrian policy to denude the countryside when conditions forbade access to the ruler in revolt. In the ninth century, for example, Shalmaneser III burnt the region of Hubushkia when its king took refuge in the mountains (Michel 1947: 9.II.9-14). Again, the population of Bit Adini dispersed at Shalmaneser's approach; its king, Ahuni, withdrew into the security of the capital. So Shalmaneser set

1. For the logic of rural devastation as a military tactic, see, for example, Polybius 2.64; 3.90-91; Thucydides 2.11, 14-16, 20; 3.26; 4.83-88; 5.83; 6.75; 8.24. For parallel thought among modern strategists, see, e.g., Kahn 1960: 165-72. For further discussion, see Eph'al 1983: 94-97.

about ravaging the landscape. Ahuni had sufficiently spared his manpower next to join a coalition of four powers against Shalmaneser. In a battle at Lutibu, on the border of Sam'al, Shalmaneser failed to destroy the enemy field force, and so levelled the town. Yet, as he advanced westward, the coalition stood, and attracted new accessions. Similarly, Shalmaneser claims to have worked out his frustration on Hamath's palaces, when decisive victory eluded him at Qarqar (all this in the Monolith, *ANET* 277-79). He pillaged hundreds of settlements in enemy territory (*ANET* 279). Similar actions accompanied the escape of Aramu the Urartean (see Hulin 1963: 63). Most vividly, Shalmaneser's unsuccessful siege of Damascus in his eighteenth year (841) led him to lay waste the entire region (*ANET* 280).

Shalmaneser's tactics survived among Sennacherib's immediate predecessors. Tiglath-Pileser III may have destroyed some districts to expedite resettlement in Babylonia (as Rost 1893: 8.39-41; 42.8–44.10; 58.15–60.22; 62.29–64.36) and punish recurrent revolt (10.51-52?). More often, he devastated districts whose kings had fled (Rost 1893: 6.28–8.34; 26.158–28.162; 44.22–46.36; 50.29–52.45; and 14.67-73; 30.173-79, with resettlement), or remained unbowed (10.51-52?). Given the scribes' poetic hyperbole (Rost 1893: 42.8) and departures from chronological sequence to end the reports with a rhetorical flourish of obliteration, we cannot always tell whether Tiglath-Pileser ruined regions during or after a siege (8.39-41) or pursuit (28.162-64). But some descriptions of widespread destruction (as Rost 1893: 32.180-83 and following) are silent about the enemy king, suggesting that the core of the army escaped. A graphic passage, of the sort Sennacherib later applied to Hezekiah, explicitly describes Tiglath-Pileser's siege of Rezin in Damascus and the demolition of his fields and orchards and rural districts (Rost 1893: 34.197–36.209); a similar passage attaches to the Sealands (60.23-25). The tactic is explicitly identified as an incentive to submission (Rost 1893: 10.42; Luckenbill 1924: 41.11-16; 42.31-43.43 with Saggs 1963: 149): it has this effect, too, on the young Merodach-Baladan (Rost 1893: 60.26–62.28).

Sargon conforms to the pattern. Deportees' towns are levelled (Lie 1929: 32.198-201; 8.58-65; cf. Gadd 1954: 183.55-58). But Raphia was torn down (Lie 1929: 8.55-57) because tactical and strategic logic forbade pursuit of the Egyptian king. The same conditions motivated later demolitions (Lie 1929: 18.106-108; 66.450–68.451). Otherwise, kings who retained strategic resources were prime targets of vandalism, including especially the elusive Merodach-Baladan.[1] Sargon's burning of Izirtu (Lie 1929: 14.87) might be exceptional; but most likely (see Winckler 1889: 104.41-42 and the parallel case of Mita, 126.149–128.153), rural devastation led the rebel to submit to vassalship there (Lie 1929: 18.108-109).

The paradigmatic instance evoked a letter to Asshur in praise of the destruction of Musasir, and Sargon's magnificent dismantling, his systematic obliteration, of the paradaisical capital of Rusa of Urartu. Sargon's song was the poetry of cataclysm, and his muse portrays it as a sort of ballet noir (esp. Zaccagnini 1981; cf. Oppenheim 1960). The text simply assumes that Rusa's withdrawal beyond Sargon's reach had precipitated the destruction of the garden (Lie 1929: 24.139–28.165; Thureau-Dangin 1912 esp. 200-32).

Outside Judah, Sennacherib was also true to type. Unable to capture Merodach-Baladan, he laid waste the southern reaches of Babylonia (Luckenbill 1924: 52.34–54.53; 35.59-70). He burnt the land of the Kassites, then rounded up the fugitive population for resettlement; he imposed the same justice in Elippi, charring the soil as he went, when the king had withdrawn (Luckenbill 1924: 58.23; 59.27-30). And, eluded by his opponents in his fifth and seventh campaigns, he again razed town upon town (Luckenbill 1924: 35.75–38.31; 39.61–40.80), being frustrated in the latter case only by the onset of winter. In the sixth campaign, he rampaged in Elam—where Chaldean refugees had established a base—before the Elamite king met him in the field (Luckenbill 1924: 38.44-46).

Assyria found a variety of uses for rural marauding as fewer antagonists offered open battle. Esarhaddon marauded to secure unconditional surrender (Borger 1956: 104–105.II.1, 16, 33-35). But Sennacherib's activity in the Judahite countryside is entirely in character. Hezekiah was insulated in the capital, and Sennacherib maintained forms by reducing as much of the country as time and his

1. For Sargonic devastation of other kings' territories, see Thureau–Dangin 1912: 14.80–16.90; Winckler 1889: 106.47; 148.25-26; Lie 1929: 22.131–24.133; 34.208-211; Lie 1929: 30.184-191, with Scythian-type tactics; Winckler 1889: 110.68-70. For Babylonia, where Sargon's frustrating failure to lay hold of Merodach-Baladan determined his policy, see Gadd 1954: 186.50-62; Lie 40.262–44.282 with 50.332-337; 62.9-10; 64.7-8 and note the scorched earth policy of 50.11-13.

troop strength allowed. Hezekiah had invited destruction, and it was a matter of Assyrian honour that the invitation be taken up. If the king and ruling classes could not be got at, the rest of the land had to go.

Fourth, deportation was the highest form of devastation, and Sennacherib was a master of both, as Oded has documented (1979: 21). He executed a resettlement identical in magnitude, of 208,000 Babylonians, in the first campaign. This figure may reflect some, but not great exaggeration. A sample of 5,000 indicates that twenty-five per cent or less were males of an age to do service (*ABL* 304), which means that Sennacherib claims to have acquired roughly 50,000 workers. How the figures were reckoned—to include casualties, or elements resettled locally—is opaque. But the number is not inflated by a factor even of, say, four (or the sample of 5,000 is ten per cent of the total). Tiglath-Pileser III claimed to have exiled 155,000 people from the Sealand, Sargon 90,000 from Bit-Yakin. Sennacherib's claim, even if bloated, is in line with the other figures (cf. Brinkman 1979: 227; for a list of over 1,200 Aramaeans, Parker 1961: 40). Survey evidence, though somewhat dirigible, puts the nadir of Babylonian demography in just this era (Brinkman 1984: 10).

Fifth, neo-Assyrian sums of western deportees are otherwise realistic (see Oded 1979: 20-22, 31-32, 37-38), and are corroborated by archaeological results (Galilee—Gal. in press 7.3, where the figure of 13,520 deportees is shown to correspond to a realistic density of 30 persons/dunam) or later events (Samaria—see Eph'al 1979a: 185-88, and p. 190 on Israelites in exile; esp. Na'aman 1989). Assyrian logistics capable of sending 30,000 Samarians to the east or their replacements westward could service a pipeline, given time, for 200,000 captives (Oded 1979: 52; Lie 1929: 12.75; Gadd 1954: 179.21-24; Luckenbill 1924: 76.102-103.). Why, then, single out the figure for Judahite captives for scorn? And what possessed Sennacherib to invent the curious number, 200,150, instead of a round (and therefore rough) figure? Exaggeration has been isolated in blanket remarks about exiling 'everyone' (Oded 1979: 21-22.) but has never been proved in relation to specific figures.[1] Any suggestion of fanciful invention must itself be contrived (as Sauren 1985).

Sixth, Sennacherib was erecting a new capital in Nineveh at the

1. Despite Oded 1979.20-21 n.5. In the case of Rost 1893: 79-83, the continuation shows that the exaggeration is metaphoric, not literal.

time, and drew enormous quantities of labour from the west (Luckenbill 1924: 95.71; 104.54-56). Westerners manned the naval force of the sixth campaign, much of it unskilled labour (Luckenbill 1924: 73.57-64 and 86.23–87.24). This is not to mention projects outside the capital (as Luckenbill 1924: 58.24; 59.32), including the Asshur temple (in a town freed from corvée), or field force requirements (see Brinkman 1979: 242 n. 28; 1984: 17-22, 52; *ABL* 304). Sennacherib's appetite for manpower was voracious, and the high pitch of his deportations reflects his need (see Oded 1979: 90; Tadmor 1975: 40-42).

Seventh, deportation had created population imbalances in the empire. Where Sennacherib settled Judahites, as distinct from earlier exiles, is not transparent.[1] The Rassam cylinder speaks of allocations of Judahites among all the districts and cities of the empire (Luckenbill 1924: 61.60): for economic exploitation, a grave concern (Oded 1979: 67-74), populations needed to be reshuffled along with provincial boundaries (2 Kgs 18.31-32). Having suffered far-reaching deportations under Tiglath-Pileser and Sargon as well as Sennacherib, Babylonia must have been experiencing a crying need for cultivators (as Stohlmann 1983: 173-74; later, *ABL* 942), and in 701 Sennacherib may have planned to locate Judahites there: a neo-Babylonian demographic resurgence (Adams 1981: 177) presumably reflects the influx of deportees to replace those Assyria removed in the late eighth century. Such a policy under Sennacherib would account for seemingly prescient predictions of Mic. 4.10 and 2 Kgs 20.17-18 (cf. Stohlmann 1983: 170-74) about exile to Babylon, which were later interpreted to refer to the events of 597–586 (as in 2 Kgs 20.19), and which some modern scholars consequently excise as secondary. Indeed, were a Judahite population already established in Babylonia, the rapid assimilation and economic success of the exiles of 597 and 586 would find an easy explanation (note Zadok 1979: 78-79). In any case, the neo-Assyrian empire could easily have digested the deportees

1. For an Israelite (Nadbiyau) in Assyria in 709, see *ADD* 234. For attempts to locate Judahites, Eph'al 1979: 190-91; Barnett 1958: 161-62 (with a depiction of Judahites in Sennacherib's guard); Zadok 1979: 35-38; Stohlmann 1983: 167-68. Note further ADD 148, where a loan contract from c. 660 involves grain measured *ina* GIŠ-BAR *ša mat Ia-ú-di* (the lender A-du-ni-ḫa-a, either Adoniyah[u] or Adonihay, presumably from Judah, the borrower Atarsuri); Parker 1963: 91, with a ^{m}Ia-u-da witnessing a contract on 1 Ab 687 (limmu of Sennacherib); BT 105.11.

from Judah of which Sennacherib speaks.

Eighth, whatever drove Sennacherib to leave Judah before consummating his victory may itself have demanded additions to his labour reserves. In any case, it was essential for Sennacherib to provide against a fresh renewal of the revolt, and a Hezekian assault on communications with the West. This concern is reflected in Sennacherib's assignment of Hezekiah's 'towns that I plundered' to Philistine city-states. Regular deportations to Samaria—under Sargon, Esarhaddon and Ashurbanipal—may also reflect a continuing nervousness about Judah. So whether Sennacherib sent 200,000 Judahites eastward, or allotted some to Philistia (repopulating Eqron?),[1] rural depopulation was a way of purchasing insurance against immediate upheaval on the Egyptian border: leaving a rebel state without taking the capital was a novel experience, though an Elamite winter later reproduced it (Luckenbill 1924: 39.61–41.11, noting the capital's evacuation). Sennacherib could not discipline the ruling classes, rout the flower of their army, or even raze their major fortress, leaving only a headless population (as he chose to do at Eqron). Exiling the population was an intelligent alternative. Sennacherib, so excellent in resettlement, will have adopted it.

Ninth, as an estimate of the rural population of Judah, 200,000 is far from being inappropriate. Thus, Samaria, long cut off from resources outside the Ephraimite hills, after a successful siege by Shalmaneser V, yielded a haul of almost 30,000 exiles to Sargon (who replaced them) in 720. Sennacherib claims to have despoiled 46 walled towns, 4,351 people per fort on average. Mesha, comparably, claimed to have taken 7,000 Israelites in Nebo (*KAI* 181.14-17; cf. Cross 1983: 154); Sargon removed 9,033 people from Raphia in 720.

1. For deportees to Philista, see Naveh 1985; but cf. Kempinski 1987; for the possibility of deportees from Israel at Eqron, see Gitin 1989a: 49; 1989: 59*-64*. Stohlmann (1983: 153-157) argues that a period of delay intervened between capture and deportation (as 2 Kgs 18.31-32), and that not all the Judahites who were captured (210, 500) were necessarily deported. He bases this conclusion in part on the Rassam cylinder, where the formal notice of deportation (Luckenbill 1924: 61.60) is separated from that of the capture. However, the record of deportations is also placed after Hezekiah's messengers and tribute arrive in Nineveh. The section is substantively, not chronologically, ordered, relating the division of spoils, not their initial acquisition. This does not, however, reduce the likelihood that some captives were sent to Philistine towns, others further abroad, and some to Assyria.

These were not the towns' standing populations. Rather, they reflect an emergency concentration of the outlying areas (cf. 1 Sam. 11.1 in 4QSam[a]; Josephus; Cross 1983). This was a corollary of abandoning the countryside to the aggressor—as the king of Elam did once Sennacherib loosed his raiders in the seventh campaign (Luckenbill 1924: 40.1–41.5), and as Pericles did in the face of Spartan land power (Thucydides 2.13-16, 65). An average of 4,000 people per enclosure, combining town and rural population, falls within the realm of reason (note Barkay 1988: 125). A mass grave at Lachish, in fact, contained the burnt, disarticulated bones of some 1,500 war dead in a pile 1.3 metres high (Tomb 120), and other tombs contained emergency burials from the same period, of up to 500 corpses (T. 107, 108); animal bones, including pig, were strewn across the tops of the piles (Tufnell 1953: 193-96; Risdon 1939). This reflects Israelite losses, as Assyrian bodies will have been recovered after each engagement and buried properly away from the mound. Allowing that the number of adult male casualties (at 45-50% based on Risdon 1939: 103-104) equates with even half the adult male population, a conservative estimate of the population of the fortress in the emergency runs to around 12,000. This is probably low.

Total population estimates based purely on archaeological samples are necessarily crude: they do not reflect fluctuations in the construction of upper stories, in the average density of settlement, squatter and wood-frame construction (as Thucydides 2.14, 52), and so on. Some idea of the complexity of these calculations can be had from the work of Shiloh (1980) and Stager (1985: 21). Nevertheless, Israel in the eighth century came as close to carrying capacity as at any time before the Roman period. Since Hezekiah had seized land and people from Philistia (Gath, and towns from Eqron, Ashdod and Gaza), Sennacherib's total is immune from gross ridicule. Indeed, evidence of marked depopulation will be adduced below.

B. *Sennacherib's Judah*

Tenth, Sennacherib's figure of 46 walled towns compares well to the physical evidence. It is not realistic to expect that Assyria levelled every town. Yet, neither will excavation determine which towns fell and which did not: some will have surrendered to threats and blandishments, others to shortages; still others (Batashi III) suffered local breaches, not general destructions. Sennacherib takes care not to say that he fired the remains—his reticence dovetails with the claim that he redistributed much of Hezekiah's domain to Ashdod, Eqron, Gaza, and, in one text, Ashkelon (Luckenbill 1924: 70.29-30; 33.30-34). Hoping to cement these vassals' loyalty, he will have spared the local architecture, where appropriate. Under the circumstances, a regional enumeration of 'walled towns' is indicated.

There should be no dispute that Assyria ravaged the northern approaches to the capital, and, though some scholars link it to other events (see Stohlmann 1983: 159-60 n. 40), Isa. 10.28-32 (with 9–12 sites) furnishes a notional itinerary—in a context directly concerned with the return of Israel's exiles from Asshur to Davidic sovereignty (10.20-27 [10.26-27 referring to 9.3-5]; 11.10-16). *lmlk* stamps are well represented in this region. At two sites, Gibeon and Tell en-Nasbeh, excavators saw no signs of a 701 destruction (Pritchard 1962: 161; McCown 1947: 151-53). However, at Gibeon, in a large cut, the uppermost level contained pottery of the Tell Beit-Mirsim A^2–Ain Shems IIc horizon (see Pritchard 1964: 44-45), implying marked contraction after 701. Na'aman has shown that the rock-cut pool, with 75 *lmlk* handles in its silt, went out of use in 701; the stepped tunnel represents the next phase of occupation on the site (1979: 74 n. 29).

Tell en-Nasbeh is more confused (McClellan 1984: 53-54). Here, there was no Babylonian destruction; but the early phase of stratum I, poorly isolated, yielded numerous *lmlk* stamps and ceramic and other parallels to Beit Mirsim A^2 (McCown 1947: 156-159, 160, 183, 246). And, even apart from those in the fill of which *lmlk* handles were found (McCown 1947: 130-32), a profusion of cisterns fell into disuse in the early seventh century.[1] Probably, Tell en-Nasbeh was depopulated in 701, before the late phase of Stratum I, a conclusion sustained by McClellan's demonstration (1984: 55) that Stratum II, with its

1. See McCown 1947: cisterns 320, fig. 27B, esp. 19, 20, 29, 30, and Assyrian ware; 368, fig. 29B.33, 10; 370, p. 139, fig. 30A-C, and cf. the jugs in Wampler and McCown 1947: 18, comparable to Ain Shems IIc; 176, fig. 25A-B (esp. B:8.10, 14); 183, p. 132; 191, fig. 25C: 3,4; 285, fig. 26A-B; 304, p. 168, with Assyrian ware, pl. 26D.33; 325, pl. 27C-D, as at Lachish III; 363, fig. 28D, 29A, with 8th–7th-century forms. Note that, if it had not already been replaced by the later gate, the early gate must have gone out of use at this time. The single *lmlk* jar handle found at Bethel (Eshel 1989) does not necessarily imply Hezekian activity there.

eighth-century pottery, is identical with the early phase of Stratum I. Any Assyrian levee striking south from the province of Samerina passed this site, and will have reduced it to secure logistical links with the north (note Na'aman 1979: 76). Subsequently, en-Nasbeh may have become the southern border of Samerina, as it was in the ninth century; this would explain why it was later elected by the Babylonians as the administrative centre of Judah—it had remained quiescent during Jerusalem's revolts in 605–586.

Similar problems surround the reconstruction of events at Tell el-Ful. Here, the pottery of Fortress IIIA has been correlated to Beth Zur III and Ain Shems IIc, both at 701 (below, and Aharoni and Aharoni 1976), but also to Lachish II, Ein Gedi V, and Ramat Rahel VA, all of which fell in the sixth century (Lapp 1981: 82-83). However, there were gaps in occupation before and after Fortress IIIA, and the later fortress, IIIB, contained *lmlk* stamps, as well as rosettes (Sinclair 1960: 32-35; 1964: 59). IIIB, then, may be a seventh-century rebuild of a ruined Hezekian fortress (IIIA). Inadequate stratification and publication forbids any secure conclusions (see Finkelstein 1988: 57); but if the identification of el-Ful with Gibeah of Saul is maintained (as Albright 1924: 28-43), texts such as Isa. 10.29 demand an eighth-century occupation.

Ramat Rahel VB was also destroyed, and reoccupied by Assyrians: here, *lmlk* stamps and associated ware appear below the Assyrian 'palace ware' that seems to mark the seventh century (Aharoni 1962: 40-41, 51; Na'aman 1979: 71-73; cf. Pratico 1982: 9; Aharoni 1962: 59-60; 1964: 123-24; 1965: 20 for the view that the Assyrian 'palace ware' is a late local imitation, leaving VA late and VB, and the *lmlk* stamps in Josiah's reign—in suppport of Lance 1971; Holladay 1976: 266-67). The Assyrian goblets, as Na'aman has observed (1979: 72) belong to the last phase of VA, and the beginning of VA therefore logically coheres, at the latest, with the period of Assyrian domination under Hezekiah and Manasseh. The destruction of the earlier phase, VB (on which see Yadin 1973: 62), is most sensibly attributed to Sennacherib (Na'aman 1979).

With Isa. 10.28-32 attesting a line of march fanning out down the spine of the hills north of Jerusalem, there is thus a case to be made out that Sennacherib encountered a large number of settlements in the region. How many were counted as 'fortified walled cities' is unsure. But to link up with the contingents in the Shephelah, and to impair

Hezekiah's communications with the Shephelah and Philistia, this cohort had also to seize the roads leading west. Towns commanding such routes included Gibeon, Khirbet el-Burj (Kochavi 1972a: 186), Beth-Horon, Ayyalon, Shaalbim, Khirbet Kefira, Qiryath-Yearim and Chesalon. A count of fifteen sites north of the capital is conservative.

How far east the Assyrian army extended itself is unclear. The force moving south through Michmash took control of the main roads to Jericho (see A. Mazar, Amit and Elan 1983). No fortified centres were to hand in the region. Smaller settlements offered targets for forage and gratuitous destruction.

The central arena of Sennacherib's assault was the Shephelah. Here, Lachish III shows how assiduous he was (Ussishkin 1976; 1978: 38, 51-53, 63-74). The destruction of this Level was followed by a gap in settlement that may have lasted half the century; tombs of a hundred years' standing suddenly go out of use (as T. 1002—Tufnell 1953: 229-36). Other defensive concentrations included Zorah, Eshtaol, Zanoah, Azekah, Sochoh, Adullam, Tell Judeideh, Tell Bornat, Maresha, and perhaps Yarmut, where Iron II is not yet attested (further Mic. 1.9-15, with Moreshet Gath and a royal centre at Achzib [for storejar manufacture?]; note Na'aman 1979: 74). Gezer, to judge from the 32 *lmlk* stamps found there, also passed from Assyrian (or Samarian or Gittite) to Judahite hands, before its reconquest (see *EAEHL* 2.428-443; Eph'al 1979b). Nor is Gezer the only town controlled by Assyria to succumb to Hezekiah's ambition between 712 and 703. Its fate had also overtaken Eqron and Gath, which Sargon had secured along with Gibbethon (el-Amin 1953: 35-37; Reade 1976: 99-102; further below), all at Assyria's expense. The status of Gibbethon in 701 has not been ascertained, the site not having been identified with any certainty. But it must have been near Gezer, and if the identification with Tel Melat is maintained, must be envisioned as being in Hezekiah's hands. In other words, between 712 and 703, Hezekiah systematically undid what Sargon had achieved in northern and central Philistia.

The excavators date the fall of Tell 'Eton to 750, but report a history of settlement after the period uncovered in their soundings (Ayalon 1985; Zimhoni 1985). However, it is certainly possible that 'Eton fell in 701, given the history of Tell Beit Mirsim and Tell Halif: the absence of *lmlk* ware on the site need not provoke remark, given the scarcity of this ware in the southern Shephelah and the limited area excavated at Tell 'Eton; the latest elements in the pottery repertoire have their closest parallels at Lachish III and Arad X-VIII, both ending in 701 or thereabouts. Halif VIB (with one *lmlk* stamp) suffered a violent destruction in 701. The same is true of Beit Mirsim A^2 (four *lmlk* impressions), and the more important Beth Shemesh IIc (Aharoni and Aharoni 1976). At Beth Shemesh, nineteen *lmlk* handles and a sealing of Elyaqim the servant of Yo/awchin accompany a major olive processing industrial centre that is probably to be attributed to the eighth century (Grant and Wright 1939: 75-84; for industrial-scale olive processing in an analogous position inland from the northern coast during the eighth century, see Gal 1990; further, Eitam 1987: 23-25). The fall of Beth-Shemesh is a premise both of the increase in deer consumption below, at Batashi, and of the industrialization of seventh-century Batashi and Eqron (see below). Some of the destruction layer attributed by the excavators to IIb may in fact have pertained to the stratum in question, and there were hints of destruction in IIc itself (Grant and Wright 1939: 13-14, 73). However, the real evidence for the fall of Beth-Shemesh is the history of the olive-processing industry, which passed decisively into the hands of Eqron after 701 (below): it is of course possible that Sennacherib captured the town without overmuch violence.

Further south, Judah's hegemony stretched out toward the plain, embracing Eqron, carried by fifth columnists, and Tell Batashi III, carried by assault (Kelm and Mazar 1985: 104-105), possibly domestic (below). Gath was under Hezekiah's sway (Na'aman 1974: 26-27), recovered, like Eqron (el-Amin 1953: 37-40) and Ashdod's territory, after Sargon's siege (as Lie 1929: 249-62). Ashdod's weakness created a power vacuum drawing both Judah and Ashkelon in. And of former Israelite possessions on the Philistine border, Hezekiah had apparently acquired Gezer and, probably, Gibbethon (above). According to 2 Kgs 18.8, Hezekiah controlled lands from Gath to Gaza (which need not imply a conquest of Gaza), suggesting he also played an active role in placing Sidqa on the throne in Ashkelon (which would account for Sennacherib's relative leniency there—Luckenbill 1924: 30.60–31.68). He may have refortified Tell 'Erani IV; but the destruction is not yet securely dated (Yeivin 1961: 6-10), and certainty must await the publication of B. Brandl's re-evaluation. This collocation raises the question whether Sennacherib reckoned some of the towns on the plain, such as Eltekeh, as Judaean. In any event, Hezekiah will also have assumed control of Tell Zayit, and, outside Lachish, Tell Hesi (Doermann and Fargo 1985; for a late eighth-century Phoenician name at the site, *lsmk*, possibly evidence of Assyrian deportation, Lemaire 1985) and Tell Najila (Bülow and Mitchell 1961). The region thus contained upward of twenty forts to which Sennacherib will have addressed his attentions.

The Negev did not altogether escape the furor (see above, and, generally, Na'aman 1979: 74-75). Tel Beersheba II was levelled (Aharoni 1973: 5-6; cf. Yadin 1976: 5-14; Aharoni and Aharoni 1976: 83), and it was levelled after the implementation of Hezekiah's reform (Aharoni 1974). It is not plain how Aroer 4 fared (see Biran and Cohen 1976): only recently built, it required extensive rebuilding in the seventh century (Biran and Cohen 1978), and two *lmlk* stamps were found at the site (Biran and Cohen 1975). The excavators now lean toward a late dating; as the next layer reflects Assyrian influence, though, their original dating, which would equally square with Na'aman's hypothesis of a Sargonic context (1986b: 13-14), was probably correct (see Biran 1987: 30-32). At Tel Malhata, there may have been contraction after the eighth century on the lower, southern part of the tell (Kochavi 1970; 1972b: 594); but in the seventh century the resettled site flourished, establishing trade links with Edom and the Mediterranean. Before a similar expansion, there are signs of an outpost at Tel Ira; and a small settlement existed at Bir a-Saba (Herzog, in correspondence). Further south, the Middle Fortress at Qadesh Barnea may have fallen; but it is doubtful whether Assyrian armies ranged quite so far without making themselves felt around Eilat (see Pratico 1985). Outside Beersheba, then, only Arad VIII shows unmistakable signs of a major conflagration, after considerable refitting at the end of the eighth century (Mazar and Netzer 1986; cf., however, Herzog 1987; Holladay 1988: 256-57). And here, the two stratified *lmlk* impressions, from stratum VII, must have arrived in the aftermath of the Assyrian destruction (whether under Sargon or Sennacherib), or, conceivably, a slightly later attack from the south. This is perhaps also true of the stamped handle at Kh. Gharreh.

In all, these regions offered something on the order of forty walled towns as potential targets. How many surrendered cannot be determined. The pattern of Assyrian tactics contradicts the assumption that more than a few were bypassed (and Saggs 1963: 151-54). Some targets, such as Halif and Beit Mirsim, seem strategically marginal;

but these may have figured in a flanking movement (below). Furthermore, there is evidence that Sennacherib penetrated the hill country as well. Three sites he assaulted lay on the verges of the hills—Halif, Beit Mirsim, and Beth Shemesh. Inside the hills, he reduced Khirbet Rabud, probably Debir (Kochavi 1974: 12-18).

The action against Rabud makes strategic sense as a manoeuvre to turn the Shephelah line from the south, a manoeuvre dictating assaults on Beit Mirsim, Halif and, if it was occupied at the time, Tel 'Eton. Such a thrust can only have been made with great circumspection and the systematic obliteration of garrisons on the path—for the hills were a region of great vulnerability to a marching field force. But even if contained south of Hebron, the invaders will have had contact with Duma, Adoraim, Eshtemoa, Khirbet Fuqeiqis (Kochavi 1972a: 65), Khirbet el-Marajim (Kochavi 1972a: 66) and several other forts.

The thrust toward Hebron may even have met with success. The excavations at Beth Zur, north of Hebron, produced few stratified remains. However, the preponderance of the published ceramic assemblage from stratum III (together with 11 *lmlk* stamps—Welten 1969: 90-91) appears to belong on the 701 horizon, with parallels at Lachish III, Beth Shemesh IIc and Tell Beit Mirsim A_2 (as Sellers 1933: 42 pl. 9.12,14; Lapp and Lapp 1957: 57, 59, 61-64, as fig. 15; 16.13-24; 19.13, 14; note Lapp 1981: 82-83). All the stratified pottery, including that beneath the only evidence of destruction uncovered in the excavations, is in this category (Sellers 1933: 37, 39 fig. 32, with the ring-burnished bowls; and, 42 pl. 9, the hole-mouth jars).

Beth Zur was occupied in the seventh century as a station on the Jerusalem–Hebron road. It may, nevertheless, have been resettled, perhaps chiefly in the citadel, on the ruins of a larger, eighth-century site (for the view that the site continued undisturbed, see Na'aman 1986b: 6). The case of Khirbet Rabud documents a tactical interest in the western slopes, and the virgate watershed, of the Judaean hills. Even if frustrated, this inroad would function as a feint, diverting resources from the Shephelah toward the centre. If successful, it will have cut all effective communications between Jerusalem, in the north, and the Shephelah, preventing flight while Sennacherib, having sealed off the northern access roads (Na'aman 1974) and then struck inland, rolled up the Shephelah from the south (2 Kgs 19.8; Mic. 1.10-12, 13-15). It will also have severed Jerusalem's lines of supply from the southern hills, the Negev, and Egypt. Most important, the settlement survey of Judah now being conducted by Avi Ofer indicates a low point in hill country occupation after 701, before resettlement in the seventh century.

That the Assyrians, then, should have reduced five to ten towns in the hill country is not too much to imagine. And the figure of forty-six walled towns is therefore probably on the mark. That Hezekiah found it necessary to stock so many garrisons is a sound indicator that his demographic resources were substantial. Should we reduce Sennacherib's captive count even by half, the result would be an average of 2,174 persons per fortress, or roughly 540 adult males. For a country in a state of emergency urbanization, this seems to fall on the low side. Sennacherib's own figure (4,351 persons, 1,080 adult males per fort) would suggest that Judah's general staff exercised a more sensible economy of scale.

IV. *The Countryside Reformed*

A. *The Depopulation of Judah*

On the record, then, Sennacherib left the countryside in ruins, and there is corroboration. Most obvious, if subject to the most dispute, are literary references. 2 Kgs 18.13, for example, makes the unusually clear, detailed statement that 'Sennacherib, king of Assyria, came up against all the fortified cities of Judah and captured them'. This ratifies explicitly the claims of the Assyrian annals, avoiding, like the annals, the claim of widespread property destruction. The verse is the more remarkable in that, in Kings, reports of campaigns that reached the capital usually omit or play down the foregoing action in the countryside.

It is worth mentioning that the summary of 2 Kgs 18.13 also corroborates Sennacherib's claims about the size of Hezekiah's tribute (18.14),[1] although it does seemingly place the payment of tribute before the fall of Lachish (18.16; cf. 19.8): 18.13-16 may be part of a reconstruction of the campaign—in two stages—so as to accommodate both the domestic tradition (2 Kgs 18.17–19.37; Isa. 14.24-27, dated

1. For Sennacherib's figures of 30 gold and 800 silver talents, 2 Kgs 18.14 has 30 (OG 300) gold and 300 silver talents. It is highly possible that the figure 'thirty' was applied mistakenly by the scribe to the quantity of silver as well (cf. the OG figure for gold, clearly displaced from MT's silver figure).

to 701 in Mettinger 1987: 139), possibly derived from a dedication (cf. *KAI* 202, where the agent of salvation is that of 2 Kgs 13.5), and the evidence from the Assyrian annals and the reliefs at Nineveh (cf. *ADD* 148 in 660). In this case, the text has little value as an independent witness; still, the report that Sennacherib destroyed 'all the fortresses' (not 46) in Judah matches the archaeological as well as the annalistic picture.

This same assertion has brothers in contemporary literature, not least in Isaiah's efforts to portray a devastated hinterland and the spared Jerusalem as an imprimatur on Hezekiah's reform (Isa. 1.7-9, 24-31; 2.5-11, 20; 3.1-4, 13-17, the 'daughters' not just suburbs, but all villages subordinate to Jerusalem, and women; 4.3, etc.). That Sennacherib's marauding was Yhwh's judgment on the rural cult (as well as government corruption) will have been the view of Hezekiah's ideologues at large (as Mic. 1.13; 5.9-13; Isa. 1.11-17), whose attacks on the cult (cf. Hos. 8.11-14) lie at the heart of the policy of centralization.[1] In fact, events in the countryside led to a prophecy that the countryside would be repopulated from the one population centre still left—Jerusalem (Isa. 37.30-32, where 37.32c reflects Isa. 9.6c, and 37.30-31 Isa. 9.2). Hezekiah's prophets used the fate of the hinterland in much the same way they had used the fate of the northern kingdom (see Mettinger 1987: 140-41)—as a judgment on others, justifying their own political programmes.

Of such non-historiographic references to the events of 701, Isa. 1.7-9 stands out (Alt 1953b: 242). After excoriating the nation as sinners (the survivors in Jerusalem are called 'captains of Sodom, people of Gomorrah' in 1.10), the prophet relates:

> Your land is desolation,
> Your towns are burnt with fire.

1. Shaw (1987) proposes instead to link such texts to a hypothetical revolt of the countryside against Jerusalem during the Syro-Ephraimite War under Ahaz, the hinterland towns joining in the Aramean revolt against Tiglath-Pileser II. But in the first place, it is Sargon, not Tiglath-Pileser, who styles himself 'subduer of Judah'. In the second, the author of Kings would have been pleased to relate a history of secession under Ahaz, a king whom he condemns roundly. For the view that the Syro-Ephraimite War never occurred, cf. Bickert 1987; but this extreme, and is based on the assumption that the two allies, Damascus and Israel, did not act in concert because only Aram earns mention in Kings.

Your soil, before you, aliens eat her,
And she is desolation like the overthrowing of aliens.

There remains the daughter of Zion,
Like a booth in a vineyard,
Like a lodge in a cucumber-patch,
Like a town preserved.

Had Yhwh of Hosts not left us a tiny remnant,
Like Sodom would we be,
Gomorrah we would resemble.

Zion's lonesome survival among the smouldering shambles of a people (cf. also Isa. 2.12-22; 3.2-4; 6.9-12) corresponds to one historical situation only—that reported in Sennacherib's annals, and expressed in 2 Kgs 18.13 (*all* the forts captured). The Isaianic concept of a 'remnant' repopulating Judah is actually a picture of the return of those sheltering behind the walls of the capital to the surrounding land in the wake of Sennacherib's departure.

That an earlier event, the Syro-Ephraimite War, could be the subject of this discourse is refuted by three considerations: first, the object of the Syro-Ephraimite coalition was to install a new dynasty (Isa. 7.6) in Judah to face Assyria, so the preservation of the indigenous population and architecture will have been a paramount consideration; second, Sennacherib alone can be said to have denuded Judah, turning it over to aliens, to the point at which Jerusalem's survival was a singular phenomenon; and, Isaiah's articulated posture on the Syro-Ephraimite threat was specifically that it was nugatory, and would be superseded by more serious Assyrian inroads (Isa. 7.5-17; 8.5-8). Isaiah thereafter applies similar imagery to the capital (as 4.3), speaking of the countryside as shaved bald (3.16-17, a reference to the hilltop settlements of the Judahite hills), as abandoned (5.5-7; 6.13), as 'flooded' with a flood to be evaded only in the capital (28.15, on which Halpern 1987a; cf. Mic. 1.9). The 701 campaign is in point (as Isa. 5.26-30), and Jerusalem is the only fortified centre Sennacherib's marauders failed to place under siege (further, Vogt 1986: 90-94; cf. van der Kooij 1986).

Similar implications emerge from 2 Kgs 19.28-32, where it is only Sennacherib's taunt of Jerusalem that provokes Yhwh's wrath, and where the resettlement of the countryside will be accomplished only by the Jerusalemite 'remnant'. This tradition, however late (see

Wilson 1980: 213-219; the argument on the resemblance of Hezekiah's to later prayers discounts the impact of modelling), is a product of Hezekian party thinking after the event. Moreover, passages and imagery similar to those in Isaiah recur in Micah, such as a section promising the rehabilitation of Judah through the depopulation of the countryside (5.9-13 after 5.1-8; cf. 7.13)—surviving the Assyrian assault ushers in a period of eschatological purity and prosperity.[1] That is, the Hezekian interpretation of the 701 campaign seems to have been that Assyria was the 'rod of [Yhwh]'s anger' until it independently turned on Jerusalem (as Isa. 10.5-34; cf. Mic. 4.8, 11-13

1. Mic. 1.2–4.7 concern Judah (1.5, 9; 3.10, 12; 4.2, 7), and Assyrian depradation, as in Israel, is at issue. Micah's prediction (3.12) of Jerusalem's destruction was located in this context no more than a century later (Jer. 26.18-19)—again, the reference is to destruction, not a Syro-Ephraimite takeover; a second prediction, of exile to Mesopotamia, comes in 4.10, probably a part of the same literary unit. So 1.10-16 allude to Shephelah destructions, 1.9 expressing the fact that the devastation reached as far as Jerusalem. Cf. also 2.8, 12-13. The 'captains' of Sodom of Isa. 1.10 (and 3.6, 7; 22.3) may be related to the 'captains' of Mic. 3.1, 9 given the term's infrequency (only six other occurrences). Note further the relationship of Mic. 4.14 (mentioning the Assyrian siege: cf. 5.4-5) to Isa. 10.24, and of Mic. 5.1 to Isa. 11.1 (and various passages in Micah, such as 3.1-3; 6.7-8, to Isa. 1.10-17). The superscriptions of Micah and Isaiah both employ the phrase, *'šr ḥzh 'l . . . wyrwšlym*. Mic. 1.2 and Isa. 1.2 invoke heaven and earth as witnesses. Mic. 1.6-9 and Isa. 1.5-9 speak of the devastation of the land up to Jerusalem, and both blame the judges (Mic. 3.1-4, 9-12; Isa. 1.21-23). And both speak of the refinement of Jerusalem effectively by suffering (Mic. 3.12 before 4 after 2.3-5; Isa. 1.18-20, 24-31). On Mic. 1.10-16 as a possible parallel to Isa. 10.28-32 in 701, cf. Shaw 1987, with the argument that rejoicing in the Shephelah reflects Jerusalem's comeuppance in the Syro-Ephraimite War; but Micah's words about rejoicing are probably ironic, as he announces the exile of the Shephelah. And Isaiah (2.2-4) and Micah (4.1-3) speak in identical terms of the necessity of returning from a war-time to a peace-time standing, in a word, of retooling (Armstrong, unpub.). Essentially, Micah and Isaiah 1–5; 9–12; 28–33 are in close agreement, and relate mainly to the events of 701. Isa. 14.24-27, holding that Assyria was broken in Yhwh's land, has been related to 701 by Mettinger (1987: 139). It seems to announce the end of Assyrian political ascendancy and to promise, later, an end to its economic demands (v 25, taking the 'yoke' as political, and the 'load' as economic, but this is notional). If so, it would be inappropriate much after 701. Nor is it unrelated to the earlier Isa. 9.3; 10.27. These texts seem to be a keystone of the 'miracle tradition' of Hezekiah's escape, which may in turn have required the later historian of Kings to reconstruct a double-campaign.

with 5.1-5, as Isa. 10.24 with 11.1-11). This view leaves the status of the countryside ambiguous: was Sennacherib's campaign a tangible divine judgment on the rural cult?

A second indication of rural depopulation is physical: fallow deer became a staple at Tel Batashi in the seventh century (Wapnish and Hesse unpub. a), where it was previously insignificant. In one household, for example, it represents thirteen per cent of the animal detritus. This change reflects unrestricted access to the hills, now, along with Tel Batashi, part of the hinterland of Eqron (so Na'aman 1987: 14 n. 21 against A. Mazar 1985: 321). The quantity of deer in the sample suggests that the consumers at Batashi were experiencing no competition from other deer hunters. Predators, chiefly human, were so depleted in the Shephelah and western hills that game could become a reliable component of the diet. The implication is that a vast preponderance of the hills population had been deported (and much competing livestock, as Sennacherib claims; cf. Isa. 5.5-6; A. Kempinski reports that fallow deer multiplied in the same region after 1948).

Third, after the invasion, Sennacherib assigned substantial portions of Judah to Philistia. His early inscriptions (the Rassam cylinder, the Oriental Institute Prism) report that he assigned the cities he had plundered to Ashdod, Eqron and Gaza; the Nineveh Bull inscription adds Ashkelon (with its new pro-Assyrian regime) to the list (Luckenbill 1924: 33.30-34; 70.29-30).

Eqron, the easternmost of these towns, bears witness to the process. Beth Shemesh, as noted above, showed signs of industrialization in connection with olives in the eighth century (Grant and Wright 1939: 75-84). In the seventh century, however, Tel Miqneh (IB), with 102 olive processing installations, 88 of them technically advanced (Eitam 1985; Dothan and Gitin 1986: 8), almost completely absorbed the Shephelah olive processing industry, with a capacity of 1.1 million litres per year. Eqron also developed an impressive wine production capacity (eight presses located to date), and was probably home to a major textile centre (Dothan and Gitin 1987: 215-218)—Eqron's textiles, too, may have flourished in the absence of serious competition for resources by Judah and several other Philistine centres (cf. Luckenbill 1924: 60.56; Tadmor 1966: a substantial portion of Hezekiah's tribute was paid in textiles). Secondary reuse of discarded olive processing equipment in stratum IB at Eqron may suggest a shrinking capacity as against the earlier IC (first uncovered in 1990 excavations—Gitin, in conversation). However, it is equally probable that the decline in production during the mid-to-late seventh century at Eqron is to be correlated with the resurgence of Judah, its repatriation and nucleation of the olive processing industry, and a simultaneous increase in Judah's southern trade diverting supplies away from the Mediterranean: the kings of Judah in the seventh century will have wanted desperately to recapture cash crops such as olives to put themselves on a sound financial footing (see further below).

With these accumulations came an unexampled prosperity: Eqron grew fat by siphoning off the olives, and the viticulture, of the western declivities; these were no longer intercepted by the Shephelah towns of Judah. Eqron availed herself of vast new markets opened up to her by the empire (note Na'aman 1987: 10-11; Gitin 1989b), burgeoning from a sleepy village into a sprawling town of fifty acres. Judaean pottery on the site (Dothan and Gitin 1985: 5; 1986: 8) may mean that Sennacherib contributed human as well as commercial resources to Eqron's floruit (Gitin [1989b] adduces evidence of deportation from Israel to Eqron); it surely signals the flow of goods from the mountains to the markets—the markets not just among Assyria's vassals, but also in the developing trade network of the Mediterranean basin unfurled in the seventh century by Phoenician mercantile resources. Eqron in particular developed a large and rich elite district (Area IV), in which East Greek pottery and Assyrian palace ware, as well as jewelry hoards, beautifully carved ivories and inscriptions, have been found (Gitin 1989a). Numerous ostraca bearing dedications to Asherah, and one reading 'to the sacred precinct', though not yet published, along with seven altars, attest that the elite area was home to a flourishing cult.[1]

1. The association of Asherah with trees (usually palms) makes her association with the olive industry at Eqron the more piquing: it may be that as Asherah gives suck to the gods, she is naturally associated with the production of liquids. Incense altars are also found in the processing area, one room closer to the street than the presses: it is thus possible that Asherah was invoked in the preparation of nourishment for the other gods. However, the burning of incense is regularly associated in Israelite (reformationist) literature with homage to gods inferior to Yhwh called baals and asherot/ashtarot, which are generic names for Israelite gods and goddesses (styled foreign in Josianic literature, but see Halpern 1987b; cf. Akk. *ilu, ištarāte*). If

That is, Judahite centres no longer stood between the benefits of highlands agriculture and the coastal plain. Further, between Eqron and the Shephelah centres, increased deer consumption (above) and a (growing?) olive industry (Kelm and Mazar 1985: 104-107; A. Mazar 1985: 310-11) at Batashi corroborate the inference. This situation—the hills and Shephelah countryside utterly denuded, the fat places preyed upon by aliens, Hezekiah's castle and environs alone spared the torch—is the one to which Isa. 1.7-9 makes such poignant reference. Overall, texts, archaeology, military history and the historiographic background of the annals all converge on what Sennacherib tells us.

It is possible, as older scholars contended, that Hezekiah's reform was a retrojection to a king favoured by Yhwh of a policy adopted by Josiah (as Wellhausen 1965: 46-47, 480-81; latterly, Handy 1988). Or perhaps Hezekiah made a virtue of necessity, and promulgated centralization in Sennacherib's wake. But most likely, Hezekiah's reform was his preparation for revolt (Rowley 1962).

Hezekiah had been waiting for Sennacherib. He suppressed rural cults (further below), whether first excepting those in the forts (as Arad VIII: Aharoni 1968: 26-27; on Lachish, Mic. 1.13), or including them (Tel Beersheba II: Aharoni 1974, above). If garrison temples were initially exempted (and here, much turns on the treatment of the altars of Arad VIII; note Holladay 1987: 256-57, esp. Ussishkin 1988; on incense altars, Gitin 1989b), subsequent events led Hezekiah's exponents to disown them. In any case, Hezekiah herded the free

Asherah (mention of whom is still restricted to ostraca found in the elite area) was the object of the incense offerings (or first fruits of the presses) in the industrial zone, we would have at Eqron the first reflex of the theology against which Israel's reformationist literature is railing. In this case, Gitin's demonstration (1989b) that incense altars of a type formerly found in Israel and Judah appear only in Eqron in the 7th century may well indicate an adoption or at least socialization, as he claims, of Israelite folk religion at the site. This would not be altogether inconsistent with the occurrence of the Phoenician (or Aramaic?) name, *ḥmlk* (A) himelek (cf. [A] hiram), on the site (but written in Aramic script!). However, the incense altars at Arad may be 7th-century—Ussishkin 1988. Note, in any case, that the situation at Philistine Eqron in the 7th century establishes the basis for later associations of Demeter with the Philistine coast. As to other gods at Eqron, an ostracon uncovered in 1990 reads 'holy to *ḥq..š*' (another reads, 'holy to Asherah'), a divine name possibly from a dialect related to that of the patronymics (?) found in the ostraca from Tel Jemme (Naveh 1985). This would tend to sustain Kempinski's views (1987) on the Jemme ostraca.

peasantry under arms into points of military concentration. The Chronicler, who either reconstructs or has information about the preparations in Jerusalem (2 Chron. 32.2-6), preserves echoes of this policy (32.27-29) without recognizing its strategic or cultic linkage (cf. 32.30). Rosenbaum (1979) has argued that the Chronicler had access to reliable sources concerning Hezekiah (see also Halpern 1981b). This argument, and the reflection of Hezekiah's countryside policies without a sense of their integration into a broader political program, tend to reinforce one another.

Sennacherib and Hezekiah between them left the Judahite countryside ravaged. Jerusalem therefore quadrupled in size, reaching a population on the order of 25,000 (Broshi 1974; Avigad 1983: 26-60; Broshi and Barkay 1985: 111-19). Outside of the bloated capital, and its immediate dependencies, little manpower could have been available for resettlement—a reality reflected in the concept of repopulation from Jerusalem that Isaiah advanced (above). Sennacherib established an Assyrian military presence in the Shephelah (as Gezer—Spieckermann 1982: 141), near Jerusalem (the ware at Tell en-Nasbeh and Ramat Rahel; cf. van der Kooij 1986), and in the plain, guarding the routes inland toward Arabia (as Tell Jemme and the enormous fortress inland at Tel Haror, in sight of Jemme and, to the east, of Tel Šera' [where a seventh–sixth-century bone sceptre parallels others found in Jerusalem and at Eqron]). An Assyrian entrepot, founded in the mid-eighth century by Sargon, and enduring into the 5th century, particularly flourished at Ruqeish (Oren *et al* 1986, identifying it with Sargon's 'sealed quay of Egypt'; cf. Reich 1984): Assyria employed Philistia as its central marketing agency, for Egypt, for the southern trade, and for the sea-lanes of the Mediterranean. Its strategy seems to have been to privilege the inland centres (Eqron, Haror) in order to retain control over the direction of resources to gateway sites (ports), and thus to determine their economic fates without engaging in siege operations proper: revolts by coastal sites were particularly dangerous, as supply by sea could protract operations for years. Indeed, it was in reaction to Assyrian expansionism that Phoenicia began to reach out toward the western Mediterranean in the first place, starting in the ninth century, creating an artificial hinterland on which to draw for resources.

Sennacherib reassigned rural Judah to Ashdod and Gaza, which remained loyal, and to loyalist kings of Eqron and Ashkelon, whom he restored—and his texts suggest the reallocation embraced the entire hinterland, which may well have been the theory (Alt 1953b: 242-49; cf. Na'aman 1979: 83-86; 1986b: 17). Sennacherib also claims to have plundered all the livestock in the country. Philistia reoccupied the western countryside (as Batashi II); Hezekiah's manpower focused in the capital. If Sennacherib left some exiles in the vicinity, no significant number remained a part of Hezekiah's domain (cf. Stohlmann 1983: 161 for the view that many fugitives eluded Sennacherib and returned home on his departure). In the circumstances, and given Manasseh's later standing, we may dismiss the suggestion that Hezekiah later renewed his revolt (Shea 1985; Begg 1987).

In sum, Judah entered the seventh century in a state of emergency urbanization. The consequences of this circumstance merit contemplation. Yet to assess the impact of the catastrophe that befell the country, we must subpoena into evidence what can be known about the traditional social fabric of Judah. Only then will it be possible to determine what revolutions in society, in royal policy, and in popular mores the changes of 701 wrought.

B. *The Traditional Organization of the Countryside*

Because Israelite kinship terminology is so plastic, the lines between different levels of tribal organization often blur. However, the skeletal structure of the old Judahite kinship system is made visible in several texts, the simplest of which is Josh. 7.14-18 (cf. 1 Sam. 10.19-21, reading with OG). Here, four segmentary levels are in evidence:

a) the 'tribe—usually referred to as the *maṭṭe*[h] or *šēbeṭ*, but sometimes called a *bêt 'āb* (lit., 'father's house') or *mišpāḥâ*;
b) the clan, or, better, patriclan—called the *mišpāḥâ* or, at times, the *bêt 'āb* —in its military incarnation this may be referred to as the *'elep*, or 'thousand' (Mendenhall 1958), as in 1 Sam. 10.19.
c) the extended family, or household—*bayit* ('house'), *bêt 'āb* (or *bêt* PN);
d) the individual adult male—*gbr*, usually married.

Thus, in Josh. 7.14-18, sortition singles out the tribe of Judah, from among all the other tribes; within the tribe of Judah, the clan of Zerah is distinguished. Zerah is reviewed by 'individuals', the 'house' of Zabdi being selected. This entity is then paraded by 'individuals', and

Achan the son of Karmi the son of Zabdi is chosen—an adult male with sons and daughters and his own establishment (7.24), all of whom share his own fate.

In a brilliant study of the Israelite family, L.E. Stager has attempted to locate kinship units in the ground, specifically in the housing patterns of Iron Age villages (1985: 17-21). Stager focused attention on the housing compounds, consisting of several houses butted one against the other, that occur in Iron I villages. Though local practice may have varied (see Goody 1969: 120-46), texts consistently indicate the predomination of patri-virilocal marriage and patrilateral inheritance. The compound, then, reflects the practice of married sons building houses abutting their father's and brothers' homes. The practice persists in modern Arab villages in Israel. Examples are reasonably abundant at small sites in the Iron Age, into Iron II at such sites as Tell Beit Mirsim (A^2; esp. Albright 1943: pl. VII), Beth Shemesh, and even some larger towns, such as Tell en-Nasbeh and Tell el-Far'ah (for which see de Vaux 1955: pl. VI; Chambon 1984: 24, plan III, 149B, 161, 163, 410A, 436, plan V, 362, 366, 336).

It is not to be presumed that such compounds were universal, as Wilson has observed on the basis of the excavations at Tel Masos (Wilson 1983: 62-63; see Fritz and Kempinski 1983: 7-91; we might add Finkelstein 1986, among others). Rather, they attest a form of kinship organization that often, but not necessarily always, articulated itself in architectural abutment. Other factors entered in, such as limitations of space, defence, urban planning, and so on (see Shiloh 1988). Still, whether consisting of adjoining houses, or houses in a single, spatially-defined area, the compound deserves investigation.

Stager concluded that the compound is at most that of an extended family, which would represent maximally some 25–40 individuals. The maximum number of abutting houses seems to be about five, with fewer more the rule. Assuming that the compound originates as an extended family unit, it is essentially a (patri)lineage, whose members can prove their common descent. The main house, that of the lineage founder (see, e.g., Finkelstein 1986: 15), may have figured in reckoning the double-inheritance of eldest male heir (Deut. 21.17), either as a double-portion of itself, or as a second house to be appropriated in the compound (as opposed to the single house of each of the younger brothers). In any event, the location of ovens at sites such as Tell Beit Mirsim A^2 NW in common courtrooms or in alleys accessible to all units of a compound (see now Vanderhooft 1990) indicates that at least some aspects of household economy were shared—minimally, fuel preparation and cooking, and maximally the main meals.

Similarly, Deut. 25.5 provides for the levirate 'when brothers live together': the widow should not be sent 'outside'. Plainly, the brothers are married, which implies that each has his own establishment. And that the eldest son of the levirate should 'arise in the name of [the levir's] dead brother' (Deut. 25.6) suggests that, to preserve the son's inheritance, the widow may typically have remained in possession of her husband's house—ideally, in polygamous households, wives occupied separate suites in any case (Rachel and Leah, for example, have separate tents, and this remains Bedouin practice today). But the principal point is, the text assumes that the brothers remain in the same compound—whether in abutting houses or in a single, defined neighbourhood. The institution of the levirate, then, in its Deuteronomic instantiation (against Ruth 4.3-6), depends on the normalcy of compound construction.

Again, in Judg. 17.4-5, Micah has a 'house', in which he installs a shrine and a priest. This is a separate 'house of God', inside Micah's compound, to which the priest is entitled as though he were one of Micah's sons (17.11). Several further references—one to Micah's 'houses', one to 'the house of the Levite lad at the house of Micah'—make it clear that this is the case (17.5, 11-12; 18.2-3, 13-15). Indeed, when the tribe of Dan as a whole 'came to the house of Micah, the five men who had gone to reconnoitre the land of Laish answered and said to their brothers, "Do you know that in these houses there is an ephod and teraphim and a carved image and its regalia?"' (18.13-15): Micah's house consists of a number of houses. The 'houses that were with Micah's house' (18.22), whose residents took Micah's part in a contretemps with the tribe of Dan, have been identified by Gottwald (1979: 291-92) and Stager (1985: 22) as those of his compound mates; in light of the evidence here, it seems more probable that neighbouring compounds are involved. In any case, 'the house of Micah' in the account is in fact 'Micah's compound'. By the same token, the compound chief in the case of Achan son of Karmi is at best Achan's grandfather ('the house' of Zabdi, Josh. 7.18). Although tents, not houses, are the idiom of discourse in this account, the social assumptions are those of Iron Age Israel, and the fact that Achan has his own tent, and household, inside Zabdi's compound is significant.

After the compound, or lineage, scholars generally identify the primary tribal section, the clan (*mišpāḥâ*, or primary kinship section) as the next rung on the kinship ladder (de Geus 1976; Gottwald 1979: 257-84; Stager 1985: 20-22; Wilson 1983: 63). This may be precipitate. Most texts enumerate between four and eight clans, in general, for each tribe, and no more than six for most (see Gottwald 1979: 239-318; Halpern 1983: 115-16)—the ten-tribe Israel of the Song of Deborah, for example, fields forty clan regiments (Judg. 5.8). Judah is always divided into four or five clans. As the Samaria Ostraca attest, the few clans named for Manasseh were indeed the functioning subunits of the tribe—and no clan name unrecorded in biblical genealogies appears in the ostraca. Yet, such large units would have been unwieldy tools for managing local political affairs, which is why scholars tend to posit a great number of smaller clans, consisting of a few extended families only—who banded together, not necessarily along descent lines—for common defence and administration. The trouble is, the texts never inform us of such entities. The temptation is therefore to identify the village as an intermediate political unit (Mendenhall 1983).

There is a great deal to be said on behalf of this alternative. Between clan names and patrilineages in Israelite genealogies, we often find the names of regional eponyms, of town eponyms, or of town founders. Of critical importance is the fact that the village is implicitly understood to be a kin-unit, with one founder (as 1 Chron. 2.24, 42-55; cf. Demsky 1971: 19). It is sometimes named for a founder or ancestor (B. Mazar 1981; Stager 1985: 23-24). It can even be called a 'mother-unit' (*'ēm*—2 Sam. 20.19; cf. Ezek. 21.26; Malamat 1979).

This usage allows a speaker to divide the patriclan into sections, just as discussion of the 'mother-units' (*'ummôt*) of the tribes (Rachel, Leah, Bilhah, Zilpah) subdivides the nation. The urge to categorize regions in terms of matrilineage echoes, too, in the expression 'daughters' for small settlements in the hinterland of a larger town (as 'daughters of Zion' for the settlements of Judah). Further, Hebrew usage assumes the consanguinity of village and town residents: settlement names, among other things, are governed by 'elders', a term almost always used with kin-units (Halpern 1981: 196-97). A. Malamat has observed (1979: 535) that Jer. 3.14, 'I will take you one from each village, two from each clan (*mišpāḥâ*)', implies that the clan is larger than the village, but that the village is a unit in the clan hierarchy. The genealogical metaphor generally reflects the fact that villages were administrative units. The metaphor is apt, though (Malamat 1979), because the reality of village life is such that agnatic and affinal ties weld the population together. Simultaneously, an Israelite could have expressed the consanguinity of the 'clan' and the even closer coherence of each of two villages by suggesting that a single male was the ancestor of both villages, by different wives.

It is important to recognize that the congruence of the village with a tightly-knit section of a clan was theoretical rather than real. In small settlements, no doubt, the denizens were all close relations (so the various genetic defects reflected in Risdon 1939 in Lachish). But in larger villages (small towns and large), various 'families' will have been represented. Thus, 1 Chron. 2.53 speaks of four *mišpāḥôt* ('families', 'clans') occupying Qiryath Yearim, and this will have been the rule rather than the exception (see below on Judg. 9).

Even the compound will not have reflected kinship bonds in towns where circumvallation limited new construction, where economic constraints dictated the sale of property, or where the accidents of fertility and of gender left housing stock available for disposal. Conversely, where there was a surfeit of male grandchildren, or as a condition of exogamous matches, new compounds might be founded, either within the village or on neighbouring hilltops. Thus a village might consist of several extended families (patrilineages), all closely related in accordance with the theory governing Hebrew usage. A town, even on the order of Tell Beit Mirsim (pop. c. 350, max. 840 on the coefficient of Broshi and Gophna 1984: 42) might comprise one or two 'expanded families'—that is, combinations of extended families—like the four represented at Qiryath Yearim. These would be local sections usually of one, but perhaps sometimes of more 'clans' of the 'tribe'. Indeed, in the cases of larger settlements, as in the case of shrines (Shechem, Jerusalem), there may even have been a tendency to spring up not just on routes of commerce, but actually at intersections of kin-group territories.

The village, in sum, was not the real intermediate kinship entity between the clans and the patrilineages. Rather, local sectors of the clans functioned as the agencies of interhousehold administration. These clan sectors—corresponding to the clans hypothesized by Gottwald, Stager and Wilson—transcended individual compounds. In short, they were much like the Arab village hamula (a word whose use is as plastic as that of biblical kinship terminology), or expanded family—a group of (real or fictional) common ancestry, traced to an eponym, in which all males of one's own generation are regarded as *ibn 'amm*, 'cousin', and all males of the older generation are regarded as *'amm*, 'uncle'.

It is a function of their identity with the large clans, and of the plasticity of the kinship terminology (as with 'hamula') that we have no lexical reflection of the clan sectors. But the existence of such forms of kinship organization finds reflection in a wide variety of texts. Ezra 8, for example, enumerates coherent kin-groups with 28–300 adult males—groups too small to be quarter-tribes, but for the most part too large (c. 110–1,200) to be lineages or compounds (for another view, not contradictory, see Smith 1988). In 1 Chron. 2.49-55, likewise, clan sectors of Hur—itself a section of the clan, Hezron—populate about eleven villages in Judah (similarly 2.42-45). Yet in some cases, a village is said to have been divided among two or more 'families' (*mišpāḥôt*: as 1 Chron. 2.43, 52-54; 4.2, 21). These were operative kin-groups intermediate between the clan and the compound, but not congruent with a whole village. If the Greek is correct (and it probably is), the compound head with the great-grandchildren in Josh. 17.16-18 is in fact the eponym of a clan sector (= Zimri of 1 Chron. 2.6).

The reference to 'the men who were in the "houses" that were "with" Micah's "house"' in Judg. 18.22 may presuppose the same social configuration. These men act in concert with Micah against outsiders. However, the awkward formulation does not restrict itself to the lineage, avoiding the simpler, 'the men of Micah's house', which is what one would expect (given 17.4-5, 12; 18.2-3, 13-15) were the compound alone in issue. And 18.22 stipulates that the 'men' had been summoned (*nz'qw*) to muster. The likelihood is that a whole clan sector is in point. Some corroboration can be found in the fact that the Danite spies, too, were lodged '"with" Micah's house', but had to 'turn aside' in order to find the Levite serving in the shrine there (18.3). Evidently, they were not lodged inside the compound, but by it—and the 'houses that were "with" Micah's compound' were those other compounds lying in the same vicinity or settlement. Alternatively, the model may be that of a settlement like Izbet Sartah II, where a large manor house was surrounded by more ordinary stock, perhaps the homes of less affluent clan-sector-mates (see Finkelstein 1986: 15). In any event, Dan's 600 warriors are imagined as cowing, not a group of five adult males, but one of, say, twenty to fifty: Micah's pursuit (of a group of five Danite ruffians who have been seen skulking about the compound) is not risible to begin with; the literary topos is, he organizes a respectable posse to pursue the five men, and then his posse encounters the main Danite detachment.

The operation of a clan-sector, smaller than a town but larger than a compound, underlies Isaiah's description of men pressing military captaincies on others in their 'father's house' (3.6-7), where the unit presumably exceeds in size an establishment such as the compound, which could produce only five or so able-bodied adult males. The same implication is even more stark in the case where Abimelek, the pretender to the throne of Shechem in Judg. 9.1, lobbies his mother's natal clan sector (*mišpaḥat bêt 'ᵃbî 'immô*) to support his enthronement. Since his mother's 'father's compound' can hardly consist of five houses and yet succeed in carrying the town as a whole, one must presume that demographic or other pressure has fissured families off from the compound, leading to the evolution of a multi-compound 'father's house' (*bêt 'ab*; cf. 2 Sam. 9.10, 12), i.e., a primary section of the clan as a whole.

To these cases may be added that of a curse on the house of Eli, and on the house of his father, against their ever producing an elder—i.e., a compound head (2 Sam. 2.31-32).[1] The curse on the house of Eli himself precludes the establishment of independent households with children in Eli's compound (lineage, house; cf. 2 Sam. 3.29; 7.19, 29). The curse on Eli's father's house addresses itself to Eli's clan sector, not his father's physical compound (part of which he no doubt inherited): hence the 85 adult males in 1 Sam. 22.11, 15-18, far too many for a single compound, and far too few for a fifth of a tribe. In this light, Jeremiah's (3.14) 'one from each village, two from each patriclan' (*mišpāḥâ*) may refer to the 'clan sector', a body numerically

1. That the expression, 'elder of the house of PN' (2 Sam. 12.17; Gen. 24.2; 50.7) refers to servants suggests that the compound head alone had the status of an elder in dealings with other compounds, at least in the first generation. Where the father was deceased, however, or even infirm, the situation is less clear: it seems inherently unlikely that one had to leave the compound in order to join in the elders' deliberations.

equivalent to one or more villages, or a part of a city.

The most vivid illustration of the clan sector at work, however, stems from a hypothetical case in the Davidic Court History. In 2 Sam. 14.7, the 'wise woman of Tekoa' presents a plea for her suppositious fratricidal son, whose death 'all the *mišpāḥâ*' demand. Now, the mother's compound-mates, her son's paternal uncles and cousins, if any, might be expected to be sympathetic to her, since they must do levirate duty, endangering their own legacies (cf. Ruth 4.6). Yet the deceased husband's *mišpāḥâ* are all for retribution. They are numerous enough to prohibit individual identification (14.7, 10). Against the *mišpāḥâ*, the mother offers to bear the guilt herself—with her *bêt 'āb*. Since the guilt cannot be taken on unwillingly, or even unknowingly, to judge from other texts, and since the *mišpāḥâ* are trying to avoid guilt by expunging it, not taking it upon themselves, it seems that the woman has introduced a distinction between her husband's *bêt 'āb,* the compound in which she resides, and her husband's *mišpāḥâ*, the local clan sector, here standing in for the clan as a whole—which is far too widely distributed geographically to take a hand in justice in a single village. This view draws confirmation from the fact that the term *mišpāḥâ* is never used to designate a mere extended family, but always refers to the clan sector, or clan, or, metaphorically, the primary section of some larger kinship unit (Vanderhooft 1990). A similar cleavage appears in Judg. 6.27, where the clan is Abiezer, but where the local compounds are divided. The clan sector (*mišpāḥâ)* enforces justice (2 Sam. 14.9); the compound in the instance resists it.

C. *Continuity in the Clan Sector*

In the clan sector, then, one can locate the functioning medium of village and town administration in the countryside. First, it is the local seat of jurisprudence: the elders are probably the compound heads, and these administer justice, with their male dependents, in matters transcending the bournes of the compound. Lawcodes and narratives sometimes presuppose the congruence of the settlement with the clan sector in juridical contexts, where the elders presided and the male dependents executed sentence (Deut. 21.18-21; 22.14-21; 25.5-10; Ruth 4.2, 9; Halpern 1981: 199-200). But these regulations would serve equally in cases involving more than a single clan sector (note Wilson 1983).

No doubt the notional equivalence of clan sector and settlement was reinforced by partial endogamy—statistical distortion in gender distribution in the clan sector's small population would prohibit a rate much higher than forty per cent—which would minimize the alienation of property. It is no coincidence, after all, that the incest taboos stop short of prohibiting (patrilateral parallel—Goody 1969: 216-34) cousin marriage (cf. 1 Kgs 15.2; Gen. 24.15; 29.10 [matrilateral cross-cousin]). Conversely, the same laws effectively prohibit wife-exchange between proprietors of residential units inside the compound in the first generation (Lev. 18.6-20; 20.11-12; Deut. 27.22; cf. Gen. 20.12; 2 Sam. 13.12-13): that is, brothers could not wed co-resident half-sisters, aunts or brothers' daughters. The fact that the incest taboos end just short of prohibiting parallel cousin marriage is an indication that that was the preferred marriage pattern. Schematically, the compound was exogamous (in the first generation) within a clan sector with a preference for endogamy.

Similarly, the clan sector is the seat of real estate title. Thus, the ideal 'redeemer' is the paternal uncle or cousin, which is to say, a former compound mate (Jer. 32.6; Deut. 25.5; Amos 6.10). But more distant relations are also eligible to fulfill the role—as Leviticus (25.47-49) and Ruth (2.1, 20; 4.4) provide. This customary complex, like that of the 'blood avenger' (2 Sam. 14.11) presumes cohesion not in the clan, but in the clan sector, otherwise village land could fall permanently into absentee hands, the very eventuality against which the practice of land redemption is directed. The Deuteronomic levirate, similarly, represents another method of keeping property within the compound.

Along with blood claims and claims on the land, the clan sector shared its ancestry. Indeed, ancestry and the common treatment of the ancestors were a language in which claims to property could reliably be lodged. If it is impossible to gauge the size of the clan sectors architecturally—compounds being liable to fracture, and some clan sectors dividing their lodgings across two or more towns or villages (1 Chron. 2.52, 54; see Stager 1985: 20)—their size is sometimes expressed through burial customs (as Humphreys 1980: 122-23; note O'Shea 1984: 3-13; Pearson 1982).

Most Israelite rock-cut tombs before the seventh century were multi-chambered. In each chamber, skeletal remains, once the bodies had decomposed, were swept from the burial benches into repositories dug out underneath them. For the extended family (the *bêt 'āb*), there was no regular need for more than three benches: even if every male for four generations had two male offspring, the tomb would house only thirty adult interments in a century, and fifteen to twenty would be more realistic. Large tombs, therefore, or crowded tombs like those at Tel 'Ira, express supra-compound relationships—the tomb of a great-grandfather is already shared by second cousins, and having the tomb in common would have reinforced solidarity in a group whose effective kinship network reached across the limits of extended families.

From this it follows that the clan sector, the hamula, was probably the focus of the ancestral cult. One text illustrates the point: David takes leave from Saul on the pretext of having an 'annual sacrifice of the whole *mišpāḥâ*' (1 Sam. 20.6). This annual event is restricted to the 'family'—it is certainly distinguished from a national festival. But it can hardly be envisioned as a sort of birthday celebration restricted to Jesse's compound (never denoted, in any case, by the term, *mišpāḥâ* 'primary [tribal] section'; see above). A clan sector celebration, a feast of the ancestors, must be in reference. Indeed, the custom of pouring the blood of one's sacrifice into the earth (Deut. 12.21-24; 15.23; Lev. 17.10-14), appropriated early as a rite for Yhwh (Exod. 23.18; 34.25; 1 Sam. 14.32-35; Deut. 12.13-28; Exod. 29.12; Lev. 3.17; 4.7, 18, 25, 30, 34; 7.26-27; 17.10-12; Ezek. 33.25), may have originated as an ancestral offering; by the time of P (probably seventh-century), it was understood to preempt ancestral ritual (construed as a communion of eating meat without draining the blood—Lev. 19.26-32). In any case, the informal sacrifice around which the patrilineal clan sectors gathered was one directed toward the ancestors.

Each hamula, then, had property (potentially) in common: stretches of land, modest herds, an altar or two (Judg. 17.4 with 18.22; note Judg. 6.25-30, where the clan sector share in Joash's altar), and one or more bench-tombs (cf. Goody 1962: 410-12 on the Lo Dagaa). The bench tombs housed those to whom the living owed their right to the use of the land. Compound fracture might occur under demographic or exogamic pressures, as extended families fissured into neighbouring compounds and sent out tendrils to nearby settlements. Under these pressures, however, the centripetal forces of endogamy, labour exchange, common property rights and descent, and common cultic and ancestral duties held the local clan sector together.

The extended family compound furnished an environment in which three to five generations of each family lived, bred, worked and worshipped together, surrounded by less proximate relations. These realities fostered the doctrine of collective reward, of a god who visits sin on children unto the third and fourth generation (Exod. 20.5), which is, on the co-residents of a compound (see Malamat 1982; note, too, *ABL* 453.13-19). The fourth generation equates to second cousins, perhaps the limit of the extended family, even the linkage across the lines of the extended family within the expanded family. Since Yhwh reserves persecution to the descendants of 'those who hate him', of traitors, the punishment represents the utter attainder of all compound-heirs (not necessarily compound-mates, except in the case of a paterfamilias) and the endangering of clan-sector mates.

The Israelite inherited the house of his ancestors, the fields of his ancestors, the tools of his ancestors, the gods of his ancestors, and, in the end, the place of his ancestors in the tomb. The continuity between generations was a reality, a grim reality for those whose inheritance was a flotsam of sour grapes. This is the environment that vanished in Hezekiah's, and Sennacherib's, reforms.

V. *The Aftermath*

Hezekiah's policies created a Judah in which the rural landowners and the clans had been stripped of their power, in which court parties and the standing army were ascendant. The rural priesthoods lost direct access to agricultural revenues as the state took formal control of the cult (cf. 2 Chron. 31.15); the state probably underwent a transition from tax farming through priests (see Ahlström 1982) and settlement heads to bureaucratic tax collection. The tradition that Hezekiah registered the priesthoods (2 Chron. 31.16-20), though possibly deduced from his registration of the lineages (1 Chron. 4.41) in preparation for their concentration in the forts, fits flawlessly into this scheme of things. With the priests and the population under crown control, countryside conservativism could no longer put the brake on royal innovation. Not to underrate the staying power of traditional modes of thought, the eighth-century elite, amid a growing accumulation of wealth that made itself felt throughout the country (e.g. King 1989), had amassed a welter of fresh doctrine, the intellectual explosion of which expressed itself both in Hezekiah's reform and in the assembly of the first written corpus of classical prophecy. But this is to address the short-lived state of things in Judah before the summer of 701. What of the aftermath of Sennacherib's spring?

The great task confronting Hezekiah's son, Manasseh, was to recover and resettle Judah. This he did, though the processes by which he did so are more or less opaque to us. The generally infertile wilderness regions of eastern Judah probably never fell under effective Philistine control, and the same may be true of the mountain ridges. In the south, the territorial competitor was not Philistia, but Edom, a power poor in population, and weakened by Assyria's Arabian campaigns (on which, Eph'al 1984: 81-169). Still, it seems likely that Edomite territorial designs on Judah in the seventh century had their ideological roots in the period when Sennacherib was dismembering Hezekiah's territory, and Edom was not explicitly included in the feast.

On the western hillslopes, Philistia retained control for a longer period. The long gap between the destruction of stratum III and the construction of stratum II at Lachish, the anchor of the Shephelah defensive system and of its southern extension around Tel Erani, Tel Hesi and Tel Nagila, suggests that Jerusalem reasserted its authority over the Shephelah no earlier than mid-century (Ussishkin 1977; 1983: 133-34; only around Jerusalem is the pottery sequence unbroken after 701). Correspondingly, the Shephelah remained sparsely settled throughout the century: the painstaking survey of Yehuda Dagan revealed that there were only a few sites, mainly 0.5–1 ha. in size (in correspondence). This is no more than we should expect: so long as Philistia was able to withstand Judah's inroads, it will have held onto the Shephelah, for military reasons as well as economic. Indeed, some of the Shephelah sites themselves may have been Philistine farmsteads.

Nevertheless, Manasseh, under Assyrian supervision (Spieckermann 1982: 307-16), accomplished an astonishing revival. By the late seventh century, almost all the sites destroyed by Sennacherib had been reclaimed. In addition, a line of small settlements was pushed out down toward the Dead Sea at Tel Goren and in the Buqeiah farmsteads (see Cross and Milik 1956; Stager 1975; A. Mazar 1982; Mazar, Amit and Elan 1983) and at Tel Masos, Tel Ira, Aroer, Horvat Uzza and Qadesh Barnea, among others, into the Aravah and through the south (see the list of settlements in the wilderness district of Joshua 15; Na'aman 1987: 5-6; Cohen 1986: 111-12).

Manasseh's resettlement was systematic. Its distribution reflects an interest in cash crops and the spice trade from the south. An Arabian presence in Jerusalem (Shiloh 1987) indicates a nexus from the south through the capital integrated with the Assyrian trade network Sargon created by locating Arabs in Samaria and Damascus, and secured by Sargonid campaigns in Arabia (Tadmor 1958: 77-78; Luckenbill 1926.2.118; Lie 1929: 20.120-22.123; Gadd 1954: 179-80; Elat 1977: 131-38; but note Yadin 1969), where Sargon himself installed a trading colony (on the identity of which, Reich 1984; Oren *et al* 1986). This interest in the southern trade was ongoing (see Eph'al 1984: 112-69), and was in some measure both reflected and, one suspects, heightened by Sennacherib's daring naval campaign in the Persian Gulf, and by the destruction of Babylon in 689. In any event, the centres of southern Transjordan flourished in this era, presumably by mediating the flow of southern goods to various reaches of Assyria's empire. Over the course of the seventh century, Edom waxed increasingly strong (Bennett 1983; 1984; Pratico 1985 on Kheleifeh IV; Hart 1986; 1988; Na'aman 1987: 10). Possibly, its growth was fed by Assyrian deportations (Hart 1986: 54-57). At Horvat Uzza, the seventh–sixth-century onomasticon includes Edomite names (Beit-Arieh and Cresson 1985); there, a seventh-century bulla depicts Sin of Harran (Beck 1986b), suggesting an Aramean presence in the vicinity, quite possibly to the south, in Edom proper. Edom expanded up to the borders of southern Judah, even erecting a temple at Horvat Qitmit (Beit-Arieh 1986; for the horned goddess there, Beck 1986a; further, below). Only the resurgence of Babylon at the end of the century initiated a period of decline.

Judahite interest in southern goods was equally strong and equally natural, which is why royal projects on the Red Sea are a staple theme in the books of Kings. Earlier, Ahaz had submitted to Tiglath-Pileser in order to avert or reverse the loss of Eilat (2 Kgs 16.5-6). With the Phoenician markets open, the south was the logical hinterland for Jerusalem (as Hiram and Solomon, and the Negev developed in the tenth century; Jehoshaphat and Ahaziah; Uzziah building Eilat during the reign of Jeroboam II). The loss of this resource, in EB III, had propelled the wealthy south of EB II into ruin, and in the Iron Age, the importance of the trade was old hat to the rulers of Mesopotamia and Egypt. Necho's confrontation with Josiah, part of the struggle for the Assyrian empire (Malamat 1973), may also have turned on local competition over trade: not long after, Necho dug a canal to secure communications with the Arabian peninsula, while Nabonidus was slightly later to transfer his residence to Teima for the same reason.

Much of the tension between Judah and Edom will have turned on competition as to whether the southern goods were to flow north or west. Nevertheless, Judah's southern stations were riddled with Edomite personnel (Arad ostraca, 'Uzza ostracon) and goods (E. Mazar 1985; Beit-Arieh and Cresson 1985; Biran and Cohen 1976; Kochavi 1970). The location of the Edomite shrine at Qitmit, too, lends support to A. Kempinski's argument that the Beersheba Valley was resettled under Edomite pressure (Beit-Arieh and Beck 1987). That this means that the region was not under Manasseh's effective control—that Edomite elements were proxies for Philistia in the south during the period when Sennacherib's territorial reassignments still held force—is not so clear. Certainly, outside of Qitmit, built at the end of the century in a period of Edomite expansion, excavations have produced only small samples of Edomite pottery (E. Mazar 1985: 264). And the forts must have furnished a conduit for merchandise passing through Jerusalem as well as to the coastal areas (so Herzog, in correspondence)—or else the Arabian connections through Jerusalem to Samaria and Damascus would make little sense. The Negev must have figured prominently in Manasseh's plans for economic recovery—the more so in that seventh-century Greek and Cypriot personnel and goods were finding their way into citadels like that at Arad (the ostraca), and forts at Tel Šera' IV (*EAEHL* 4.1062) and Tel Ira (Biran 1987: 27). No such powerful a figure as Manasseh could sit idle while fortunes were being made on his borders.

The commodities in which seventh-century Judah dealt are identifiable in part. This was an era of mass production, of scale. Other than the southern goods, such as sesame, streaming up from the Negev, several intensive agricultural programmes can be identified. At the Dead Sea, therefore, herbs used in the production of perfumes will have been raised (B. Mazar, Dothan and Dunayevsky 1966, esp. pp. 20-21; Herzog et al 1984: 19; note Patrich and Arubas 1989). At Gibeon, an enormous wine industry developed (Pritchard 1962: 92-99; 1964), a more modest counterpart of which is attested in the storage facilities of rooms 376 and 380 in Building 379 at Tell en-Nasbeh (McCown 1945). In the west, olive oil production developed multiplication of incense altars at Eqron suggests that here, local production and the southern trade may have been intertwined, scented oils, among other things, being produced for export (Gitin, 1989b). And, on the coast, a Judahite onomasticon and an administrative appeal at Mesad Hashavyahu indicate that corvée labour was applied to intensive cash-crop agriculture, at least in the vicinity of the shipping lanes.

Na'aman has brilliantly thrown into dispute the association of Mesad Hashavyahu with Josiah (1987: 7, 12-14). The onomasticon there, however, is Israelite (see Naveh 1962). Too, the seventh-century forts at Tell el-'Erani (Yeivin, above; Kempinski, in correspondence), Tel Masos (Fritz and Kempinski 1983: 124-30), and possibly that at Tel Hesi (Petrie 1891: 32) attest expansion in the direction of Philistia. Na'aman, who also situates Judah's efflorescence in the context of the Assyrian trading empire, bases his argument on the principle that Egypt was the successor state in Canaan in the era of the empire's decline (Malamat 1983: 228-34): Judah could not have expanded into the plain, which was under Egyptian control.

Still, Egypt's dominance on the coast was achieved only after a long conflict with Ashdod (Herodotus 2.157), in the territory of which Mesad Hashavyahu probably belonged. That Judah should have taken the opportunity to expand at Ashdod's expense is entirely possible—indeed, the fort may even have been ceded to Manasseh: Josiah, at least, seems to have moved with freedom in the neighbouring province of Samaria (2 Kgs 23.15-20). Nor is the Greek pottery at the site an indication of direct Egyptian control (as Naveh 1962: 97-99), for the Judahite commander of Arad stratum (VII–)VI had Greek subordinates of his own, possibly including troops based at Tel Malhata (Aharoni 1981: 12-13). Greek pottery, in the trading world of the seventh century, is as likely an economic as an ethnic indicator.

In any event, integration into the Assyrian empire entailed palpable advantages: Assyria had opened huge markets to Judah (note Saggs 1969: 19-21), which Manasseh was quick to exploit. Nor was his work unavailing. Trade in wine, oil and balms thrived—and much of the processing of the imported materials may have been done either in Judah or on Judah's borders. On the archaeological record, it is no great surprise that Manasseh is ranked second, after Baal of Tyre, in all lists of Assyria's western tributaries. Under (Hezekiah and) Manasseh, Judah crossed over from a traditional economy based in extensive agriculture to a cash-cropping, industrial economy, a transition that implied and produced a centrally-directed state (note Flannery 1972: 418).

Still, even meticulous central planning could not resuscitate the status quo ante-bellum. Under Manasseh, Jerusalem remained bloated, the lineages off the land. What population could be spared from the capital and from the work of meeting Assyrian demands was meted out to agricultural and strategic endeavours—it was spread thin—and Judah became a sort of Assyria in miniature through a policy of internal deportation.

Systematic exploitation of agricultural and industrial resources was standard Assyrian strategy (Oded 1979: 67, 70-74, with bibliography; esp. Postgate 1974: 381-82; Saggs 1955: 139-40). Adherence to this strategy, especially in the south, repaid Manasseh's efforts with a mild demographic recuperation. That the recuperation did not entirely relieve the limitations constricting Jerusalemite policy should be clear: the gap at Lachish after 701 speaks to a failure to translate human resources into territorial recovery. The resettlement at Lachish, and the contemporary resettlement at Gezer, was small (see Dever 1974: 73-84), and the Shephelah as a whole remained relatively empty (Dagan, above). Internal sites such as en-Nasbeh, Beth-Shemesh, Beth Zur, and Tel 'Eton never regained their earlier stations. Some of this comports, as well, with what we should guess of Assyrian military demands, including troops for Asshurbanipal's invasion of Egypt.

But where did Manasseh find the manpower even for resettling the hills and south? On Sennacherib's record, natural increase is ruled out; no significant population of undetected fugitives can be posited (contra Stohlmann 1983: 161); further, one looks in vain for evidence of deportations to Judah (cf. pp. 34-35, and Horvat Uzza, above), never an Assyrian province. The systematic repopulation was orchestrated by the court. With the north, Shephelah, western hills and south in ashes, the only possible source of settlers was the population Hezekiah had safeguarded within the walls of the capital—a deduction the mortuary evidence sustains (below). Repopulation took place from Jerusalem, as the Isaianic prophecy had it. The policy can only have been implemented at the cost of fragmenting the large kin-groups from rural areas near the capital that had been assembled in Jerusalem for the siege.

With the rehabilitation of rural areas, we should expect the reopening of old shrines, a policy to which Assyria can only have been indifferent (contrast Spieckermann 1982). This, like much else, we charge to Manasseh, the scapegoat of the books of Kings. It is to Manasseh, that Josiah's scribes and an exilic editor (Cross 1973: 275-89) attribute a diametrical reversal of Hezekiah's policies: collaboration with Assyria, redevelopment of the rural cult, apostasy (2 Kgs 21). How far this went is uncertain. Rural reclamation demanded resacralization (Ahlström 1982: 75-81). But to a considerable extent, the renewal may have been inaugurated by the kin-groups. What was the contribution of the state?

The argument that Manasseh presided over a cultic reaction has stark political implications: Hezekiah's had been a cargo cult. It is no coincidence that the first king known to have adopted holing up in Jerusalem as a first line of defence—Ahaz—is also the first to have removed metal imagery from the temple nave (2 Kgs 16.17): for all that Kings convicts Ahaz for an apostate (for introducing a larger altar and taking the old one for his personal use), he removed both the bulls or oxen supporting the bronze sea, and the wheeled basin stands, on which were impressed lions, bulls and cherubim (1 Kgs 7.29; see Holladay 1987: 295-96; these are the template of the vision in Ezek. 1). Like his son, Ahaz must have adopted a line, or exploited one, developed from the start of classical prophecy—the assault on iconography. Possibly, the bovine imagery in particular gave offence in the aftermath of the Syro-Ephraimite War. It is equally likely, however, that aniconic ideology rationalized the royal expropriation of temple resources.

Hezekiah expanded the range of Ahaz's iconoclasm, not just to the serpent, Nehushtan, but also to other aspects of the cult. But for all that Hezekiah's elite remained at the court, Sennacherib, and a forlorn vassalage, had rendered his cultic policy inexpedient. Manasseh's men may have scoffed at the claim that religious reform had produced Sennacherib's withdrawal and later death, that the rural areas were laid waste because the high places were there (as Isaiah, Micah). Assyria had left Judah a rump state, and deported the population of the north, the south, the Shephelah and the western hills. Manasseh's reign, then, would bear the marks of political pragmatism.

Nevertheless, Hezekiah's ideologues remained. They attributed Sennacherib's withdrawal, and his death, much later, to Hezekiah's reforms. They even acceded to power, seven or eight decades after

Hezekiah's revolt, implementing a doctrinaire programme characterized by a dogmatism transmitted with Hezekiah's dogma. It is hard to imagine that the party of revolt was sealed off from policy-making for almost a century, to materialize without warning in Josiah's (eighth or) eighteenth year.

In fact, the only hard evidence for state-directed resacralization under Manasseh is the reform of Manasseh's grandson, Josiah, around 622. It is out of this reform that the literature slandering Manasseh for an apostate emerged. However, it is reasonably clear that Hezekiah's measures had been far less radical than Josiah's were. Thus, Hezekiah left standing shrines at Lachish and at Arad; at the latter he may have eliminated some iconography.[1] He did dismantle an

1. Aharoni (1986: 26-27) held that the main, earth-and-fieldstone altar for burnt offerings at Arad went out of use after stratum VIII, as a result of Hezekiah's reform (and remained out of use until Josiah ruined the sanctuary): he reports an intact floor of stratum VII, with an oven, on the spot where the altar stood, with the altar's last phase belonging to stratum VIII; probably, in the same phase, two 'incense altars' (see generally Gitin 1989b, esp. n.4 where an association with 'meal offerings' is suggested) were buried in the steps of the holy of holies, and two stelae plastered over inside the holy of holies (the removal of the incense altars was originally attributed to stratum IX, but it is now clear that the sanctuary cannot have been built before stratum IX, sometime in the 8th century). Aharoni also reported that Josiah subsequently buried the holy of holies under a casemate wall (further Herzog *et al.* 1984); but this stemmed from the Hellenistic period, not the 7th century (Mazar and Netzer 1986; cf. Herzog 1987). Nevertheless, there may be, signs of Josiah's reform in some Iron Age partition walls above the holy of holies (Mazar and Netzer 1986), which would imply that the temple was in disuse. Ussishkin (1988), however, has shown that the incense altars may have been discarded only at the final destruction of the shrine in stratum VI. This in turn implies that only the covering over of the large, courtyard altar, and the plastering over of the pillars inside the Holy of Holies could possibly antedate Josiah; it may even be that the entire complex survived Josiah's reform, or that the large altar and pillars then went out of use. Should the two (small) incense altars be correlated to the two stelae, and associated with oblations to (male and female) classes of intermediate divinities—the baals and asherot (or ashtarot)—chiefly served through the burning of incense, according to our contemporary texts? The huge altar of burnt-offering would then pertain to Yhwh, the main object of meat sacrifices. In any event, Hezekiah certainly left the temple standing as a functional structure. It is difficult to imagine his leaving the priesthood intact there, or enrolling rural priests there, without making some provision for sacrifice or at least ritual slaughter. Some of the ambiguities in the interpretation of the data will be clarified with the final publication of the site, which Herzog promises (1987). For the interim,

altar at Beersheba (Aharoni 1974), but not an altar in a formal temple, like those at Lachish and Arad. Further, the account of Josiah's reform indicates that the high places Solomon built on the Mount of Olives opposite Jerusalem survived Hezekiah's reform (1 Kgs 11.1-3; 2 Sam. 15.30-32; 2 Kgs 23.13). Nor is this all. The account of Josiah's reign notes that he destroyed 'the altars that Manasseh built' (2 Kgs 23.12); but the same verse speaks of 'altars that were on the roof of Ahaz's upper chamber that the kings of Judah made'. That is, various kings supplied these altars, just as 'the kings of Judah' in general provided the 'horses...for the sun' (23.11). But between Ahaz and Josiah, only Hezekiah, Manasseh and Amon reigned—did Hezekiah build one or more of the altars? Certainly, he let Ahaz's altars survive (contrast the inference of 2 Chron. 28.23-25; 29.18-19).

Solomon's high places were dedicated to a variety of gods that Israelite theology regarded as subordinate to Yhwh (as Deut. 32.8-9; Job 1–2) and that the author of Kings regarded as foreign, alien—deities located in the traditional theology among the host of heaven (Halpern 1987b). Did the paraphernalia of the host of heaven (2 Kgs 23.4) come into the temple under Manasseh? Or was this paraphernalia never suppressed? Did the priests hired by the 'kings of Judah to burn incense on the high places in the towns of Judah' all find work first under Manasseh? Or were the 'high places' Hezekiah removed different establishments from those which Josiah squelched? Did Hezekiah tolerate state-sponsored centres of worship, in temples in major fortresses?

The altar at Beersheba had a serpent inscribed on its side (Aharoni 1974: 4). The ophite motif (note Stern 1984: 21-22; Dever 1987: 230) recalls Moses' serpent, Nehushtan, which Hezekiah destroyed (2 Kgs 18.4); it also raises questions as to the significance of Isaiah's image of the seraphim by the altar, instead of cherubim (Tadmor, oral observation). Possibly, Hezekiah dismantled the Beersheba altar, then, as an assault on a 'Levitic' or Mosaic (see Cross 1973: 195-215) countryside priesthood, whereas public shrines served by other priests (Aaronides?) were left standing.

with the final publication of the site, which Herzog promises (1987). For the interim, it seems most conservative to suggest that any marked reform of the temple at Arad be associated with Josiah, or with the Babylonians.

It is more likely, however, that Hezekiah removed the Beersheba altar because it lay outside a formal sanctuary (Yadin 1976). Hezekiah's policy may have been consistent, and consistently less fanatical than Josiah's (Halpern 1987b: 93-98). No report indicates that Hezekiah centralized the rural priests in the capital (2 Chron. 31.15-20). Conversely, Josiah executed the priests of Samaria (2 Kgs 23.20), and herded those of Judah into the temple (2 Kgs 23.8-9). Josiah seems to have taken the business of centralization a good deal more seriously than Hezekiah. Unlike Hezekiah, he allegedly suppressed all worship outside the temple, not just sacrifice outside Jerusalem and the state forts.[1]

Hezekiah's measures may thus have been directed principally against the old rural cult of the lineages. Of this, archaeological attestation is relatively rich (see Holladay 1987: 275-80). In texts, only meagre traces survive. One associated complex is the altar law of Exod. 20.20-23, forbidding expensive metal figurines, expensive hewn altars, and expensive altar platforms: a pile of dirt will do for sacrifice; 'any place where I cause my name to be called, I will come to you and bless you' (Exod. 20.21; cf. Judg. 6.19; 1 Sam. 7.9; 14.32-35, etc.). No trained ritual specialists are necessary (Judg. 17.5; 1 Kgs 12.31; 2 Kgs 16.15). Any Israelite anywhere will do—truly a 'nation of priests'.

This distributive theory of sacrifice dovetails into the circumstance that Yhwh's sacred mountain, Sinai, is extraterritorial: yet Amos articulates a tradition that sacrifice began only in Canaan (5.25; cf. Jer. 7.22); in Canaan, then, Yhwh was peripatetic (*drk*, *mthlk*), no more concentrated geographically than the Levites, and his sacred mountain is the hill country as a whole in Exod. 15.17—no particular locus in Canaan assumes, in popular religion, a supreme sanctity. Jeroboam I articulated the same theology by placing his bulls at Dan and Bethel, such that if the Yhwh thought to sit between the cherubim stood upon the bulls, he bestrode the whole of the land.

Again, Deuteronomy 33, which fondly cites local mountain sacrifices (vv. 18-19), playfully portrays Israel's conquest with the line, 'on their 'high places' you will tread/dominate' (v. 29)—a line with which the whole litany culminates (cf. Hab. 3.19), no doubt in immi-

1. Thin walls above the holy of holies may suggest he destroyed a shrine at Arad [VII–]VI, for which see the previous note.

nent expectation of participation in a sacrificial meal. In Deut. 32.13, Yhwh himself brings Israel to the 'high places' to enjoy the fruits of 'the hills/Shadday'; here the implication of sacrifice is palpable, and the hills are designated with an epithet pertaining to Yhwh. And in Amos 4.13, Yhwh, who fashions the hills, the wind, and humanity, and controls the dawn, 'treads on/dominates the 'high places' of the land/ earth'—it is he that Israel, in the cultic context of Amos 4–5, should expect to 'meet' (Amos 4.12).

The phrase, 'who treads on/dominates the 'high places' of the land/ earth' (Amos 4.13) is the one that Micah levers into a picture of the destruction of the high places (Mic. 1.3-5); but in the countryside, the suggestion is, Yhwh's frequenting the high places was usually experienced as an endorsement of the informal religious practices of the clans (as 1 Sam. 20.6; 9.12; Judg. 11.40; 21.19). Thus, Yhwh was not, as the Arameans are lampooned for thinking, a 'god of mountains' (1 Kgs 20.23); rather, it was in the hills that Yhwh was to be encountered (*bhr yhwh yr'h*, reappropriated now to mean, 'On the mountain of Yhwh he appears', Gen. 22.14, to validate Zion's cultic exclusivism).

The traditional cult, then, was probably distributive, spread across the entire land. Shrines in the home (Judg. 17) were probably compound-bound, which would perhaps explain the fitful distribution of figurines by house (Holladay 1987: 276); like ovens, icons served the extended family as a whole. Clan sector and civic shrines (does Judg. 6.27-31 reflect such an institution?) may have been more public (1 Sam. 9.12; 1 Kgs 3.4), or, in some cases, may have been associated with the tomb. In all, the popular religion, mirrored in state 'high places' like those of Dan, Beersheba or Bethel (*bātê bāmôt*?), seems to have been the principal object of Hezekiah's reform. If Ahaz had cleaned the bull iconography (or most plastic iconography) out of the temple, differentiating the Judahite cult from that of the north, Hezekiah's intolerance for high places could also be portrayed as a rejection of Israelite practice (Mic. 1.5, 13; Isa. 28.1-15; the assault on multiplication of sacrifice in Isa. 1.10-17).

Josiah's historians presumed the ideological congruence of Hezekiah's and Josiah's cultic policies. They attributed deviant iconography largely to Manasseh, though antiquarian precision prohibited their imputing specific items specifically to that king (generally Halpern 1988). But the congruence is not sustained by the evidence:

Hezekiah's measures appear to have been geared more directly toward his general approach toward defence, his need to sever the lineages from the land, his need to deconsecrate the land on the 'high places' of which Yhwh 'trod'. In sum, how far Manasseh reversed Hezekiah's policies, and how far he merely retained them, will probably never be known.

The material aspect of Manasseh's policy, however, is its impact on the old kinship structures of Judah. The diminutive settlements established outside the vicinity of Jerusalem were centrally designated and designed. This meant sending out smallish work-groups from the capital, fracturing the patrilineages—and achieving in the process one of the incidental objectives of Hezekiah's policies by establishing the unchallengeable ascendancy of the throne.

Several factors suggest that clan sector disintegration was extensive. Thus, lineage compounds do reappear in the seventh century. But the new wilderness settlements, like Tel Goren V, were mostly too small to house whole clan sectors. Second, the new settlements, nearly all of them forts, have been called 'paramilitary'. Their layout and location seems to reflect a new economic order, geared mainly to state trade (on Eqron, Gitin 1989a, 1989b; on the Negev and the Buqeiah, above). They are hierarchical in nature, military in organization—the impression is strong at Mesad Hashavyahu, Lachish II, Arad VII, Qadesh Barnea, Masos 'post-I', Aroer, Ira and even Beersheba I. At Beit Mirsim, the only structure that may have survived into the seventh century was the public West Tower and Gate. Not to overestimate the survival of epigraphs from the eighth century (epigraphs tend to survive more abundantly from just before a destruction layer), weights seeem to have been standardized around the end of that century, suggesting increasing state intervention in commerce (Cross, in conversation). And extant epigraphs support the same conclusion (Aharoni 1981: 24-25, 88, 111; *KAI* 194; Talmon 1986: 80-86): administrative ostraca suddenly abound as well (Aharoni 1981; Beit-Arieh and Cresson 1985); an unpublished bulla from southern Judah, from Manasseh's or Josiah's reign, reads, *b-26 lmlk 'ltld*, 'in the twenty-sixth (year) of the king, Eltolad' (N. Avigad, public lecture, 1990), providing the earliest example of a date or village name already cut into the seal. The transition from the eighth to the seventh century for Judah was a transition, as McClellan (1978) called it, from 'Towns to Fortresses'. Nor could Manasseh afford, in the light of his integration into the imperial economy (Reviv 1979: 200; Elat 1977: 223-25), to undo the military administrative model Hezekiah had imposed.

The crown's relations with the nuclear family in this era were direct, unmediated by the clans, which the state had in effect supplanted, without, however, discarding the ideology and language of kinship (as Deut. 16.18-20; 25.1-3; see below). The first kings had attacked the clans to cement a central government in power (Mettinger 1971: 112-21; Halpern 1974: 528-31; 1981: 237-49). Hezekiah rendered them politically and administratively marginal by herding them off the land. By god's grace and Sennacherib's, he and Manasseh polished them off.

Material–cultural indicators point toward the same conclusion. Thus, cooking pots and ovens diminish in size in the seventh century, without marked change in functional design. This is a typical reaction to a change in the number of those being fed at one time, since villagers economize on the number of ovens in use in order to save fuel (Kramer 1982: 120). But the change occurred on a massive scale. Evidently, most cooks were serving the same cereal gruels to fewer people than before.[1] The indication of reduced table fellowship matches the architectural residue.

Even more important, however, is the change in burial customs. In the seventh century, the old multi-chambered Israelite rock-hewn tombs with several burial benches in each chamber persisted in use at a number of sites, such as Khirbet el-Kom (Dever 1969; cf., e.g., Naveh 1963). However, a marked shift took place toward single-chambered rock-hewn tombs in the countryside in this era. These were often square in plan, most often with three benches; they sometimes also had an antechamber (A. Mazar 1976: 5-8, with the prototypes at Tell 'Eton and the seventh-century parallels in the countryside; Waldbaum 1967 for a Philistine origin of the burial type; Ussishkin 1986: 86-87), and only two benches in some instances (see Loffreda 1968). That is, the ancestral community, the kin

1. The observation and the inference concerning the numbers of those dining is that of S. Gitin (orally, 1984). A. Kempinski kindly called my attention to the diminished capacity of 7th-century ovens. For a parallel, note that Graves and Hodge (1985: 352) remark a decline in oven size, and in the size of butchers' joints, as family size dwindled in Britain after the First World War.

corporation, had moved decidedly in the direction of smaller units, probably centred on the nuclear family.

In the seventh century, for the first time, examples of single burials, headrests on burial benches, and burial benches with ridges on the outside, occur outside Jerusalem, where the urban and royal burial system had already developed such features (note Barkay and Kloner 1986: 29; Ussishkin 1969; Abercrombie 1984; Kloner 1982; Barkay 1986a: 51; 1986b: 19-20). Though double-chambered (Davis and Kloner 1978) and multi-chambered (A. Mazar 1976: 2-4; Barkay and Kloner 1986) tombs occur even in the capital, the former, some without repositories, appear to have been small, extended-family, not clan-sector, accommodations that were expanded after long use (esp. Davis and Kloner 1978: 19; Arensburg and Rak 1985; Mazar 1976: 4); in some cases (e.g. Kloner 1982), three-bench square tombs were expanded to include a second three-bench square room.

Of the multi-chambered tombs in use in the capital in the seventh century, one, at St Etienne (Barkay and Kloner 1986: 37-39), probably stems from Judaean royalty, with founders' sarcophagi preserved in the innermost chamber (the case may be similar with Mazar 1976: 2-4; Barkay 1986a: 56). Further, the richly-appointed Siloam tombs, nearly all with only a single burial bench (but some allowing twin interment), bear more than a passing resemblance to those of St Etienne (Ussishkin 1986: 257-60).

All the Siloam and St Etienne installations reflect the mores of the urban elite. The architecture is alien to the earlier rural mortuary repertoire: particularly noteworthy is the absence of bone repositories at Siloam (Ussishkin 1986: 262-64), and the prevalence of single (or paired) burials there. The individual had been divorced from the clan sector. Concepts of the afterlife must have been in upheaval, as ancestral ties were loosed; and the notion of Job that the dead do not know of or care for their descendants' welfare (14.21-22) will already have been forming.

Many of the Jerusalem tombs stretch back, to judge from the epigraphs and from the numbers of interments, into the eighth century or earlier. The funerary practices of the capital, in short, had skewed from traditional interment customs, chiefly in lavishing attention on and in isolating the individual or married couple, or perhaps the nuclear family. With the spread of cash-crop and trade-generated wealth in the eighth century, some fresh ideological winds will have swept into the hinterland, but evidence for their impact is exiguous. In the seventh century, however, funerary practices in the countryside began assimilating to those of the capital (Eshel 1987: 16; Barkay and Kloner 1986: 36): the transfer of population from the capital to the land is in evidence. With this population travelled an elite ideology concerned not with expressing the segmentation of the elite into competitive clan-sectors, but with articulating spatially the integrity of the individual against the claims of traditional kinship bonds; and this new configuration, at least at Siloam, expressed the camaraderie of all the individuals joined in the necropolis, rather than in family crypts, in the service of the true and broader collective, the nation, the state.

Of all Hezekiah's and Sennacherib's legacies, this last element may have had the most enduring intellectual effects. Resettlement, after all, severed the physical links to the ancestors, the material token of that old, pervasive continuity. As part of Hezekiah's reform, Isaiah had developed a fierce polemic against the ancestral cult (28.5-22, on which see Halpern 1987a; 2.6; 5.1-10 with 11-15; 8.19; 14.9-11; 19.13; contrast the only other early comment on ancestral sacrifice in Amos 6.6-7). One might even suspect that the phrase, 'the living god' ('ᵉ*lōhîm ḥayyîm*), found in Isa. 37.4, 17, was a coinage meant to contrast Yhwh not to the 'dying and rising god' of second-millennium Canaanite myth, but to the ancestors of the living Israelites.[1] The clan cults were centrifugal, conspiring to frustrate national policy. The ideologues at the court had to offer Hezekiah's garrison equivalent of the New Model Army—and any rural priesthoods now being put on the state payroll in the forts—a cogent rationale for forcing the peasantry into their points of concentration. This Isaiah (and others)

1. Contrast, however, Mettinger 1987: 82-91. Though the earliest reference to the 'living god' in Israel comes from Hosea (*'ēl ḥāy*), the emphasis on the 'living god' (Isa. 37. 4, 17; 2 Kgs 19.4, 16) comes principally at the end of the 7th century: Deut. 5.23 (cf. 5.3); Jer. 10.10; 23.26; possibly, 1 Sam. 17.26, 36. The expression is related to the oath formula, 'As Yhwh lives' (for the linkage, cf. Kreuzer 1983: 260-299), and is thus multivalent. However, it seems more likely that inside Israel it erects a contrast with the chthonic ancestors than that it represents a polemic against practice abroad. Significantly, Jer. 2.13; 17.13 contrast Yhwh as the 'source of living waters' with other gods, 'broken cisterns that do not hold water'. The cistern, like the chthonic god, is subterranean, which may have inspired the comparison. This is not to say, however, that Jeremiah is not lumping together ancestral spirits with heavenly subordinate gods.

fate; even worse, they were cultically competitive with Yhwh. The cult of the ancestors was no more than a foul delusion.

For Hezekiah's purposes, it had been essential to amputate the ancestors, those responsible for the bestowal of rural property on their descendants: they, and they alone, consecrated the possession of land (see Goody 1962: 400-403). They stood between Hezekiah and a population herded into fortresses: if Israelites failed to feed their ancestors, the ancestors were condemned to a diet of excrement (Xella 1980), one likely to excite their displeasure; if the family left them, too, how could one be gathered to the ancestors, in the clan-sector tomb? The assault on ancestral practices, which survived the jetsam of Hezekiah's other programmes (Deut. 14.1-2; 18.10-14; 26.14; Lev. 19.31; 20.6), helped justify dissolving the clan sectors—spreading them thin in the systematic resettlement of Judah. It also issued in a proscription on child sacrifice (2 Kgs 23.10), a rite quite logically associated with the ancestral cult in Josiah's time, and possibly earlier (Lev. 18.21; 20.2-8; Deut. 18.10). Josiah's suppression of ancestral worship (2 Kgs 23.10, 16, 20) reacts, thus, against the minimal retribalization of Judah under Manasseh and reflects a heightened stridency about deviation from the state cult (as Lang 1984, mainly interpreting Deut. 13; 17.2-7), now defined as morally normative and radically analeptic rather than as a refinement of the traditional religion. Indeed, the assault on the clans grew more radical still: repopulating the land had meant cutting not just ancestral ties, but the bonds of contemporary kinship as well.

So outside Jerusalem, the seventh century rang in the disintegration of the clans—and therefore of their local incarnations, the clan sectors—structures that until this time constituted a channel of authority parallel to that of the crown. Zion's contemporary expansion was a by-product of Hezekian strategy, probably unrelated to those unfortunate but unattested Samarian refugees whom scholars tag as the couriers of Deuteronomy (see Broshi 1974; Stohlmann 1983: 161). Even in Jerusalem, conditions would not have permitted the physical articulations of kinship that characterized the village—abutting houses, nearby tombs, adjoining fields. The capital was the special stomping ground of the king, and the newcomers to it had no economic share in it. All this is not to mention the ecumenical pressures life in the capital imposed, pressures that had already promoted individual or nuclear-family interment. Indeed, after the eighth century, even the old royal cemetery was closed, as changes in the royal burial formulae of Kings and Chronicles suggest (Rahmani 1981: 232-34).

So, in the countryside, the clans were gone. In Jerusalem, they were reduced to powerlessness. Y. Suzuki (1985) has argued in fact that for all its references to adjudication by elders and people (Halpern 1981: 198-206; Reviv 1983: 48-127), Deuteronomy reflects a pass at which the state has supplanted the kinship system as the administrator of justice. Despite its probable overvaluation of *KAI* 200 as a source on the administration of Judah, this view has much to commend it: the emphasis on stamping out elements of the traditional religion (Deut. 13; 17.2-7; 14.1; 26.14); the creation of a central cult (12; 16.5-6, 16); the erection of a centralized judiciary and appellate court (17.8-13 and 16.18-20; 25.1-3); and, while there is little to support Suzuki's hypothesis that laws in the second person singular address the administrator of justice, both the laws insisting on denunciation of relatives (13.7; see esp. the article by Dion in the present volume) and the predominantly second person singular address contribute to an impression of a devaluation of kinship segmentation: the lawgiver speaks directly to the individual, his voice unmediated by lineage usage. Scripture has supplanted tradition.

Deuteronomy stresses the homogeneity of the people, Israel, and attempts to impose upon this undivided people the social control elements of a 'shame-culture', as David Daube has demonstrated (1969). Noteworthy—to take only one of the many cases Daube adduces—is the Deuteronomic idea of deterrence: 'all Israel shall hear and fear' when capital punishment is imposed (13.12; 17.13; 19.20; 21.21). That is, the individualization imposed by Deuteronomy is, ironically, a collectivization, an attempt to impose a common code of moral indignation throughout the country, a cultural identity that outstrips the obligations of kinship—the obligations of the village—in its claims on individual loyalty.

Not surprisingly, what M. Weinfeld calls the 'humanism' of Deuteronomy—its revaluation of the status of women, slaves, debtors, resident aliens, war-captives and the like (Weinfeld 1972: 282-97)—precisely levels the distinctions of gender, class, ethnicity and even cultic status that lead to factionalization in the nation. It enlists the aid of the underclasses, and of establishment sympathy for them; it particularly lobbies women, among all those who passed from one to another kinship status, to join in forging a national agenda divorced from the (male) politics of the lineage. Daube rightly disputes the linkage of Deuteronomy to 'wisdom' literature, characteristically concerned to teach an elite the key to social success (1969: 51). Like Josiah's cultic centralization, which proscribed access to Yhwh except through the king, the levelling urges of Josiah's lawbook are those of a statist out to 'cut down the high corn' in the interest of imposing uniformity and unity on the people as a whole.

Deuteronomy's retribalization of the old kinship structures and of land tenure, its appeal to covenant forms, reflects nostalgia, an ideological commitment to the traditional organization of Judah's patrilineages. Yet the reality of village life never again approximated that of the eighth century—indeed, P's constant focus on the acknowledged lineage chiefs, the *n*^{e}*śî'îm*, rather than the elders, indicates an assumption that the kin-groups operate only through state recognition. The statist treatment accorded Josiah's reforms in Kings reflects the same tension (so Cross, in conversation): the state, now, acted as a surrogate for the old tribal institutions, while professing all the while the ideology of those institutions.

Indeed, the more the social context broadened, and became national, no longer respecting the lines of the old clan sector, the more differentiated the individual became within it. Individuation, first among the elite, and subsequently among the citizenry at large, reflected the citizen's membership first not in a local clan sector, but in a national collective. This development eventuated in the social creation of the individual in Israel—and of the self-consciousness, alienation and loneliness that necessarily attended that creation—matters to be explored in greater detail in the closing section (see Frankfurt Institute 1972: 37-48 for the correlation of individuation with state control, and the breakdown of primary groups). It is understood, of course, that here, one speaks in terms of degree, not in terms of absolutes.

In the late seventh century, the clans having been demolished, nothing but the nominal sovereignty of Assyria impeded royal plans for expansion. A certain amount of retribalization had no doubt occurred. Against these, even while embracing the ideology of the lineages, Josiah directed his reforms—and against any cultural elements that reinforced symbolically the cohesion of the lineage against the state. The state's relations with the nuclear family, and more specifically with its adult male heads were direct, now, unmediated—precisely individual.

VI. *The Seventh Century: Renaissance and Reformation*

A. *The Road to Josiah*

How far and how fast the old patterns of kinship revived is unclear. Their recrudescence will have been encouraged by traditional patterns of thought and language, which manifested itself in the survival of an ideology of kinship organization even among the elite. Yet the regeneration of the old kinship patterns will have been retarded by the hierarchical, state-oriented administration of the resettlement programme.

Regimented administration followed from the military and economic exigencies facing Hezekiah. The military model also went hand in hand with the court's assault on the lineages, the land, the ancestral cult—on continuity. The perspective informing all these policies betrays an origin in court life: concentrated in the capital, lacking a psychological or direct economic basis in the land, Hezekiah's congeries struggled not for subsistence or the accumulation of wealth, but for influence. In this struggle, lineage mates were the danger: half-brothers were rivals, cousins competitors, affinals potential foes. Hezekiah's courtiers expressed their rapacity in the rasp of *Realpolitik*. They were quintessentially detribalized men. This same elite probably had a hand in Manasseh's rural planning, though of this we cannot be sure.

It was only toward the end of the seventh century that the reform party shed all shadows of restraint in dealing with the capital's hinterlands. Their programme by this time had assumed a polarized, virulent form, the more so in that the rural clan sectors were in no position to resist. Hezekiah had left various shrines intact (Arad, Lachish) and had spared a good deal of Judahite iconography (Solomon's high places, the 'horses' given to the sun, probably the regalia of the 'host of heaven' in the temple). Josiah's iconoclasm was Cromwellian in scope, directed against any plastic art that could remotely be construed as cultic.[1] Josiah probably removed the temple that had survived

1. It is not yet clear whether Josiah's reform in Jerusalem extended to the realm of private religion. The City of David excavations uncovered numerous zoomorphic and fertility figurines, scattered in houses rather than concentrated, except for a single

Hezekiah at Arad, and, more certainly, the shrines of Solomon opposite the walls of Jerusalem.

This policy represents the ultimate triumph of Hezekiah's elite—no cultic activity was to be tolerated outside the temple, and the temple itself was purged of subordinate gods. Under Hezekiah, countryside worship had been banned, but not state temples. After 701, however, the judgment of god had been passed on the rural cult as a whole; centralization now meant sacrifice only in the Jerusalem temple, and the suppression of the 'host of heaven', identified as the stuff of foreign cults (as Deut. 4.19-20; 32.8-9 [read 'god' for 'Israel' with LXX, Qumran]; 17.3; Jer. 8.2; 19.13; Zeph. 1.4-5; Noth 1966: 52-55).

How early the avant-garde developed this exclusivist logic to its logical extreme is unsure—the events of 701 licensed the interpretation, but no text before Josiah's era reflects such views,[1] and some sources of the Deuteronomistic History even reflect favourably on the 'host' (Josh. 5.14-15, with Joshua prostrating himself to the captain of the 'host'; Judg. 5.20; 1 Kgs 22.19). The nature and the extent of Josiah's centralization speak volumes about the party's doctrinaire theology, ruthless fanaticism, and long-standing frustration.

Josiah's elite entertained no delusions as to the fact that it was revising Judah's traditional way of life. In the Deuteronomistic History, in fact, it traced the old rural cult to the aboriginal Amorites (Halpern 1988: 134-37, 220-28), identifying the cult as a paradigm of

cache of some 80 figurines. Nearly all were disarticulated in the destruction layer of stratum X (586 BCE; Shiloh, in conversation). For the 27 figurine fragments found in the Temple Mount excavations, see Nadelman 1989. In essence, there is not yet any way of knowing whether these figurines, or the Jerusalem Cave 1 deposits (most recently, Holladay 1987: 259-60) were deliberately spared Josianic iconoclasm.

1. Note Isa. 13.4; 14.13; Ps. 148.3; Job 38.7; also, Israel's comparability to the stars, as Gen. 15.5; 22.17; 26.4; 37.9; Exod. 32.13; Num. 24.17, later a demythologized cliche, as reflected in P's identification of Israel as the 'hosts' of Yhwh of Hosts—Exod. 7.4; 12.17, 41; contrast Gen. 2.11. Note the depersonalization of natural phenomena this configuration implies—no longer is the 'host of heaven' an active group of gods: the depersonalization of nature is a phenomenon typical of Renaissance-type literate thinking, placing a society on the road to a Reformation (see below, VI B, and Tawney 1938: 24). For Europe, further, see Hoffman 1985: 886-87, on mediaeval sports, fishing and especially fishing manuals. Essentially, nature is alienated from the realm of the divine, which is thus less accessible to the individual. A reaction enabling the individual to deal with the divine, rather than the community, is thus precipitated.

backsliding into the sins of the peoples who by their sins had earned eradication at Israel's hands (in P, note Lev. 18.25, 28; 20.22). Constrained neither by tradition nor by veneration of the ancestors, concerned to liberate the denizens of the present from the tyranny of the past, confined to stylite seclusion from the social fabric of an agrarian hinterland, these sophisticates now repudiated the whole notion of corporate existence, of collective liability.

The innovation refined the calibre of divine retribution. But against the larger background, philosophical considerations recede. The kings of Judah and Assyria had all but minced the old vertical and horizontal corporations. The grapes of reform soured into the vinegar of extremism; the bouquet of Isaianic hope dissipated, leaving the grim lees of dessicated desperation.

B. *Individuation and Literalism*

In this context, two factions of Josiah's coalition—represented, respectively, by Jeremiah and Ezekiel—loosened the ties between the fates of individuals and those of their ancestors and collaterals. The Babylonian exile can only have accelerated the intellectual and social processes. The relationship between state authority and the individual was now direct. The clan sector was no longer a seat of jurisprudence, though, curiously, a consciousness of its value may have been one result of the deportations to Mesopotamia. But this was the period of extensive legal codification—Deuteronomy and P (Friedman 1987: 204-11)—and, no doubt, of systematic royal administration of law in the village.

The circumstances reviewed to this point contributed to the phenomenon of individualization in the Western religious tradition. The whole of the story would have to include the impact of cultural discontinuity and exile on the ongoing socialization of the new dogma. But two points deserve emphasis. First, as propaganda, it appears that Hezekiah commissioned the first collection of literary prophecy—consisting of four books with near-identical superscriptions and related intellectual profiles: Amos, Hosea, Isaiah and Micah (Andersen and Freedman 1980: 53-56, 145-47). The literary product, significant only to the court elite and to the Reformist army, was the tip of an iceberg. Traditional Judahite culture was gone for good, swept away in the scheme of Assyrian deportations that removed the population of Israel and the rural population of Judah in the last half of the eighth century. The ratification of theology in writing was symptomatic of the change from a traditional to a literate culture (note Weippert 1981: 101, citing urbanization as a factor).

Indeed, with Deuteronomy, sacred text itself was introduced as an object into ritual (2 Kgs 23.2-3) in Judah, quite possibly for the first time: Judah thus took an enormous stride toward the transformation of Israelite religion into an elite religion of the letter, of what was fixed in writing. Even the ratification in P of priestly procedure, the codification of Deuteronomy, as canonical documents represented a significant step away from traditional and toward elite culture, the culture of literacy, of a common national norm. To introduce a fixed text into the cult—to fix a liturgy—is, after all, to establish the national standard over against the local, and thus to establish the primacy of wide (and thus individuated) social relations over against local: as Goody has observed, literacy levels social distinctions because what is written, at a remove from the various segments of society, must apply to the segments universally, regardless of local history and conditions; lawcodes in particular homogenize society below the level of the central authority (Goody 1986: 11-13; cf. Flannery 1972). One index of such homogenization is amelioration in the lot of women and others whose legal standing is marginal; accordingly, Deuteronomy equalizes all citizens and residents against the hierarchical classification characteristic of the patri-lineages (Weinfeld 1973: 282-93). In the instance, the need to maximize the pool of economic agents after 701 was a contributing factor. However, evolution in custom to the point where women naturally inherited even land (as Job 42.13-15) is a reflection of the social atomism that attends the Levelling of Reformation.

Second, Hezekiah is the earliest king under whom literary activity is documented (Prov. 25.1; *KAI* 189), although earlier monuments (2 Sam. 18.18) and texts did exist (generally Lemaire 1981b). Still, it was in the eighth century that Israel began to make the transition from a traditional to a literate culture. This is the era in which the written forms of the Yahwistic prose epic in the Pentateuch (the J source) and its Elohistic alloform (E) were probably produced (Friedman 1987: 87; forthcoming). From this period the earliest extant written prophecy (Amos, Hosea) survives. This is also the period from which ostraca and other inscriptions are first recovered at sites in Israel, but that may be a function of the fact that texts recovered archaeologically tend to be products of the decades preceding a site's abandonment or destruction. More telling is the fact that, starting in the eighth century, Israelite personal seals more frequently than before exhibit text—the name of their owners. With increasing frequency, starting in this period, they can be distinguished one from the other on the basis of the specific text alone (Demsky 1988). The texts even include occupations, such as the seal of Hanan, son of Hilqiyahu the priest (Elayi 1986). Why include such elements, except to establish one's status? Although pre-exilic Hebrew orthography does not often represent vowels, and is thus best fitted out as an aid to *oral* transmission rather than as a tool of purely written communication, the evolution of seals from early pictures to later pure texts surely indicates the spread of literacy among the propertied classes. Simultaneously, by no coincidence, individual interment burgeoned in the capital.

As part of the transition to a widely literate culture, the elite culture, as reflected in the early prophetic corpus, developed a critique of traditional culture on which Reformation critiques of traditional Catholicism were closely patterned. Icons, in this critique, were not symbols of gods, but were worshipped as gods themselves. Rituals were empty gestures, so that between the festivals, worshippers could sin against Yhwh's norms with impunity. The temple, taken as a guarantee of Yhwh's protective presence, was an empty symbol. Subordinate gods—the baals, the host of heaven—were powerless, empty cisterns as distinct from the living waters of the high god. Yhwh was the reality, but the Israelites were misled to revere mere representations of him. Yhwh's will was the way, but the Israelites turned right and left to perform empty gestures of compliance with it.

It was on this critique that Ahaz must have seized when removing metal imagery from the temple nave. Hezekiah's men used it in order to isolate the rural cult from that of the state—Yhwh did not want sacrifice, after all, but the obedience of his people. Isaiah and Micah articulate this view, in treating Sennacherib's deportations as Yhwh's verdict on the rural cult, the cult that the Deuteronomistic History exposes as Amorite, as foreign. And Josiah's Puritan aniconism, and Jeremiah's radical monotheism both presuppose the same ideology, the very ideology that produced a doctrine of moral individuation: monism, the one, and not the many, was the order of the day (Halpern 1987b).

The intellectual logic actuating the prophetic critique sharply distinguishes a representation from the thing it represents. It further indicts others (idolaters) for failing to make the same distinction. Thus, icons, ritual, temples are misunderstood by the worshippers, taken to have a life of their own. This *Sprachkritik* reflects a literalistic mentality, a semantic deflation that fails to engage the poetic dimension of metaphor. What is portrayed in metaphor as beautiful, is perceived, in reality, as tainted. Expressions of devotion are mere lip service (as Amos 8.4-6; Hos. 6.1-6; Isa. 1.15-17), so that feasts will be transformed into mourning (Amos 8.10; Hos. 9.4) or eliminated (Amos 5.21-27; Hos. 2.11). Icons represent gods, but are not gods (as Amos 4.4-5; Hos. 4.12; 8.4-6; 2.5-8; 11.1-4; 12.5-11; Isa. 2.6-22; 10.11; 19.3), so the icons, with the altars, will be destroyed (Amos 3.14-15; Hos. 12.11; 8.6). Appearances are deceiving—and wealth proceeds not from piety, but from oppressing the poor (Amos 2.6-7; 4.1; 6.12; Isa. 1.23; 5.7-10; Mic. 2.1-2).

So all things beautiful in appearance must be defaced to reflect their hideous essence (Amos 4.2-3; Hos. 2.9-10; Isa. 1.7, 22; 3.16-24; 5.1-6; 7.23; Mic. 1.6; 3.12). Even military security is a sham, when based on alliance with other powers than Yhwh (Hos. 2.5-8; 5.13-15; 7.8-12; Isa. 7.7-11; 8.5-8; 10.5-6; 30; 31): evanescent political alliances are lures in which to snare a fickle people. And Israel's election by Yhwh is not the same as immunity from correction: Israel must be treated as others have been, broken down, defeated, destroyed (Amos 2.4–3.15; 9.7; Hos. 1.9; Isa. 1.9-10).

The *Bauhaus* character of the critique is unmistakable: the law does not deliver justice (text itself originates in the lying pen of the scribes), because centrally-imposed written law cuts across the grain of local customary usage; 'law' and 'custom' (*mišpāṭ*) are suddenly in conflict (Goody 1986: 127-32). Any communication, any action or representation, is a deception. Paranoia reigns.

Hezekiah deconsecrated the land, assaulted the resonance of its timeless ancestral associations; the reform ideology rejected the resonance of language, of gesture, of religious and non-religious metaphor, as mere hypocrisy covering a lack of substance. As Hapsburg ornamentation seemed to the Bauhaus movement, as Catholic iconography seemed to the Reformationists, all symbol was deceit, or at least, any symbol was liable to be seized on as a deception. Between the reality of human manipulation and the environment on the one hand, and, on the other, the perception of that reality, there should ideally be no softening, metaphoric medium, no expression—symbolically (Armstrong unpub.), no intermediary between God and the individual, between the king and the people. No intermediary gods, and no intermediary ancestors or lineage institutions.

Under this anti-poetic programme, Kantian reason also operates upon the multiplicity of reality; thus, other divine beings are merely Yhwh's representatives; reality is the One, the underlying cause and unifying will, and the many are mere epiphenomena—useless, deceptive intermediaries. By Josiah's time, the host of heaven were identified with the baals,[1] or were demythologized (Deut. 4.19; in P, Gen.

1. 'The baal', Hebrew *hab-ba'al*, does not refer to a single god, Baal, by name, but is a title, sometimes applied to Yhwh (as Hos. 2.18; Isa. 1.3; and in the onomasticon in the case of Saul's sons Ishbaal and Meribbaal or the judge Jerubbaal—see Cross 1973: 263-64), specifically 'master'. As the word for 'husband', its application to Yhwh fathered and disseminated Hosea's imagery of apostasy as adultery, or whoredom. The title never refers to a god unless qualified, most often by the definite article, to indicate which particular god of this class is in point. In 8th-century and later literature, however, *hab-ba'al,* 'the baal', is often a collective plural, 'the baals', 'the gods of the class, baals'. Thus, Jeremiah, who speaks regularly of the baals in the plural (as 2.23; earlier in Hos. 2.15, 19; 11.2), identifies child sacrifices as a rite directed toward 'the baal', yet identifies the 'host of heaven' as beneficiaries (7.32–8.3; 19.5, 13), and in a parallel text (32.29, parallel to 19.13) speaks of the baals. 2 Kgs 23.4-5 speaks of those 'who burn incense to *hab-ba'al*, to the sun and to the moon and to the constellations and to all the host of heaven', where hab ba'al is set into apposition with the succeeding objects of worship. And Zephaniah includes priests and worshippers of the host of heaven among the 'remnant of *hab-ba'al*,' an expression that itself suggest a collective plural (1.4-5). These and other texts suggest that the baals were included, at least in Josianic theology, among the host of heaven. The baals were perhaps popularly identified with the planets, as gods enjoying greater independence than those represented by the other stars (but the identification of the baals with gods of all the foreign nations—Spieckermann 1982: 201-11; Noth 1966: 52-55; Halpern 1987b—speaks to a more inclusive club in certain circles, perhaps like the fifty great gods in Mesopotamia). The customary cult practice was to burn incense in their honour on rooftops—Jer. 19.13; 32.29—where various cultic activities took place (1 Sam. 9.25-26, the designation of Saul; 2 Sam. 16.2 after 11.2, Absalom entering unto David's harem on the spot where David had spotted Bathesheba; Isa. 22.1, 13, sacrificial feasting in the face of Sennacherib's destruction of the countryside; Neh. 8.16, tabernacles on the roofs; Isa. 15.3; Jer. 48.38, Moabite mourning on the roofs [and squares]; Judg. 16.27, Philistines watching Samson from the temple roof; cf. Josh. 2.6, Rahab's roof with *pšty h'ṣ* spread out; Prov. 21.9; 25.24). This was also the locus of sacrifice to the host (Zeph. 1.5), suggesting that Ahaz's roof with the altars built by 'the kings of Judah'

2.1; see Spieckermann 1982: 224-25, though his view that the host was Assyrian, as p. 273, fails to reckon with such texts as Josh. 10.10-13; Judg. 5.20). Here, the reformists reached the intellectual stage at which adulation directed to the host was not merely pointless, but pernicious, where Jeremiah could imagine a divine realm wholly devoid of gods other than the One (Halpern 1987b: 98-101), where P could rewrite the folk history suppressing all mention of angels (Friedman 1981: 84, 88, 92, 97), where the very insignia of the host had to be suppressed from the cult (2 Kgs 23.4-5). The gods, along with nature, were alienated from Yhwh, identified as alien. The contrast is to the old theology (Deut. 32.8-9; Mic. 4.5; Judg. 11.24; Num. 21.29), which lived comfortably with their stewardship of other nations in subordination to Yhwh. It was an era of alienation—from land, gods, kin, tradition.

This critique, like Protestantism, gathered momentum from cultural integration into a world economy. The eighth century saw the dawning of the first truly international age, principally in Western Asia and Egypt. During the eighth and seventh centuries, Phoenician colonization reached a feverish pitch in the western Mediterranean (Carthage having been founded around 814, with the prospect of Assyrian monopoly on the eastern trade already realized). Assyria, too, brought prosperity to the west, as Phoenicians plied the western routes and Judah and Aram competed for commercial influence over the southern spice trade. The Assyrians also adopted a vigorous policy of deportations, sometimes with devastating implications for ethnic identity and

was an astral installation—in other words, again, that the cult of the host survived Hezekiah's measures unimpaired. The cultic activity attested for the host is the same as that attested for the baals, chiefly burning incense (and, for the latter, child sacrifice); and it is worth noting that Spieckermann (1982: 83-85) identifies the *kmrym* of Hos. 10.5; Zeph. 1.4; 2 Kgs 23.4 with the astral priests of *KAI* 225-226 (see *KAI* 2.275). Exod. 23.19 already proscribes animal sacrifice for any god but Yhwh, and this rule may have been honoured traditionally, though sometimes, no doubt, as with child sacrifice, in the breach as much as in the observance. On the identification of the baals as gods of the nations, and the equation of these with the host under Josiah, see Halpern 1987b. The dynamic may have been different under Hezekiah, Mark Smith reminds me. But Hosea's polemic against baals and alliances is suggestive. The equation of what is foreign with what is evil is a chief point of the method of the historian who produced DtrH. The likelihood is that this was a tendency inherited from earlier members of the Jerusalem elite, starting at least with Hezekiah.

for the preservation of traditional culture. The alienation was world-wide.

Christopher Hill, writing of the English Reformationists, observes that before Puritanism, 'Sin, like poverty and social inferiority, was inherited'. The fathers had eaten sour grapes, and the teeth of the poor were set on edge. As the Church, however, offered indulgences for sale in order to cash in on the growing wealth new technologies were generating, a reaction set in among the wealthy: sacraments and priestly mediation were rejected as fraudulent; and salvation, 'justification' were internalized, liberating the community of the elect, particularly the self-made middle classes, from their humble roots and encouraging them to seek salvation on an individual basis (Hill 1975: 151-58). New wealth, combined with widespread landlessness, the breakdown of the multi-generational family, and theological scepticism based on the circulation of printed canons—these are elements that affected Britain in the seventeenth century. The Israelite elite, with its new prophetic canon, J, E and other literature, was in a similar position in the eighth–seventh centuries BCE—although the landlessness may in the main have been Assyria's doing.

The relationship of the Protestant programme to capitalism has been extensively plumbed (esp. Tawney 1938): the depersonification of reality, the desacralization of nature, leads to an analysis of the economy and of physics as impersonal objects (Tawney 1938: 24). Industrialized urban Judah of the seventh century was as receptive to the monadic critique as, later, Cromwell's England or Roman Greece were to be. Individuation both of the god and the person was an adaptive intellectual strategy in an era of lineage fissure, of economic expansion, of industrialization. It was, as Mikhail Gorbachev acknowledged in firing the bullet of glasnost toward the target of perestroika, a strategy that promoted profitable innovation, flexible personal effort: it placed one's fate firmly in one's own hands, and thus labour and puritanical morals promised capital and divine favour. The diet of the fathers no longer determined the orthodonture of the man.

And all this promised to benefit two parties, the meritorious, industrious individual, and the central state. Centralization and the prophetic critique thus conspired to keep down the old entrenched interests, the old establishment, that stood in the way of radical economic and military policies. The tolerant, heterodox, unselfconscious folk religion of an age of relative prosperity—the eighth century (cf. Tawney 1938: 206-207)—gave way to self-conscious radicalism (Halpern 1987b), as the elite theology adapted to an environment in which individual mobility was possible. Josiah, and probably Hezekiah, turned countryside conservatism back on itself, accusing the worshippers on the high places of apostasy, of foreign practice, the very charge no doubt levelled earlier against Solomon, who introduced the principle of a central temple, a royal chapel, into a rural culture. What, after all, was the rural view of the capital, if not that it was a hotbed of syncretism and alien custom, where foreign craftsmen, foreign architectural forms, foreign cultic objects and foreign emissaries accumulated? Hezekiah's or Josiah's tactic was calculated to appeal to a meritocratic, individuated urban elite, the servants of the king and not their kin (cf. Nabonidus's alienation of the capital by revaluing the hinterland).

The parallels here to other Reformations run deep, but a description of the situation in the eighth–seventh centuries should suffice to suggest them. Along with an increasingly extensive and increasingly intensive pattern of contacts across land and sea there developed, not unnaturally, a sense of *Kulturkampf*. The elite were those engaged in defining the essence of their own cultures—at the same time as a sort of international culture arose, with such Western phenomena as prophecy burgeoning in Assyria (Weippert 1981: 101-105; Tadmor 1975). The job of self-definition persisted through the seventh century. One obvious way to consolidate a conceptual grip on one's identity is appeal to the past, and Mesopotamian chronicles and historiography multiply in this period as in no other (Van Seters 1983: 79-92; Grayson 1980). The annals of the kings of Judah and those of the kings of Israel must also have been compiled at this time, as Van Seters has shown (1983: 298-302; Halpern 1988: 213-18). At the end of the period, Josiah's court party produced the Deuteronomistic History, probably rewriting an older Hezekian document in order to do so (Halpern 1988: 114-15, 134-36 and *passim*; Halpern and Vanderhooft, forthcoming).

The extent to which appeal to the past permeated Near Eastern cultures in the era is reflected, too, in the spate of 'founders'' names that suddenly appear as throne-names—Jeroboam II in Israel, Hiram II at Tyre, Rezin II at Damascus—all three commemorating figures from the tenth century (cf. also Amos 6.5)—and Sargon II in Asshur. At Asshur, an update of the Assyrian King List was drawn up, and new claims to hoary dynasty advanced (Tadmor 1981: 26-30); royal dress fossilized while other fashions continued to change (Reade 1981: 152; cf. Zeph 1.8). More obviously, Asshurbanipal's library consolidated Mesopotamia's literary heritage (Streck 1916: 256.17-18); and we might add the systematic collection, especially under Esarhaddon, of omens and the erection of a network of scholars (see Parpola 1980), excavations at ruined temples continuing down through the sixth century, the appropriation of Babylonian culture in such works as Sennacherib's *akītu*-house, and a host of other, related activities. Assyria was grasping for its identity against the denaturing impact of empire (Spieckermann 1982: 306). The systematic approach to omens and astronomical observation suggests that the historical enterprise, too, was an experiment with empirical modes of investigating a (theological) cosmology.

Yet the very act of defining their identity led the elite in Israel to a consciousness of the dissonance between elite and traditional culture. The Priestly source in the Pentateuch, for example, set out to correct the distortions in anthropomorphism, distributive sacrificial ritual, and angelology that earlier national epics had created (Friedman 1981). 'Classical' (i.e. literary) prophecy is another sign of the new situation, with its daring critique of the traditional cult, and its movement toward a distinctive aniconic monotheism.

Literary prophecy, too, is riddled with appeals to the past, reviews of the nation's heritage. Israelite covenant theology, if it antedated the literary prophets (as Levenson 1988: 131-48), predisposed divines to rehearsal of Israel's history—Yhwh's 'righteous acts on behalf of Israel' (Judg. 5.11)—were, after all, the focus of the paschal cult and the reason one executed his commands; literary prophecy thus conforms to an established pattern in its citations of national history. Still, the idea that a textual record could be as authoritative as a spoken oracle, the idea that history could be a proving ground for the revisionist theology, for an elite philosophical system, was new. The past, however distant, was now to be construed as a model on which to revolutionize present practice, to correct the peasant deviation from elite norms.

No more telling evidence of this fact could be adduced than the pseudepigraphic attribution of Deuteronomy to Moses. This, like Hezekiah's canon of literary prophets (and Asshurbanipal's redefined canon of Mesopotamian literature), reflects the urge to inject a new 'literacy', a 'literacy' of a second order, into elite society. Textual records offer the possibility of establishing that there are contradictions in the tradition (see Goody and Watt 1968). Conversely, a literary canon, like literacy proper, creates a common frame of reference, a treasury of common points of reference, of common symbols and language, to which the literate can be expected to refer—which is why canon guilds sometimes attempt to monopolize literacy (Eisenstein 1969; Goody 1987: 140-43), and why literacy and canon travel hand in hand (Goody 1986: 3-4).

In the eighth–seventh centuries, canons formed, and even genealogies—so plastic, polyvalent and protean in peasant hands (Malamat 1968; 1973b; Wilson 1977)—were recorded (1 Chron. 4.41; 5.17). Tradition lost its fluidity, and its fixity, as in other literate cultures, left traditional culture open to critical scrutiny (Goody and Watt 1968: 44-48; Goody 1986: 10) and rejection. Administration fell to a (doubly) literate elite. Those who retailed the 'righteous acts of Yhwh' in the cult could now be checked up on and compelled to admit the authority of one or another standard version. And thus the literacy of the elite made public knowledge a control on one's assertions about the past (for a parallel, Eisenstein 1969: 55, 63, 75-76). Yet all of these developments presuppose a desperation to hold onto the authentic elements of Judah's past; a despair, 'of creating a human world out of freedom and consciousness' of the sort that might drive one to model history on vegetable life and decay, or to isolate culture and the spiritual from the externalities of a civilization, to 'set...up culture against the latter and render...it absolute. And often enough in so doing it opens the gate to the true enemy, barbarism' (Frankfurt Institute 1972: 92-93). Any Reformationist attempt to create cultural preserves, in sum, is fraught with opportunities for Torquemadas. After all, what is the Western tradition of Inquisitionism, except the discovery of hidden cabals of those who cling or are said to cling to earlier traditions—Judaizers, peasant witches, worshippers of olden gods now demonized (see generally Ginzburg 1989)? With Deuteronomy turning the very idea of a Holy War inward against members of one's own nuclear family (13.2-18), with the Josianic program, the state/church of ancient Judah reached its own inquisitorial, cultural Jacobin stage. To paraphrase a recent analysis of Islamic culture (Pryce-Jones 1989), Judah's social organization passed from a stage in which individuals were housed within kinship and patronage groups to one in which their links to central authority and to their god were immediate, unmediated, without having the opportunity to develop any significant institutions or customs of civil society, of moderate political culture.

In the same period, in Greece, similar processes were under way (esp. Vernant 1966: 267-314). The eighth century was the Homeric era, in which Mycenaean tombs became shrines, and were imitated, an era in which the alphabet was widely appropriated, the city-state developed, and figurative art imported. In the cult, links to the Bronze Age were forged. At the same time, reverence of the founders—a hero-cult—ascended new heights (Snodgrass 1982: 114-17), and into the seventh century, the systematization of theogonic cosmology was the result (Hesiod: Cornford 1950: 95-116). This was the period in which colonization and integration into the network of international trade effectively began. Simultaneously, poets happened onto the first person, and asserted the worth of the individual in the context of a rejection of dominant cultural values (Archilochus).

The rest of the development in Greece was episodic, unlike that in Israel. The Homeric epic was canonized, fixed in written form, at the end of the sixth century, under Peisistratos. Meanwhile, the Pythagorean and Orphic doctrines of the soul repudiated ancestral reward; the state legislation under Solon in Athens restricted the authority of the family; further, an individuated notion of purity, of morality, gradually overtook that of generalized guilt, such that the internalized concept of intention came to be the determinant of guilt in the Draconian code. At this point, logic and law replaced tradition as the governing factors in elite life (Barbu 1960: 90-122), and 'law' and 'custom' once again stood in opposition to one another (*Antigone*). Indeed, philosophers such as Antiphon and Plato even came to see the State itself as an enactment of human society, much like the revolutionary views expressed in Judges 8–9; 1 Sam. 8; 10.17–12.25 and, tellingly, Deut. 17.14-20. No longer were state laws necessarily divine. Antiphon went so far as to suggest that Natural Law, a concept manipulated by self-appointed spokesmen of the 'oppressed' against those in power, was Truth, state law mere opinion. The consequence was that the needs of the state might lead it to pervert natural justice (see Frankfurt Institute 1972: 19)—precisely the view expressed among the literary prophets, in stories in the Deuteronomistic History, and in the Deuteronomic concern to make the 'oppressed' the social equals of the propertied classes.

The philosophical tradition, too, came to recognize the one god, different from the others, who has no cult, is invisible and unchangeable and unlike any representations of the gods (see Jaspers 1968); Anaximander even uses 'god' as the term for the stuff of the universe (Cornford 1950: 11). In part this progression responds to increasing literacy, and increasing legal codification in which the state singles out the individual as legally liable. In part it reflects the increasing desacralization of politics in the eighth to seventh centuries BCE, culminating in the conviction that humans, the citizens of the polis, control right and wrong (Vernant 1982: 68-105), stand in a position, that is to say, to determine their fate.

That legal codification should characterize the new era in Israel (as in Greece) is only to be expected: such codification permitted the definition of the culture. Enshrinement of (reconstituted) custom in law represented an attempt to maintain it in stasis, against the inroads of alien customs; again, fluidity was sacrificed, both in terms of change in usage over time and in terms of synchronic heterogeneity. Again, codified law, not specific to particular locales, broke down segmentary distinctions (Goody 1986: 11-12).

At the same time, the publication of written law creates the opportunity for conflict between the law's letter and its unseen spirit, the reality it represents (Jer. 8.8; generally, Goody 1986: 127-70). Similarly, the rise of Jeremianic prophecy, based on the 'word' and denying the visibility of the only god (as Deut. 4.12; Levenson 1985: 147-51; Halpern 1987b: 98-99 and 114 n. 99), is a predictable outcropping of a literal, monadic consciousness: a multifarious visible reality is the epiphenomenon of the unseen unifying cause. Further, the use of written registers to determine the status of those who returned to Judah from the Babylonian exile (Ezra 2, esp. vv. 59-63; 8.1-14; and note the status of archival materials in Ezra 1; 2; 3.7; 4.6-22; 5.6–6.12; 7.6, 11-28; 8.34, etc.) reflects the valorization of the same mindset throughout an entire community.

However, the new literate mentality was fundamentally that of an elite. In classical Greece, therefore, the philosophical tradition remained confined, with the exception of Socrates, to the elite. The introduction of a semi-monadic programme under Nabonidus in sixth-century Babylon was wholly abortive. In Judah, on the other hand,

Sennacherib had deported the entire rural population, leaving a society concentrated in the capital, under the watchful eyes of the royal house and its army.

The process of literalization, of elite alienation, of moral and legal individuation, began with Hezekiah's centralization and Sennacherib's response. It was carried through, and in the form of monotheism became a distinguishing mark of Judahite culture, because Judah survived as an industrial rather than agrarian society, an urbanized rather than rural organism, for a century amid the *Kulturkampf* and ethnic chaos of the seventh century. In the absence of a restraint in the hinterland, the elite theology sacrificed the comfort of the collective on the altar of the individual; it flattened the security of the unchanging past on the anvil of economic and scientific progress. It successfully defined traditional culture as un-Israelite, as pagan, as inferior, a position that Western literary religions have continued to maintain ever since.

BIBLIOGRAPHY

Abercrombie, J.R.

1984 A Short Note on a Siloam Tomb Inscription. *BASOR* 254: 61-62.

Adams, R. McC.

1981 *A Heartland of Cities: Surveys of Ancient Settlement and Land Use on the Central Floodplain of the Euphrates*. Chicago: University of Chicago Press.

Aharoni, M.

1981 Inscribed Weights and Royal Seals. In Y. Aharoni 1981: 126-27.

Aharoni, Y.

1962 *Excavations at Ramat Rahel. Seasons 1959 and 1960*. Rome: Centro di studi semitici, University of Rome.

1964 *Excavations at Ramat Rahel. Seasons 1961 and 1962*. Rome: Centro di studi semitici, University of Rome.

1965 The Citadel of Ramat Rahel. *Archaeology* 18: 15-25.

1968 Arad: Its Inscriptions and Temple. *BA* 31: 2-32.

1973 *Beer-Sheba I*. Tel Aviv: Tel Aviv University Press.

1974 The Horned Altar of Beersheba. *BA* 27: 2-6.

1975 *Lachish V. The Sanctuary and Residency*. Tel Aviv: Tel-Aviv University Press.

1981 *Arad Inscriptions*. Jerusalem: Israel Exploration Society.

Aharoni, Y., and M. Aharoni.

1976 The Stratification of Judahite Sites in the 8th and 7th Centuries BCE. *BASOR* 224: 73-90.

Ahlström, G.W.
1982 *Royal Administration and National Religion in Ancient Palestine*. Studies in the History of the Ancient Near East, 1. Leiden: E.J. Brill.

Albright, W.F.A.
1924 *Excavations and Results at Tell el-Fûl (Gibeah of Saul)*. AASOR, 4 (1922–23). New Haven, CT: Yale University Press.
1943 *The Excavation of Tell Beit Mirsim*. III. *The Iron Age*. AASOR, 21–22. New Haven, CT: American Schools of Oriental Research.

Alt, A.
1953a *Kleine Schriften zur Geschichte des Volkes Israel*. I. Munich: Beck.
1953b *Kleine Schriften zur Geschichte des Volkes Israel*. II. Munich: Beck.

el-Amin, M.N.
1953 Die Reliefs mit Beischriften von Sargon II. in Dûr-Sharrukîn. *Sumer* 9: 35-59, 214-28.

Andersen, F.I., and D.N. Freedman.
1980 *Hosea*. AB, 24. Garden City, NY: Doubleday.

Arensburg, B., and Y. Rak.
1985 Jewish Skeletal Remains from the Period of the Kings of Judaea. *PEQ* 117: 30-34.

Armstrong, D.
unpub. The Excluded Middle: Hezekiah and the Leaders of the Lineages. Seminar paper at York University, 1989.

Avigad, N.
1983 *Discovering Jerusalem*. Jerusalem: Shiqmona.

Ayalon, E.
1985 Trial Excavation of Two Iron Age Strata at Tel 'Eton. *Tel Aviv* 12: 54-62.

Barbu, Z.
1960 *Problems of Historical Psychology*. New York: Grove.

Barkay, G.
1986a The Garden Tomb: Was Jesus Buried Here? *BAR* 12.2: 40-57.
1986b *Ketef Hinnom. A Treasure Facing Jerusalem's Walls*. Catalogue 274. Jerusalem: Israel Museum.
1988 Jerusalem as a Capstone City. In *Settlements, Population and Economy in the Land of Israel in Ancient Times*, 124-25. Ed. S. Bunimowitz, M. Kochavi and A. Kasher. Tel Aviv: Institute for Archaeology, Tel Aviv University.

Barkay, G., and A. Kloner.
1986 Jerusalem Tombs from the Days of the First Temple. *BAR* 12.2: 23-39.

Barnett, R.D.
1958 The Siege of Lachish. *IEJ* 8: 161-64.
1969 Layard's Nimrud Bronzes and their Inscriptions. *Eretz Israel* 8: 1-7.

Beck, P.
1986a A Head of a Goddess from Qitmit. *Qadmoniyot* 19: 79-81.
1986b A Bulla from Horvat 'Uzza. *Qadmoniyot* 19: 40-41.

Begg, C.
1986 2 Kings 20: 12-19 as an Element of the Deuteronomistic History. *CBQ* 48: 27-38.

1987 'Sennacherib's Second Palestinian Campaign': An Additional Indication. *JBL* 106: 685-86.

Beit-Arieh, Y.

1986 An Edomite Temple at Horvat Qitmit. *Qadmoniyot* 19: 72-79.

Beit-Arieh, Y., and P. Beck.

1987 *Edomite Shrine. Discoveries from Qitmit in the Negev*. Jerusalem: Israel Museum.

Beit-Arieh, I., and B. Cresson.

1983 Horvat 'Uza. *IEJ* 33: 271-72.

1985 An Edomite Ostracon from Hurvat 'Uza. *Tel Aviv* 12: 96-101.

Bennett, C. M.

1983 Excavations at Buseirah (Biblical Bozrah). In *Midian, Moab and Edom*, 9-17. Ed. J.F.A. Sawyer and D.J.A. Clines. JSOTSup, 24. Sheffield: JSOT Press.

1984 Excavations at Tawilan in Southern Jordan, 1982. *Levant* 16: 1-23.

Bickert, R.

1987 König Ahas und der Prophet Jesaja. Ein Beitrag zum Problem des syrisch–ephraimitischen Krieges. *ZAW* 99: 361-384.

Biran, A.

1987 Tel Ira and Aroer in the Last Days of the Kingdom of Judah. *Cathedra* 42: 26-33.

Biran, A., and R. Cohen.

1975 Aroer. *IEJ* 25: 171.

1976 Aroer, 1976. *IEJ* 26: 139-40.

1978 Aroer, 1978. *IEJ* 28: 197-99.

Borger, R.

1956 *Die Inschriften Asarhaddons Königs von Assyrien*. AOB, 9. Graz: E. Weidner.

Brinkman, J. A.

1979 Babylonia under the Assyrian Empire, 745–627 B.C. In *Power and Propaganda. A Symposium on Ancient Empires*, 223-50. Ed. M. T. Larsen. Mesopotamia, 7. Copenhagen: Akademisk.

1984 *Prelude to Empire. Babylonian Society and Politics 747–626 B.C.* Occasional Publications of the Babylonian Fund, 7. Philadelphia: University Museum.

Broshi, M.

1974 The Expansion of Jerusalem in the Reigns of Hezekiah and Manasseh. *IEJ* 24: 21-26.

Broshi, M., and G. Barkay.

1985 Excavations in the Chapel of St. Vartan in the Holy Sepulchre. *IEJ* 35: 108-128.

Broshi, M., and R. Gophna.

1984 The Settlements and Population of Palestine During the Early Bronze Age II–III. *BASOR* 253: 41-53.

Bülow, S., and R.A. Mitchell.

1961 An Iron Age II Fortress on Tel Nagila. *IEJ* 11: 101-10.

Chambon, A.
1984 *Tell el-Far'ah. I. L'Age du fer. Paris*: A.D.P.F.

Clayburn, W. E.
1973 The Fiscal Basis of Josiah's Reform. *JBL* 92: 1-22.

Cogan, M.
1974 *Imperialism and Religion: Assyria, Judah and Israel in the Eighth and Seventh Centuries BCE*. SBLMS, 19. Missoula, MT: Scholars Press.

Cohen, R.
1986 Negev Emergency Project, 1984-1985. *IEJ* 36: 111-15.

Cornford, F. M.
1950 *The Unwritten Philosophy and Other Essays*. Ed. W.K.C. Guthrie. Cambridge: Cambridge University Press.

Cross, F.M.
1973 *Canaanite Myth and Hebrew Epic*. Harvard Semitic Studies. Cambridge, MA: Harvard University Press.
1983 The Ammonite Oppression of the Tribes of Gad and Reuben: Missing Verses from 1 Samuel 11 Found in 4QSamuel[a]. In *History, Historiography and Interpretation*, 148-58. Ed. H. Tadmor and M. Weinfeld. Jerusalem: Magnes Press.

Cross, F.M., and J.T. Milik.
1956 Explorations in the Judaean Buqê'ah. *BASOR* 142: 5-17.

Daube, D.
1969 The Culture of Deuteronomy. *ORITA* 3: 27-52.

Davis, D., and A. Kloner.
1978 A Burial Cave from the End of the First Temple Era on the Slopes of Mount Zion. *Qadmoniyot* 11: 16-19.

Dearman, J. A.
1988 *Property Rights in the Eighth-Century Prophets*. SBLDS, 106. Decatur, GA: Scholars Press.

Demsky, A.
1971 The Genealogy of Gibeon (I Chronicles 9: 35-44): Biblical and Epigraphic Considerations. *BASOR* 202: 16-23.
1988 Writing in Ancient Israel and Early Judaism. Part One: The Biblical Period. In *Miqra. Text, Translation, Reading and Interpretation of the Hebrew Bible in Ancient Judaism and Early Christianity*, 2-20. Ed. M.J. Mulder. CRINT, 2.1. Assen: Van Gorcum.

Dever, W. G.
1969 Iron Age Epigraphic Material from the Area of Khirbet el-Kôm. *HUCA* 40: 139-204.
1974 *Gezer*. II. Jerusalem: Hebrew Union College.
1987 The Contribution of Archaeology to the Study of Canaanite and Early Israelite Religion. In *Ancient Israelite Religion. Essays in Honor of Frank Moore Cross*, 209-47. Ed. P.D. Miller, P.D. Hanson and S.D. McBride. Philadelphia: Fortress Press.

Doermann, R.W., and V.M. Fargo.
1985 Tell el-Hesi, 1983. *PEQ* 117: 1-24.

Donner H., and W. Röllig (eds.)
1971 *Kanaanäische und Aramäische Inschriften.* 3 vols. 3rd edn. Wiesbaden: Harrassowitz.

Dothan, T., and S. Gitin.
1985 *Tel Miqne-Ekron. Summary Report of the 1985 Excavations.* Jerusalem: Albright Institute of Archaeological Research and Institute of Archaeology, Hebrew University.
1986 *Tel Miqne-Ekron. Summary Report of the 1986 Excavations.* Jerusalem: Albright Institute of Archaeological Research and Institute of Archaeology, Hebrew University.
1987 The Rise and Fall of Ekron of the Philistines: Recent Excavations at an Urban Border Site. *BA* 50: 197-222.

EAEHL
The Encyclopedia of Archaeological Excavations in the Holy Land. 5 vols. Jerusalem: Israel Exploration Society and Massada, 1975.

Eisenstein, E.L.
1969 The Advent of Printing and the Problem of the Renaissance. *Past and Present* 45: 19-89.

Eitam, D.
1985 *The Oil Industry in the Iron Age at Tel Miqne.* Jerusalem: Albright Institute of Archaeological Research and Institute of Archaeology, Hebrew University.
1987 Olive Oil Production During the Biblical Period. In *Olive Oil in Antiquity. Israel and neighbouring countries,* 16-35. Ed. M. Heltzer and D. Eitam. Haifa: University of Haifa, Israel Oil Industry Museum and Dagon Museum.

Elat, M.
1977 *Economic Relations in the Lands of the Bible.* Jerusalem: Bialik and Israel Exploration Society.

Elayi, J.
1985 Les relations entre les cités phéniciennes et l'empire assyrien sous le règne de Sennachérib. *Sem.* 35: 19-26.
1986 Le sceau de prêtre ḥanan, fils de ḥilqiyahu. *Sem.* 36: 43-46.

Eph'al, I.
1979a Israel: Fall and Exile. In *The Age of the Monarchies: Political History,* 180-91. Ed. A. Malamat and I. Eph'al. World History of the Jewish People 4.1. Jerusalem: Massada.
1979b Assyrian Dominion in Palestine. In *The Age of the Monarchies: Political History,* 276-89. Ed. A. Malamat and I. Eph'al. World History of the Jewish People 4.1. Jerusalem: Massada.
1983 On Warfare and Military Control in the Ancient Near Eastern Empires: A Research Outline. In *History, Historiography and Interpretation. Studies in biblical and cuneiform literatures,* 88-106. Ed. H. Tadmor and M. Weinfeld. Jerusalem: Magnes Press.
1984 *The Ancient Arabs.* Jerusalem: Magnes Press.

Eshel, H.
1987 The Late Iron Age Cemetery of Gibeon. *IEJ* 37: 1-17.

1989 A *lmlk* Stamp from Bethel. *IEJ* 39: 60-62.

Evans, C.D.
1980 Judah's Foreign Policy from Hezekiah to Josiah. In *Scripture in Context*, 157-78. Ed. C.D. Evans, W.W. Hallo and J.B. White. Pittsburgh: Pickwick.

Fales, M. (ed.)
1981 *Assyrian Royal Inscriptions: New Horizons in Literary, Ideological, and Historical Analysis*. Orientis Antiqui Collectio, 17. Rome: Istituto per l'Oriente.

Finkelstein, I.
1986 *'Izbet Sartah. An Early Iron Age Site near Rosh Ha'ayin, Israel*. BAR International Series, 299. Oxford: British Archaeological Reports.
1988 *The Archaeology of the Israelite Settlement*. Jerusalem: Israel Exploration Society.

Flannery, K.V.
1972 The Cultural Evolution of Civilizations. *Annual Review of Ecology and Systematics* 3: 399-426.

Frankfurt Institute for Social Research
1972 *Aspects of Sociology*. Boston: Beacon. (ET, of *Soziologische Exkurse*. Frankfurt: Europäische Verlagsanstalt, 1956).

Friedman, R.E.
1981 *The Exile and Biblical Narrative*. Chico, CA: Scholars Press.
1987 *Who Wrote the Bible?* New York: Summit.
forthcoming *Introduction to the Hebrew Bible*. Anchor Bible Reference Library. Garden City, NY: Doubleday.

Fritz, V.
1981 The 'List of Rehoboam's Fortresses' in 2 Chr 11: 5-12—A Document from the Time of Josiah. *Eretz Israel* 15: 46-63.

Fritz, V., and A. Kempinski.
1983 *Ergebnisse der Ausgrabungen auf der Ḫirbet el-Mšāš (Tēl Māsōs) 1972–1975*. 2 vols. Wiesbaden: Harrassowitz.

Gadd, C.J.
1954 Inscribed Prisms of Sargon II from Nimrud. *Iraq* 16: 173-201.

Gal, Z.
in press *The Settlement of the Lower Galilee*. ASOR Dissertation Series. Winona Lake, IN: Eisenbrauns.
1990 A Phoenician Fort at Horvat Rosh Zayit. In *Highlights of Recent Excavations*, 15. Jerusalem: Israel Antiquities Authority.

Garfinkel, Y.
1984 The Distribution of Identical Seal Impressions and the Settlement Pattern in Judaea before Sennacherib's Campaign. *Cathedra* 32: 35-52.
1988 2 Chr 11: 5-10 Fortified Cities List and the *lmlk* Stamps—Reply to Nadav Na'aman. *BASOR* 271: 69-73.

Geus, C.H.J., de
1976 *The Tribes of Israel*. Studia Semitica Neerlandica, 18. Assen: van Gorcum.

Ginzburg, C.
1989 *Storia Notturna: Una Decifrazione del Sabba*. Turin: Einaudi.

Gitin, S.
1989a Tell Miqne-Ekron: A Type-Site for the Inner Coastal Plain in the Iron Age II Period. *AASOR* 49: 23-58.
1989b Incense Altars from Ekron, Israel and Judah: Context and Typology. *Eretz Israel* 20: 52*-67*.
Gonçalves, F.J.
1986 *L'expédition de Sennachérib en Palestine dans la littérature hébraïque ancienne*. Louvain: Institut Orientaliste.
Goody, J.R.
1962 *Death, Property and the Ancestors*. London: Tavistock.
1969 *Comparative Studies in Kinship*. London: Routledge & Kegan Paul.
1986 *The Logic of Writing and the Organization of Society*. Cambridge: Cambridge University Press.
1987 *The Interface between the Written and the Oral*. Cambridge: Cambridge University Press.
Goody, J.R., and I. Watt.
1968 The Consequences of Literacy. In *Literacy in Traditional Societies*, pp. 27-68. Ed. J.R. Goody. Cambridge: Cambridge University Press.
Gottwald, N.K.
1979 *The Tribes of Yahweh*. New York: Orbis.
Grant, E., and G.E. Wright.
1939 *Ain Shems Excavations*. V. Haverford: Haverford College.
Graves, R., and A. Hodge.
1985 *The Long Weekend. A Social History of Great Britain 1918–1939*. (Orig. Pub. 1940.) London: Hutchinson.
Grayson, A.K.
1980 Histories and Historians of the Ancient Near East: Assyria and Babylonia. *Ori*. 49: 140-95.
Greenberg, M.
1960 Some Postulates of Biblical Criminal Law. In *Yehezkael Kaufmann Jubilee Volume*, 5-28. Ed. M. Haran. Jerusalem: Magnes Press.
1983 *Ezekiel 1–20*. AB. Garden City, NY: Doubleday.
Halpern, B.
1974 Sectionalism and the Schism. *JBL* 94: 519-32.
1981 *The Constitution of the Monarchy in Israel*. HSM, 25. Chico, CA: Scholars Press.
1981b Sacred History and Ideology: Chronicles' Thematic Structure—Intimations of an Earlier Source. In *The Creation of Sacred Literature. Composition and Redaction of the Biblical Text*, 35-54. Ed. R.E. Friedman. Near Eastern Studies, 22. Berkeley: University of California Press.
1983 *The Emergence of Israel in Canaan*. SBLMS, 29. Chico, CA: Scholars Press.
1987a 'The Excremental Vision'. The Priests of Doom in Isaiah 28. *Hebrew Annual Review* 10: 109-21.
1987b 'Brisker Pipes than Poetry: ' The Development of Israelite Monotheism. In *Judaic Perspectives on Ancient Israel*, 77-115. Ed. J.A. Neusner, B.A.

Levine and E.S. Frerichs. Fs. H.L. Ginsberg. Philadelphia: Fortress Press.

1988 *The First Historians. The Hebrew Bible and History.* San Francisco: Harper & Row.

Halpern, B., and D.S. Vanderhooft

unpub. The Editions of Kings in the 8th–7th Centuries B.C.E. Forthcoming in HUCA 63.

Handy, L.K.

1988 Hezekiah's Unlikely Reform. *ZAW* 100: 111-15.

Harper, R.F. (ed.)

1892–1914 *Assyrian and Babylonian Letters.* 14 vols. Chicago: University of Chicago Press.

Hart, S.

1986 Some Preliminary Thoughts on Settlement in Southern Edom. *Levant* 18: 51-58.

1988 Excavations at Ghrareh, 1986: Preliminary Report. *Levant* 20: 89-99.

Herzog, Z.

1987 The Stratigraphy of Israelite Arad: A Rejoinder. *BASOR* 267: 77-79.

Herzog, Z., M. Aharoni, A.F. Rainey, and S. Moshkovitz.

1984 The Israelite Fortress at Arad. *BASOR* 254: 1-34.

Hesse, B.

1986 Animal Use at Tel Miqne-Eqron in the Bronze Age and Iron Age. *BASOR* 264: 17-28.

Hill, C.

1975 *The World Turned Upside Down. Radical Ideas During the English Revolution.* Harmondsworth: Penguin.

Hoffmann, R.C.

1985 Fishing for Sport in Medieval Europe: New Evidence. *Speculum* 60: 877-902.

Holladay, J.S.

1976 Of Sherds and Strata: Contributions toward an Understanding of the Archaeology of the Divided Monarchy. In *Magnalia Dei: The Mighty Acts of God*, 260-68. Ed. F.M. Cross, W.E. Lemke and P.D. Miller. Garden City, NY: Doubleday.

1986 The Stables of Ancient Israel. Functional Determinants of Stable Construction and the Interpretation of Pillared Building Remains of the Palestinian Iron Age. In *The Archaeology of Jordan and Other Studies*, 103-66. Ed. L.T. Geraty and L.G. Herr. FLC. S. Horn. Berrien Springs, MI: Andrews University Press.

1987 Religion in Israel and Judah under the Monarchy: An Explicitly Archaeological Approach. In *Ancient Israelite Religion. Essays in Honor of Frank Moore Cross*, 249-99. Ed. P.D. Miller, P.D. Hanson and S.D. McBride. Philadelphia: Fortress Press.

Hulin, P.

1963 The Inscriptions on the Carved Throne-Base of Shalmaneser III. *Iraq* 25: 48-69.

Humphreys, S. C.
1980 Family tombs and tomb cult in ancient Athens: tradition or traditionalism. *JHS* 100: 96-126.

Jaspers, K.
1968 Xenophanes. In *Aneignung und Polemik. Gesammelte Reden und Aufsätze zur Geschichte der Philosophie*, 32-42. Ed. H. Ganer. Munich: R. Piper.

Johns, C.H.W. (ed.)
1901 *Assyrian Deeds and Documents Recording the Transfer of Property*. 7 vols. Cambridge: Deighton Bell.

Kahn, H.
1960 *On Thermonuclear War*. Princeton: Princeton University Press.

Kelm, G.L., and A. Mazar.
1985 Tel Batash (Timnah) Excavations. Second Preliminary Report (1981–1983). In *Preliminary Reports of ASOR Sponsored Excavations*, 93-120. Ed. W. Rast. BASOR Supplements, 23. Winona Lake, IN: Eisenbrauns.

Kempinski, A.
1987 Some Philistine Names from the Kingdom of Gaza. *IEJ* 37: 20-24.

King, P. J.
1989 The Eighth, the Greatest of Centuries. *JBL* 108: 3-15.

Kloner, A.
1982 A First Temple Burial Cave at Ṣobah. *Hadashot Archaeologiyyot* 78–79: 71-72.

Kochavi, M.
1970 The First Season of Excavations at Tel Malhata. *Qadmoniyot* 3: 22-24.
1972a (Ed.) *Judaea, Samaria and the Golan: Archaeological Survey 1967–1968*. Jerusalem: Carta.
1972b Tel Malhata. *RB* 79: 593-96.
1974 Khirbet Rabûd = Debir. *Tel Aviv* 1: 2-34.

Kooij, A. van der
1986 Das assyrische Heer vor den Mauern Jerusalems im Jahr 701 v. Chr. *ZDPV* 102: 93-109.

Kramer, C.
1982 *Village Ethnoarchaeology. Rural Iran in Archaeological Perspective*. New York: Academic Press.

Kreuzer, S.
1983 *Der lebendige Gott*. BWANT, 6.16. Stuttgart: Kohlhammer.

Kümmel, H.M.
1981 *Texte aus der Umwelt des Alten Testaments*. I. *Rechts- und Wirtschafts-urkunden. Historisch-chronologisch Texte*. Gütersloh: G. Mohn.

Lance, H.D.
1971 Royal Stamps and the Kingdom of Judah. *HTR* 72: 315-32.

Lang, B.
1984 George Orwell im gelobten Land. In *Kirche und Visitation*, 21-35. Ed. E.W. Zeeden and P.T. Lang. Stuttgart: Klett-Cotta.

Lapp, N.
1981 *The Third Campaign at Tell el-Ful: The Excavations of 1964*. AASOR, 45. Cambridge, MA: American Schools of Oriental Research.

Lapp, P., and N. Lapp.
1968 Iron II-Hellenistic Pottery Groups. In *The 1957 Excavation at Beth-Zur*, 54-79. Ed. P.W. Lapp. AASOR, 38. Cambridge, MA: American Schools of Oriental Research.

Lemaire, A.
1981a Classification des estampilles royales Judéennes. *Eretz Israel* 15: 54-59.
1981b *Les écoles et la formation de la Bible dans l'ancien Israël*. OBO, 39. Göttingen: Vandenhoeck & Ruprecht.
1985 Notes d'épigraphie nord-ouest sémitique. *Sem.* 35: 13-17.

Levenson, J.D.
1985 *Sinai and Zion. An Entry into the Jewish Bible*. Minneapolis: Winston.
1988 *Creation and the Persistence of Evil*. San Francisco: Harper & Row.

Lie, A.G.
1929 *The Inscriptions of Sargon II, King of Assyria. Part I: The Annals*. Paris: Geuthner.

Loffreda, S.
1968 Typological Sequence of Iron Age Rock-Cut Tombs in Palestine. *Liber Annuus Studii Biblici* 18: 244-287.

Luckenbill, D.D.
1924 *The Annals of Sennacherib*. Oriental Institute Publications, 2. Chicago: University of Chicago Press.
1926 *Ancient Records of Assyria and Babylonia*. 2 vols. Chicago: University of Chicago Press.

McClellan, T.L.
1975 'Quantitative Studies in the Iron Age Pottery of Palestine.' PhD dissertation, University of Pennsylvania.
1978 Towns to Fortresses: The Transformation of Urban Life from the 8th to 7th Century BC. In *Society of Biblical Literature Seminar Papers 1978*, 277-86. Ed. P.J. Achtemeier. Missoula, MT: Scholars Press.
1984 Town Planning at Tell en-Nasbeh. *ZDPV* 100: 53-69.

McCown, C.C.
1945 The Long-Room House at Tell en-Nasbeh. *BASOR* 98: 2-15.
1947 *Tell en-Nasbeh. I. Archaeological and Historical Results*. Berkeley: Pacific School of Religion.

Machinist, P.
1983 Assyria and its Image in the First Isaiah. *JAOS* 103: 719-37.

Malamat, A.
1968 King Lists of the Old Babylonian Period. *JAOS* 88: 163-73.
1973a Josiah's Bid for Armageddon. *JANESCU* 5: 267-79.
1973b Tribal Societies: Biblical Genealogies and African Lineage Systems. *Archives Européenes de Sociologie* 14: 126-36.
1979 *Ummātum* in Old Babylonian Texts and its Ugaritic and Biblical Counterparts. *UF* 11: 527-36.

1982 Longevity: Biblical Concepts and Some Ancient Near Eastern Parallels. *Comptes rendus des rencontres assyriologiques* 28: 215-24.

1983 *Israel in Biblical Times. Historical Essays*. Jerusalem: Bialik.

Mazar, A.

1976 Iron Age Burial Caves North of the Damascus Gate, Jerusalem. *IEJ* 26: 1-8.

1982 Iron Age Fortresses in the Judaean Hills. *PEQ* 114: 87-109.

1985 Between Judah and Philistia: Timnah (Tel Batash) in the Iron Age II. *Eretz Israel* 18: 300-24.

Mazar, A., D. Amit, and Z. Elan.

1983 'The Border Road' between Michmash and Jericho and the Excavations at Horvat Shilha. *Eretz Israel* 17: 236-50.

Mazar, A., and E. Netzer.

1986 On the Israelite Fortress at Arad. *BASOR* 263: 87-91.

Mazar, B.

1981 The Early Israelite Settlement in the Hill Country. *BASOR* 241: 75-85.

Mazar, B., T. Dothan and I. Dunayevsky.

1966 *En-Gedi. The First and Second Seasons of Excavations 1961–1962*. 'Atiqot, 5. Jerusalem: Department of Antiquities.

Mazar, E.

1985 Edomite Pottery at the End of the Iron Age. *IEJ* 35: 253-69.

Mazar, E., and B. Mazar.

1989 *Excavations in the South of the Temple Mount. The Ophel of Biblical Jerusalem*. Qedem, 29. Jerusalem: Institute of Archaeology, Hebrew University.

Mendenhall, G.E.

1958 The Census Lists of Numbers 1 and 26. *JBL* 77: 52-66.

1983 Ancient Israel's Hyphenated History. In *Palestine in Transition: The Emergence of Ancient Israel*, 91-103. Ed. D.N. Freedman and D. F. Graf. Social World of Biblical Antiquity Series, 2. Sheffield: Almond Press.

Mettinger, T.N.D.

1971 *Solomonic State Officials. A Study of the Civil Government Officials of the Israelite Monarchy*. ConBOTS, 5. Lund: Gleerup.

1976 *King and Messiah. The Civil and Sacral Legitimation of the Israelite Kings*. ConBOTS, 8. Lund: Gleerup.

1987 *In Search of God. The Meaning and Message of the Everlasting Names*. Philadelphia: Fortress Press.

Michel, E.

1947 Die Assur-Texte Salmanassars III. (858–824). *WO* 1: 5-20.

Millard, A. R.

1985 Sennacherib's Attack on Hezekiah. *TynBul* 36: 61-77.

Mommsen, H., I. Perlman and J. Yellin.

1984 The Provenience of the *lmlk* Jars. *IEJ* 34: 89-113.

Na'aman, N.

1974 Sennacherib's 'Letter to God' on His Campaign to Judah. *BASOR* 214: 25-39.

1979 Sennacherib's Campaign to Judah and the Date of the LMLK Stamps. *VT* 29: 61-86.

1986a *Borders and Districts in Biblical Historiography*. Jerusalem: Simor.

1986b Hezekiah's Fortified Cities and the LMLK Stamps. *BASOR* 261: 5-21.

1987 The Negev in the Last Days of the Kingdom of Judah. *Cathedra* 42: 4-15.

1988 The Date of 2 Chronicles 11: 5-10—A Reply to Y. Garfinkel. *BASOR* 271: 74-77.

1989 Population Changes in the Land of Israel in the Aftermath of the Assyrian Deportations. *Cathedra* 54: 43-62.

Nadelman, Y.

1989 Iron Age II Clay Figurine Fragments from the Excavations. In Mazar, E. and Mazar, B. 1989: 123-27.

Naveh, J.

1962 The Excavations at Mesad Hashavyahu: Preliminary Report. *IEJ* 12: 90-113.

1963 Old Hebrew Inscriptions in a Burial Cave. *IEJ* 13: 74-92.

1985 Writing and Scripts in Seventh-Century BCE. Philistia: The New Evidence from Tell Jemmeh. *IEJ* 35: 9-21.

Noth, M.

1966 *The Laws in the Pentateuch and Other Studies*. London: SCM Press.

Oded, B.

1979 *Mass Deportations and Deportees in the Neo-Assyrian Empire*. Wiesbaden: L. Reichert.

Oppenheim, A. L.

1960 The City Assur in 714 BC. *JNES* 19: 133-47.

Oren, E.D., N. Fleming, S. Kornberg, R. Feinstein, and P. Nahshoni.

1986 A Phoenician Commercial Center on the Egyptian Border. *Qadmoniyot* 19: 83-91.

O'Shea, J. M.

1984 *Mortuary Variability*. Orlando: Academic Press.

Paine, T.

1945 *Complete Writings*. Ed. P.S. Foner. New York: Citadel.

Parker, B.

1961 Administrative Tablets from the North-West Palace, Nimrud. *Iraq* 23: 15-67

1963 Economic Tablets from the Temple of Mamu at Balawat. *Iraq* 25: 86-103.

Parpola, S.

1980 *Letters from Assyrian Scholars to the Kings Esarhaddon and Assurbanipal*. Kevelaer: Butzon and Bercker.

Patrich, J., and B. Arubas.

1989 A Juglet Containing Balsam Oil(?) From a Cave Near Qumran. *IEJ* 39: 43-59.

Pearson, M.P.

1982 Mortuary practices, society and ideology: an ethnoarchaeological study. In *Symbolic and Structural Archaeology*, 99-113. Ed. I. Hodder. Cambridge: Cambridge University Press.

Petrie, W. F.
1891 *Tell el Hesy (Lachish)*. London: Palestine Exploration Fund.

Postgate, J.N.
1974 *Taxation and Conscription in the Assyrian Empire*. Studia Pohl, Series Maiora 3. Rome: Pontifical Biblical Institute.

Pratico, G.D.
1982 A Reappraisal of Nelson Glueck's Excavations at Tell el-Kheleifeh. *American Schools of Oriental Research Newsletter* 6 (March) 6-11.
1985 Nelson Glueck's 1938–1940 Excavations at Tell el-Kheleifeh: A Reappraisal. *BASOR* 259: 1-32.

Pritchard, J.B.
1962 *Gibeon Where the Sun Stood Still*. Princeton: Princeton University Press.
1964 *Winery, Defenses, and Soundings at Gibeon*. Museum Monographs. Philadelphia: University of Pennsylvania Museum.

Pritchard, J.B. (ed.)
1969 *Ancient Near Eastern Texts Relating to the Old Testament*. 3rd edn. Princeton: Princeton University Press.

Pryce-Jones, D.
1989 *The Closed Circle: An Interpretation of the Arabs*. New York: Harper & Row.

Rahmani, L.Y.
1981 Ancient Jerusalem's Funerary Customs and Tombs. Part Two. *BA* 44: 229-35

Reade, J.E.
1972 The Neo-Assyrian Court and Army: Evidence from the Sculptures. *Iraq* 34: 87-112.
1976 Sargon's Campaigns of 720, 716 and 715 B.C.: Evidence from the Sculptures. *JNES* 35: 95-104.
1981 Neo-Assyrian Monuments in their Historical Context. In Fales 1981, 143-67.

Reich, R.
1984 The Identification of the 'Sealed *kāru* of Egypt'. *IEJ* 34: 32-38.

Reviv, H.
1979 The History of Judah from Hezekiah to Josiah. In *The Age of the Monarchies: Political History*, 193-204. Ed. A. Malamat and I. Eph'al. World History of the Jewish People, 4.1. Jerusalem: Massada.
1983 *The Elders in Ancient Israel. A Study of a Biblical Institution*. Jerusalem: Magnes Press.

Risdon, D.L.
1939 A Study of the Cranial and Other Human Remains from Palestine Excavated at Tell Duweir (Lachish) by the Wellcome–Marston Archaeological Research Expedition. *Biometrika* 31: 99-166.

Roberts, J.J.M.
1983 Isaiah 33: An Isaianic Elaboration of the Zion Tradition. In *The Word of the LORD Shall Go Forth*, 15-25. Ed. C.L. Meyers and M.P. O'Connor. Fs. D.N. Freedman. Winona Lake, IN: Eisenbrauns.

Rosenbaum, J.
1979 Hezekiah's Reform and the Deuteronomistic Tradition. *HTR* 72: 24-43.
Rost, P.
1893 *Die Keilschrifttexte Tiglat-Pilesers III*. Leipzig: Eduard Pfeiffer.
Rowley, H.H.
1962 Hezekiah's Reform and Rebellion. *BJRL* 44: 395-431.
Saggs, H.W.F.
1955 The Nimrud Letters, 1952—Part II. *Iraq* 17: 126-60.
1963 Assyrian Warfare in the Sargonid Period. *Iraq* 25: 145-54.
1969 *Assyriology and the Study of the Old Testament*. Cardiff: University of Wales Press.
Sauren, H.
1985 Sennachérib, les Arabes, les déportés Juifs. *WO* 16: 80-99.
Sellers, O.R.
1933 *The Citadel of Beth Zur*. Philadelphia: Westminster Press.
Shaw, C.S.
1987 Micah 1: 10-16 Reconsidered. *JBL* 106: 223-29.
Shea, W.H.
1985 Sennacherib's Second Palestinian Campaign. *JBL* 104: 401-18.
Shiloh, Y.
1970 The Four-Room House: Its Situation and Function in the Israelite City. *IEJ* 20: 180-90.
1980 The Population of Iron Age Palestine in the Light of a Sample Analysis of Urban Plans, Areas and Population Density. *BASOR* 239: 25-35.
1984 *Excavations at the City of David I. 1978–1982*. Qedem, 19. Jerusalem: Institute of Archaeology, Hebrew University.
1987 South Arabian Inscriptions of the Iron Age II from Jerusalem. *Eretz Israel* 19: 288-94.
1988 The Casemate Wall, the Four-Room House, and the Beginnings of Planning in the Israelite City. In *Settlements, Population and Economy in the Land of Israel in Ancient Times*, 145-65. Ed. S. Bunimowitz, M. Kochavi and A. Kasher. Tel Aviv: Institute for Archaeology, Tel Aviv University.
Sinclair, L.A.
1960 *An Archaeological Study of Gibeah (Tell el-Fûl)*. AASOR, 34-35 (1954–1956). New Haven, CT: American Schools of Oriental Research.
1964 An Archaeological Study of Gibeah (Tell el-Fûl). *BA* 27: 52-64.
Smith, D.L.
1988 The Politics of Ezra. Seminar paper for Society of Biblical Literature consultation on the Sociology of the Second Temple Period. *SBLSP*. Decatur, GA: Scholars Press.
Snodgrass, A.
1982 Les origines du culte des héros dans la Grèce antique. In *La mort, les morts dans les sociétés anciennes*, 107-19. Ed. G. Gnoli and J.-P. Vernant. Cambridge: Cambridge University Press.
Spieckermann, H.
1982 *Juda unter Assur in der Sargonidenzeit*. FRLANT, 129. Göttingen: Vandenhoeck & Ruprecht.

Stager, L.E.
1975 Ancient Agriculture in the Judaean Desert: A Case Study of the Buqe'ah Valley in the Iron Age. PhD dissertation, Harvard University.
1985 The Archaeology of the Family in Ancient Israel. *BASOR* 260: 1-35.

Stern, E.
1984 *Excavations at Tel Mevorakh (1973–1976). Part Two: The Bronze Age.* Qedem, 18. Jerusalem: Hebrew University Press.

Stohlmann, S.
1983 The Judaean Exile after 701 B.C.E. In *Scripture in Context II*, 147-75. Ed. W.W. Hallo, J.C. Moyer and L.G. Perdue. Winona Lake, IN: Eisenbrauns.

Streck, M.
1916 *Assurbanipal und die letzten assyrischen Könige bis zum Untergange Ninevehs.* 3 vols. Vorderasiatische Bibliothek, 7. Leipzig: Hinrichs.

Suzuki, Y.
1985 Juridical Administration of the Royal State in the Deuteronomic Reformation. *Seishogaku Ronshuu* 20: 50-94.

Tadmor, H.
1958 The Campaigns of Sargon II of Assur: A Chronological–Historical Study. *JCS* 12: 22-40, 77-100.
1961 Azriyau of Yaudi. *Scripta Hierosolymitana* 8: 232-71.
1966 Philistia under Assyrian Rule. *BA* 29: 86-102.
1975 Assyria and the West: The Ninth Century and its Aftermath. In *Unity and Diversity*, 36-48. Ed. H. Goedicke and J.J.M. Roberts. Baltimore: Johns Hopkins University Press.
1981 History and Ideology in the Assyrian Royal Inscriptions. In Fales 1981: 13-33.
1982 Traditional Institutions and the Monarchy: Social and Political Tensions in the Time of David and Solomon. In *Studies in the Period of David and Solomon and Other Essays*, 239-57. Ed. T. Ishida. Tokyo: Yamakawa-Shuppansha.
1985 Sennacherib's Campaign to Judah: Historical and Historiographical Considerations. *Zion* 50: 65-80.

Talmon, S.
1986 *King, Cult and Calendar in Ancient Israel.* Jerusalem: Magnes Press.

Tawney, R.H.
1938 *Religion and the Rise of Capitalism.* West Drayton: Pelican.

Thureau-Dangin, F.
1912 *Une relation de la huitième campagne de Sargon (714 av. J.-C.).* Textes cunéiformes du Musée du Louvre, 3. Paris: Geuthner.

Tufnell, O.
1953 *Lachish III. The Iron Age.* London: Palestine Exploration Fund.

Ussishkin, D.
1969 On the Shorter Inscription from the 'Tomb of the Royal Steward'. *BASOR* 196: 16-22.
1976 The '*lmlk*' Store Jars and the Excavations at Lachish. *Qadmoniyot* 9: 63-68.

1977 The Destruction of Lachish by Sennacherib and the Dating of the Royal Judaean Storage Jars. *Tel Aviv* 4: 28-60.

1978 Excavations at Tel Lachish—1973–1977. *Tel Aviv* 5: 1-93.

1983 Excavations at Tel Lachish 1978–1983—Second Preliminary Report. *Tel Aviv* 10: 97-185.

1985 Reassessment of the Stratigraphy and Chronology of Archaeological Sites in Judah in the Light of Lachish III. In *Biblical Archaeology Today*. Jerusalem: Israel Exploration Society: 142-44.

1986 *The Village of Silwan. The Necropolis from the Period of the Judaean Kingdom*. Jerusalem: Yad ben-Zvi and the Israel Exploration Society.

1988 The Date of the Judaean Shrine at Arad. *IEJ* 38: 142-57.

1989 Schumacher's Shrine in Building 338 at Megiddo. *IEJ* 39: 149-72.

Vanderhooft, D.S.

1990 Kinship Organization in Ancient Israel. MA thesis, York University.

Van Seters, John.

1983 *In Search of History*. New Haven: Yale University Press.

Vaux, R. de

1955 Les Fouilles de Tell el-Far'ah Près Naplouse. *RB* 62: 575-89.

Vernant, J.-P.

1966 *Mythe et pensée chez les grecs*. Etudes de psychologie historique. 2nd edn. Paris: Francois Maspero.

1982 *The Origins of Greek Thought*. Ithaca, NY: Cornell University Press.

Vogt, E.

1986 *Der Aufstand Hiskias und die Belagerung Jerusalems 701 v. Chr*. AnBib, 106. Rome: Pontifical Biblical Institute.

Wäfler, M.

1975 *Nicht-Assyrer neuassyrischer Darstellungen*. AOAT, 26. Neukirchen: Neukirchener Verlag.

Waldbaum, J.

1967 Philistine Tombs at Tell Fara and their Aegean Prototypes. *AJA* 80: 331-40.

Wampler, J.C., and C.C. McCown.

1947 *Tell en-Nasbeh. II. The Pottery*. Berkeley, CA: Pacific Institute of Religion.

Wapnish, P., and B. Hesse.

unpub. a Philistine/Israelite Animal Use in Iron Age Canaan. Annual Meeting, Society for Ethnobiology, March 1987.

unpub. b Faunal Remains from Tell Dan: Perspectives on Animal Production at a Village, Urban and Ritual Center.

Weinfeld, M.

1972 *Deuteronomy and the Deuteronomic School*. Oxford: Clarendon Press.

Weippert, M.H.E.

1981 Assyrische Prophetien der Zeit Asarhaddons und Assurbanipals. In Fales 1981: 71-115.

Wellhausen, J.

1965 *Prolegomena to the History of Israel*. Cleveland, OH: Meridian (= 2nd edn; Berlin: G. Reimer, 1883).

Welten, P.
1969 *Die Königs-Stempel. Ein Beitrag zur Militärpolitik Judas unter Hiskia und Josia*. ADPV. Wiesbaden: Harrassowitz.

Wilson, R.R.
1977 *Genealogy and History in the Biblical World*. Yale Near Eastern Researches, 7. New Haven, CT: Yale University Press.
1980 *Prophecy and Society in Ancient Israel*. Philadelphia: Fortress Press.
1983 Enforcing the Covenant: The Mechanisms of Judicial Authority in Early Israel. In *The Quest for the Kingdom of God: Essays in Honor of George E. Mendenhall*, 59-75. Ed. H.B. Huffmon, F.A. Spina and A.R.W. Green. Winona Lake, IN: Eisenbrauns.

Winckler, H.
1889 *Die Keilscrifttexte Sargons I*. Leipzig: Eduard Pfeiffer.

Wiseman, D.J.
1951 Two Historical Inscriptions from Nimrud. *Iraq* 13: 21-26.

Xella, P.
1980 Sur la Nouriture des Morts. Un aspect de l'eschatologie mésopotamienne. In *Death in Mesopotamia*, 151-60. Ed. B. Alster. Mesopotamia, 8. Comptes rendus des rencontres assyriologiques, 26. Copenhagen: Akademisk.

Yadin, Y.
1969 An Inscribed South-Arabian Clay Stamp from Bethel? *BASOR* 196: 37-45.
1973 The 'House of Baal' in Samaria and in Judah. In *Eretz Shomron*. 30th Archaeological Convention. Jerusalem: Israel Exploration Society: 58-66.
1976 Beer-Sheba: The High Place Destroyed by King Josiah. *BASOR* 222: 5-17.

Yaron, R.
1980 Biblical Law: Prolegomena. In *Jewish Law in Legal History and in the Modern World*, 27-44. Ed. B.S. Jackson. Jewish Law Annual Supplement 2. Leiden: Brill.
Forthcoming Social Problems and Policies in the Ancient Near East. In *Law, Politics and Society in the Ancient Mediterranean World*. Ed. B. Halpern and D.W. Hobson. Sheffield: Sheffield Academic Press.

Yeivin, S.
1961 *First Preliminary Report on the Excavations at Tel 'Gat'*. Jerusalem: The Gat Expedition.

Zaccagnini, C.
1981 An Urartean Royal Inscription in the Report of Sargon's Eighth Campaign. In Fales 1981: 259-95.

Zadok, R.
1979 *The Jews in Babylonia during the Chaldean and Achaemenian Periods*. Haifa: Haifa University.

Zimhoni, O.
1985 The Iron Age Pottery of Tel 'Eton and its Relation to the Lachish, Tell Beit Mirsim and Arad Assemblages. *Tel Aviv* 12: 63-90.

The Function of the Law in the Development of Israel's Prophetic Traditions[1]

Brian Peckham

There was a time when prophecy, history and law were considered to be separate and quite incompatible things. Law is a constant feature of historiography, but it was thought to be late and intrusive in historical texts, its present narrative context a far cry from its discrete origins and enactments.[2] History runs the gamut of genres from epic to archive (Van Seters 1983; Fornara 1983), but it was considered an approximation to past events in their original setting and sequence, and it acquired an air of authenticity from its anonymity and amalgamation of sources that together seemed to reflect the very process of tradition and transmission (Noth 1943, 1948). Prophecy is personal and speaks in the future tense, but it was traced to some social setting, to an acute perception of contemporary events, to some momentary inspiration and impassioned delivery, and included the obvious consternation of its audience, that are all still evident in the awkward and unruly written version (Lang 1984; McKane 1979; Wilson 1979, 1980). In that time, prophecy was always primary, law was alternately first or last in time and importance, and real history was sifted out of

1. Collections of laws such as the 'Book of the Covenant' in Exod. 20.22-23.33, or the 'Cultic Decalogue' in Exod. 34, or even the entire legislative section of the book of Deuteronomy, are usually supposed to have arisen independently of the narrative contexts in which they take shape: see, for example, Noth 1962:173; Halbe 1975; Levenson 1979.

2. In practice prophecy was considered the source or inspiration of normative Israelite religion (von Rad 1965), the law was thought to have been revealed early in the history of the nation even though it only gradually surfaced in the literature (Paul 1970), and the sequence of events in the history of Israel seemed to correspond pretty well to the sequence of biblical books (Albright 1963).

its casual editorial accretions and accepted as an innocent bystander.[1]

That time in the history of biblical scholarship is complex and recurrent. It was the time of Higher Criticism when historical documents could be denuded of their troublesome aspects and aligned in chronological order; when the law was not Mosaic but a symptom of incipient Judaism; when prophets were the nonpareils of ethical monotheism (e.g. Wellhausen 1878). It was the time of Form Criticism when historiography was a cultic art and Sinai was a separate legal tradition that had no significance for the salvation of the nation (von Rad 1938). It was more recent times of Literary Criticism when covenant became both the literary form that could combine historiography and legislation, and the ideology that explained the institution and publication of the prophets (Clements 1965, 1975). Or it was still more recent times of Redaction Criticism when covenant suddenly reverted to its late and artificial role in the rationalization of national unity (Perlitt 1969; Phillips 1982; Nicholson 1986; Oden 1987). It was the time, in fact, of historical-critical theory when literature was thought to reflect reality and when the sequence of literary works was taken as the image of historical development.

That time is past. The historical-critical theory did all it could to define likely elements of tradition and their probable sequence of transmission.[2] But it moved too easily from literary to historical data, from evidence to event, and it soon suppressed every avenue of its own verification.[3] It became compatible with any variant that accounted for all the pieces and it finally made literary and historical reconstructions seem anything from haphazard to totally arbitrary. The result was that it seemed better to leave everything pretty much

1. This aspect of the method is evident in the publication of the form-critical project, including such works as Coats 1983.

2. The existence of a premonarchic Israelite amphictyony, for instance, was projected from the existence of invariable and presumably early tribal lists and has continued to bedevil historical reconstruction (cf. Chambers 1983:39-59). Or similarly, references to Assyria in the book of Isaiah led to the conclusion that there was a redaction of his work that merely reflected the contemporary historical reality (cf. Barth 1977).

3. In post-critical times the historicity of the text is taken for granted and literary criticism is directed to some sort of holistic appreciation. In effect, historical reconstruction becomes a form of exegesis (Weinfeld 1987:303-314), theology (Childs 1979) or narrative analysis (Alter 1981).

the way it was, to suppose that the history of Israel corresponded more or less with the actual sequence of events recorded in the biblical books, to imagine that literary values really coincided with the canonical expectations of a believing community.[1]

However, the achievements of the historical-critical method in the delimitation of historiography, law and prophecy are permanent and secure, and they are not impugned by ignorance or desuetude. The problem lies not in the literary achievement of the method, but in its historical presumption, the sense that it did not have to test its results, but could simply apply them to reality. It really does not do to suppose that the order of literary works reflects the progress of history, and this suppostition is especially difficult to accept when the order itself has been established by guesswork and historical verisimilitude.

But there is a test of the literary evidence that corrects itself as it goes, without imagining some ineffable and parallel order of events to which the words correspond, and without supposing that every distinct interpretation is the product of a different occurrence. The test concerns literary integrity and dependence, the composition of simple texts from insight and information, the composition of complex literary works from text and commentary on sources, the sequence of literary works through analogous systems of recognition and citation. The test of the literary evidence produces literary results; not history or the truth of the matter, but data to be considered in historical reconstruction.

The systems of recognition and citation used to compose complex texts include repetition and cross-reference. Repetition is the re-use of literary elements from the original simple composition in an opposite order, or in a contrary, or contradictory sense.[2] Cross-reference is the restatement of these secondary and already intrusive elements in further incongruous contexts.[3] Together they create a complex and non-sequential bond of text and commentary. In a sequence of such complex texts, the establishment of a literary tradition depends on an

1. The principles of repetition were recognized in 1955 by M. Seidel and have been elaborated most recently by Beentjes (1982).

2. The editorial use of cross-reference was recognized by Kuhl (1952).

3. An interesting corollary of law's origin in historiography is the Deuteronomistic Historian's (Dtr^2) use of extant historical sources in the framing of laws (Carmichael 1974, 1985).

analogous system of quotation and allusion. Quotations are a form of repetition. They consist of one or more words (1) that are unusual or anomalous in their present context, and (2) that are repeated in an opposite order or contrary sense from another text, (a) which explains both them and the present context, and (b) is quoted again or alluded to elsewhere in the present text. Allusions are a form of cross-reference comprising groups of one or more words that are distributed in their present context, but are peculiar to another context where they are combined and explained. Together these systems of recognition and citation create a sequence of literary works whose interpretation reveals the cumulative wisdom of the ages.

The effect of this test, when it is applied to the historical-critical notions of historiography, law and prophecy, is that historiography is primary, that it always includes some form of law as a constitutive element,[1] that prophecy protests not just against real events but against the justification that the facts received in some prior history and legislation, and that prophecy finally was overtaken by the law and succumbed to historical theory. Specifically, it means that prophets from Isaiah to Ezekiel knew and criticized the laws and legal institutions propounded by J, Dtr, P and E,[2] but that those who revised their

1. The sigla refer to the Yahwist (J), the Deuteronomist (usually Dtr1, to be distinguished from the later Deuteronomistic Historian, Dtr2), the Priestly Writer (P), and the Elohist (E). The order and delimitation of these sources is described in Brian Peckham, *The Composition of the Deuteronomistic History* (HSM, 35; Atlanta: Scholars Press, 1985). In what follows the sequence of prophets is assumed to have been: Isaiah, Amos, Hosea, Micah, Jeremiah, Nahum, Habakkuk, Zephaniah, Ezekiel. The combined order of prophetic and narrative works, consequently, is presumed to have been: J, Isaiah, Dtr1, Amos, P, E, Hosea, Micah, Jeremiah, Nahum, Habakkuk, Zephaniah, Ezekiel, Dtr2.

2. The law includes (a) common or judge-made law that establishes the principles of fundamental justice and protects basic rights by restricting ordinary individual behaviour, (b) the legislation, organization, and codification of positive and negative responsibilities affecting society or specific segments of society, and (c) the theory and interpretation of law. Common law corresponds to *mišpāt* and *ṣĕdāqāh* in Israel and probably included the commands (*miṣwôt*) of the forefathers and the words (*dĕbārîm*) of the prophets: the stipulations of the J covenant are called the words (*dĕbārîm*) that Yahweh spoke to Moses (Exod. 34.27); Isaiah criticized the city that rejected his word (*dābār*) and indulged in extortion and fraud (Isa. 30.12), and he looked forward to a society established on *mišpāt* and *ṣĕdāqāh* (Isa. 28.17); Dtr1 referred to the stipulations of the contemporary covenant as the words (*dĕbārîm*)

works were influenced by the recent promulgation of the Law in the Deuteronomistic History[1] and tried to bring them into line with the Law and historical theory,[2] while their successors were limited to satire, the analysis of current affairs or the witty propositions of apocalyptic.[3]

One of the clearest examples is Isaiah, whose work went through

that Yahweh spoke to Moses (Deut. 1.1) and the commandment (*miṣwāh*) that Moses gave (Deut. 11.22; 12.14); Amos blamed the fall of Samaria on its rejection of fundamental justice (Amos 5.7, *mišpāt* and *ṣĕdāqāh*) and on its refusal to accept judicial or prophetic correction (Amos 5.10), and he cited in evidence of his claim the numerous crimes committed against the poor, the helpless and the dispossessed (e.g. Amos 2.6-8; 3.9-10; 4.1-3; 5.10-12; 8.4-6); Micah condemned the leaders of Jerusalem for perverting justice (*mišpāt*, 3.1, 9, 11; 6.8) and presented himself as the prosecutor in God's case against them (3.8; 6.1-5). Legislation falls under the general heading of a divinely sanctioned *tôrāh* and probably included elements of common law as well as customs and decrees (*ḥuqqîm*): in Isaiah it refers to Yahweh's promulgation of a civic order based on justice and contained in the words of the prophet (Isa. 28.9-19; 30.8); in E *ḥuqqîm* and *tôrāh* refer to the responses that Moses received from God (Exod. 18.20-26) that were promulgated as the words (*d*^e*bārîm*) of God (Exod. 20.1); in Hosea *tôrāh* is the written law (Hos. 8.1, 12); in Jeremiah it is the written law that has been falsified in transmission (Jer. 8.8-9); in the Deuteronomistic History (Dtr2), and in all subsequent writings, it is the codification of the law in the Book of Deuteronomy. The basic theory and interpretation of the law is that it expressed the rights and obligations of covenant partners. The notion of a divine covenant was inspired by Assyrian political treaties and in Israel seems to have been a novel idea peculiar to Judaean historians. As it was introduced by J and endorsed by Dtr1 it entailed a unique parity relationship between the nation and its God. The later Deuteronomistic Historian, influenced by prophetic criticism, abandoned the pretension and identified covenant with the obligations defined in the Decalogue and with the willingness to obey expressed in the New Covenant. All subsequent writers followed suit.

1. Although it is usual to refer to a Deuteronomistic revision of prophecy—in Amos, for instance, and especially in Jeremiah—it seems that all the prophecies were revised by different writers who endorsed the 'Law of Moses' in the Deuteronomistic History.

2. These works include Joel, Jonah, Haggai, Zechariah, Malachi. The suppression of prophecy coincided with the emergence of wisdom literature some of which, like Job, railed against the awful pretensions of the Law.

3. The revisions of Isaiah by II Isaiah and III Isaiah are not restricted to the later parts of the book (chs. 40–55; 56–66) but, as has been established in Ivan Friesen's unpublished thesis (University of Toronto), are introduced from the very beginning: cf. also Ackroyd 1977; Clements 1980; Sweeney 1988; Vermeylen 1977.

several editions, each one composed in conjunction with a contemporary interpretation of history, each one confronted by some legal formality or institution that seemed to undermine the principles of fundamental justice.[1]

Isaiah is the first of the prophets whose prophecies were preserved. His writings were known to all his successors who quoted him and alluded to his words, but they do not depend in the same way on any prophetic precedent. However, although his work is original and influential, it is not devoid of an urgent literary context, and although his images and allegories are fresh and self-explanatory, they are etched with ideologies and ideas first devised for the contemporary national epic (J).

I. *Isaiah*

The text of the prophecy composed by Isaiah can be established according to the criteria of repetition and cross-reference inherent in the editorial procedures followed in the commentaries on his work. Isaiah wrote poetry which followed grammatical and syntactic rules;[2]

1. Poetry is often identified with parallelism and poems are analysed as parallel lines, usually in pairs or triads, sometimes in larger groupings of lines distinguished by sense or complex parallel patterns. But poetry, in fact, seems to be composed in sentences whose elements are related to one another by sequence, subordination, coordination, or parallelism—with the distinction between sentences marked by the absence of these features—and whose lines are separated from one another by some form of cadence or pause. In translation, therefore, poetry is composed in stanzas which, like lines, are not graphic elements but patterns of rhythm and sound. Parallelism, consequently, is not a basic principle of poetic composition but one of its more obvious characteristics and the only feature which demonstrates without a doubt that poetry was composed in lines and stanzas.

2. Stanzas contain between three and six lines or multiples of the same types. Three-line stanzas are matter-of-fact statements that function as introductions, transitions, or conclusions. Four-line stanzas contain opposite or contrasting images or ideas and have an explanatory function in the development of the text. Five-line stanzas are descriptive and combine some image or idea and its interpretation. Six-line stanzas are narrative and follow a logical, chronological or dramatic sequence. The multiples are rare and correspond to the base types. Strophes may contain any number of stanzas of one or two types arranged in a few patterns: the repetitive pattern contains stanzas of the same type (i.e. A-A, A-A-A, etc.); the consecutive pattern contains one stanza of any type at the beginning or the end preceded or followed by

he also observed prosodic conventions which organized his work in stanzas, strophes and lessons and gave it a manageable structure.[1] It becomes evident, as the text is read continuously from the beginning, that his commentators recognized the structure and organization of his work and inserted their comments and interpretations by changing his stanzas or adding others, by responding to his strophes with others of their own, and by inserting other lessons or creating entirely new segments in his book. There are no idle words, and every editorial remark is justified both by further comment and by subsequent interpretation.

The text composed by Isaiah contains six lessons distributed equally in two complementary parts, and comprises very little of the biblical text. Much of the book was composed by II Isaiah who expanded the six lessons into five separate treatises, two of them devoted to commentary on Isaiah's work,[2] the other three detailing its implications for a later time.[3] Most of the book, however, was written by III Isaiah who redid what Isaiah and II Isaiah had done and divided the book into ten parts.[4] How and why this was accomplished can be seen in the expansions on Isaiah's original work.

A. *The First Lesson (Isa. 1.1aα, 2-7abα, 8, 18-20)*

The lesson contains four strophes (1.1aα, 2-4; 1.5-6; 1.7abα, 8; 1.18-20), each composed of two stanzas (1.1aα + 2, 3, 4, 5-6, 7abα, 8, 18a, 18b-20). The coherence of the lesson is marked by its insistence on the

any number of another type (i.e. A-B-B-, A-A-A-B, etc.); the iterative pattern contains one stanza of one type, any number of another, and a final iteration of the first type (i.e. A-B-A, A-B-B-A, etc.). Stanzas are on particular topics. Strophes have some sort of thematic integrity and are combined in chapters or lessons or some other larger unit that completes a scene or resolves an issue.

1. There are in Isa. 1–12 and in Isa. 28–30; 36–39, each commenting on a different part of the original work; cf. Clements 1985.

2. These include elements of Isa. 13–23; 40–47; 49–55, each dealing with some aspect of the restoration such as the submission of the nations (13–23), the return of the exiles (40–47) and their reunion with Sion (49–55).

3. These are Isa. 1–6; 7–12; 13–19; 20–27; 28–32; 33–39; 40–45; 46–51; 52–59; 60–66.

4. Isa. 6–8 (9) has always been considered essentially an authentic part of Isaiah's prophetic work reflecting actual historical conditions in the eighth century BCE. However, it is clearly a commentary on his work initiated by II Isaiah and revised by III Isaiah: cp. Bickert 1987; Nielsen 1986; Roberts 1985; Werner 1985.

guilt and corporal punishment of Yahweh's children, the people living in Sion, and its boundaries are clearly indicated by emphasizing at the beginning and the end that it is Yahweh who is admonishing them (1.2aα, 20bβ). The commentaries by II and III Isaiah were inserted by adding a remark or two in imitation of the original and then explaining what was meant (cf. Fohrer 1962; Niditch 1980; Willis 1984, 1985).

II Isaiah was concerned with the Davidic kings who ruled in Jerusalem and therefore added comments that gradually shifted the focus of the text from the people to the city and its leaders. The comments repeat the language or style of the original: the principal topic is introduced at the beginning by defining the content of Isaiah's vision (1.1aβb *'ᵃšer ḥāzāh*... = 1.1aα *ḥāzôn*); the main issue is introduced at the end of the first lesson by modifying Isaiah's appeal for reconciliation with a list of imperatives that mimic its form but appeal for justice (1.16-17 *rāḥăṣû hizzakkû*... cf. 1.18 *lᵉku nā'*...). Once these comments were affixed to the original text it was possible for II Isaiah to add an interpretation of Isaiah's lesson by simply including a few cross-references to his own text: recent rulers have ruined the city with their injustice, specifically by their neglect of widows and orphans (1.21-23; cf. 1.17), but eventually Yahweh will reinstitute good government and restore the city (1.24-26). The interpretation has only the vaguest lexical, stylistic and thematic links to the original version but it is corroborated in the immediate sequel composed by II Isaiah, in which he describes in detail the restoration of the city (2.1-5) and the indictment of its former leaders (3.13-15).

III Isaiah had no interest in Davidic kingship and was not too concerned with problems of injustice, but he was eager to trace the city's guilt and punishment to its ritual observances. This version gets started with a completely artificial verbal link: Isaiah saw the land in ruins, devoured by aliens (1.7abα *šᵉmāmāh, zārîm*), and III Isaiah took the occasion to call the ruin an overthrow (1.7bβ *ûšᵉmāmāh kᵉmahpᵉkat zārîm*). But the word 'overthrow' is a technical term for the destruction of Sodom and Gomorrah and this crude insertion allows III Isaiah to add a stanza that explicitly mentions Sodom and Gomorrah and introduces the issue of the purified remnant that will occupy much of his work (1.9). Once this stanza has been added he can continue with cross-references to Sodom and Gomorrah and develop his ritual and cultic interpretation (1.10-15). At the end of the lesson he summarizes his point in a text filled with repetitions of Isaiah (1.28 = 1.2, 4) and II Isaiah (1.27 = 1.17, 21, 26) and includes anticipatory references to the following stages in his argument. This mass of commentary confirms the relevance and urgency of Isaiah's prophecy, but it pretty well smothers his point that the people in Jerusalem were acting like spoiled children.

B. *The Second Lesson* (*5.1-2, 4-5, 11-12, 18-19, 26-29*)

The second lesson is composed of the song of the vineyard (5.1-2, 4-5), its interpretation (5.11-12, 18-19), and its historical application (5.26-29). The lesson is that the vineyard will be destroyed because its grapes were not good and its wine stupefied the people (cf. L'Heureux 1984; Niehr 1986).

II Isaiah repeats a couple of words from the original, gives the song a forensic context, reapplies it from Israel to Judah and Jerusalem (5.3), and adds another strophe to explain that the bad grapes are injustice (5.6-7). In still another strophe he anticipates the style of Isaiah's interpretation of the song (5.8 *hôy* = 5.11, 18), includes another allusion to the song itself (5.10) and a cross-reference to his own text (5.9; cf. 3.14), to explain that the injustice consists of amassing wealth and oppressing the poor. Another cross-reference to the same text (5.13 *'ammî* = 3.15) allows him to understand as exile the impending calamity that Isaiah described as invasion (cf. 5.26-29). He ends with insistence on the injustice that fills the city, undermines the judicial system, and can be traced to rejection of the Law (5.20-25a).

III Isaiah, again, uses a strikingly artificial form of repetition to insinuate a different interpretation: his point, as he has argued in the intervening sections (2.6–3.12; 3.15–4.6), is that the proud will be humbled and that God alone will be exalted (5.14-17), and he makes it by repeating two words from the adjacent II Isaiah text (5.14 *lākēn*, *h^{a}môn* = 5.13) and by referring to his own material. He uses the same bold technique again to introduce the refrain that will establish a link between the disparate parts of his work (5.25b = 5.25a [II Isaiah] = 9.11, 16, 20; 10.4), and again a third time in an obscure text for the same reason (5.30 *yinhom* = 5.29; cf. 8.22).

II Isaiah breaks the connections between the allegory, its interpretation and its application, but stays more or less with the imagery established by Isaiah. III Isaiah inserts a few remarks that are obviously out of place and whose function is to maintain links with his own work.

C. *The Third Lesson* (*10.5-7, 13-14, 28-32*)

The third lesson (cf. Christensen 1976; Machinist 1983) develops the historical application of the second by identifying the destroyers of the vineyard as the Assyrian invaders (10.5-7) who are accomplishing Yahweh's purpose (10.13-14) and are almost at the gates of Jerusalem (10.28-32). II Isaiah, in the intervening biography of Isaiah that he wrote, has already predicted the restoration of the Davidic monarchy and the end of Assyrian domination (6.1-11; 7.1-3aαb, 4-7, 9b-16; 8.1-15; 8.23–9.6),[1] and therefore his few comments merely play with some of Isaiah's words (*šēbeṭ* and *maṭṭeh*, 10.15, 24) and consist mainly of cross-references to his own text (10.15-19, 24-27). III Isaiah corrected the biography by dismantling its Davidic expectation and putting in its place the restoration of a purified remnant under the direct government of God (6.12-13; 7.3aβ, 8-9a, 17-25; 8.16-22; 9.7-20). In redoing this lesson, therefore, he attaches his material in the usual way to the existing text (10.1-4, cf. 10.5; 10.8-12, cf. 10.13; 10.20-23, cf. 10.19, 24) but he essentially reiterates his negative attitude to the monarchy (10.1-4) and the cult (10.8-12) and reaffirms his own idea of a purified remnant (10.20-23).

The disagreement between the two revisions continues in the immediate sequel where II Isaiah reaffirms his expectation of a Davidic king (10.33–11.10; 12.1-6) but where III Isaiah again counters with the restoration of the remnant (11.11-16). Isaiah's text is gradually overwhelmed by intricate interpretations, and the subtle dialectic that connects his lessons is almost lost in the requirements of

1. The prelude to the covenant is the arrival of the people at Sinai (Exod. 19.1b, 2b, 10-11, 14b-15a, 16aα, 18, 20). The covenant itself includes a preamble (Exod. 34.6-7, 10), the agreement (34.11-12, 14), the obligations of the covenant (34.19, 20b, 22, 24), and provisions for its maintenance (34.27). Moses appeals to it in the J story of rebellion in the wilderness (Num. 14.13-21, 23). It is quoted by the Deuteronomist in the same sense but in a different order in Deut. 5.6-7, 9-11, and in a contrary sense by the Deuteronomistic Historian in Deut. 7.9-11. The Priestly writer tried to ignore it and gave precedence to the construction of a national shrine and the inauguration of the Sabbath (Exod. 24.15-18; 25.1-5, 8, 9aαb; 26.1-20; 31.12-17). The Elohist surrounded it with the rules of good government and replaced it with the provisions of the law (Exod. 18–24*). Hosea refers to it (Hos. 1.6, 8-9), Nahum quotes it (Nah. 1.2-4), Ezekiel disputes it (Ezek. 18.2; 20.25-26). Clearly, the J text was published and known and represented an opinion that could not be ignored. Cf. Dentan 1963; Peckham 1985.

complex and continuous argumentation. These difficulties were recognized by the revisors, and since the problem was aggravated by their interpolation of oracles about or against the nations (13–27) between the first and second parts of his work, II and III Isaiah were careful to restore some vestige of the original unity that their interpolations obscured. III Isaiah, in his final comment on the third lesson, uses key words from the first lesson in the next part (10.22b *šôṭēp ṣᵉdāqāh* = 28.15, 17, 18) and from II Isaiah's commentary on it (10.23 = 28.22); similarly, in his introduction to the next lesson he repeats one of the same key words (28.2 *šṭp*), and fabricates a fanciful connection to his understanding of the earlier lessons with bombastic reminiscences of the song of the vineyard (28.1-7 *hôy*, *škr*, *šmn*, *rms*, *yyn*; cf. 5.1, 5, 11, 18) and recollections of his theory of the remnant (28.1-7 *tp'rt*, *q'h*, *ṣby*, *zrm*, *ṣ'h*, *š'r*; cf. 4.1-6). Similarly, II Isaiah maintained the general sense of the original by including in his biography of Isaiah elements taken from the second part composed by Isaiah. Isaiah's mission is to make sure that the people do not listen or understand (6.8-11) as in fact they did not (28.9-19); the trust and faith and firm resolution that Isaiah demanded of Ahaz (7.4, 9b) are the trust and faith and resolution that the people of Isaiah's time lacked (28.16; 30.15); in the biography and in fact Isaiah is told to write down his words (8.1; 30.8); in both cases the Assyrians are compared to a raging torrent overrunning the country (*šṭp*, 8.8; 28.15, 18); both writers refer to the corner stone laid in Sion (*'bn*, 8.14; 28.16) and both see miscreants stumbling against it, falling, being broken, trapped and captured (8.14-15 = 28.13); both refer to David (9.5-6; 29.1-4) and both foresee the effects of law and justice (9.5-6; 28.17). The revisions hold Isaiah's text in abeyance, but its sequence is maintained in anticipation.

D. *The Fourth Lesson* (*28.9-19*)

This follows, in Isaiah's version, on the Assyrian advance against Jerusalem (10.28-32) and describes the reactions of the inhabitants (cf. Exum 1982; Halpern 1986). III Isaiah introduced it and referred to it by repeating some of its key terms (28.1-8, *šṭp*, *mym*, *q'*, *ṣ'*) but saved his commentary for later (30.18–32.19). II Isaiah is intent on showing that the affliction will not last forever and adds his comments by repeating some terms from the adjacent text (*lyṣ*, *šm'*, 28.14, 19, 22).

E. *The Fifth Lesson* (*29.1-4, 9-14*)
This describes a siege of the city, the panic of the inhabitants, and the complicity of God (cf. Clements 1980a). II Isaiah remarks on the sudden lifting of the siege (29.5-8), the involvement of God (29.15-21) and the final conversion and salvation of the people (29.22-24). His version confronts or contradicts Isaiah's and is related to it by very tenuous verbal links.

F. *The Sixth Lesson* (*30.1-3, 8-17*)
Isaiah ends his prophecy with the people relying on Egypt and armaments instead of on Yahweh and with a prediction of delayed but inevitable catastrophe. II Isaiah repeats key terms from Isaiah's text to insert a comment and another oracle that shift the blame away from the city to the Egyptians (30.4-7). He then responds to Isaiah's warning by quoting the Deuteronomist's history of the reign of Hezekiah when Jerusalem was preserved but the Babylonian captivity was foretold (36–39 = 2 Kgs 18–20; cf. Clements 1980b).

It is a tribute to Isaiah that most of his book was composed by II and III Isaiah. They found his vision original, disconcerting, controversial and, after the fall of Jerusalem and the Babylonian exile, a little vague and out of date. But what he wrote was the motive for their revision and, however much they concurred or disagreed with his view, they were determined to keep his text intact and make their own additions cling to his meaning in a few artificial and fairly obvious ways. They had for their task, besides recent events, subsequent prophecies and schools of interpretation that made their contributions seem less bold. Isaiah claimed to be a visionary and had nothing much to go on except the partial and erroneous interpretation of tradition that was familiar from the national epic (J).

II. *Isaiah and J*

Isaiah's familiarity with J is clear from persistent quotations and allusions to the covenant that the epic proposed as the norm of national existence.[1] These references are stark and conceptual and stand out

1. The Deuteronomist adopted the J covenant and adapted it to the ideology of the Davidic dynasty by adding the requirement of centralization. The covenant is contained in the Deuteronomist's version of Deuteronomy: it repeats the first part of

from the visionary context that Isaiah composed by combining vivid imagery and allegory.

In the first vision Isaiah prefixes a metaphor of wounds that will not heal (1.4-6) to a look at the invasion that has left Sion totally isolated in a devastated land (1.7abα, 8), and frames both the image and the allegory in another story of wilful children who are less intelligent than domestic animals and will not do what they are told (1.2-3, 18-20). It is a dense and novel portrayal without any adequate parallel, except that every non-imaginative thing that it says is taken from the prologue to the J covenant on Sinai. In that text Yahweh declares that he will forgive wrongs and transgesssions and sin (*'āwon, peša'*, and *ḥaṭṭā'āh*) but that he will not ignore them and will punish the perpetrators and their children (*'awon 'ābot 'al bānîm w^e'al b^enê bānîm*) to the third and fourth generation (Exod. 34.7). In Isaiah's text this is reflected in inverse order in the charge that the nation is sinful and burdened with wrong (*ḥṭ'*, *'wn*), the offspring of bad parents, children (*bānîm*) who have transgressed (*pš'*) and are being punished for their crimes (1.2, 4, 18). In the J text the covenant consists in the words that Yahweh speaks and concerns the land presently occupied by aliens (Exod. 34.11-12, 24, 27); Isaiah, similarly, insists that it is Yahweh who is speaking (1.2, 20) and he makes it clear that what is at stake is the land now overrun by foreigners (1.7abα, 8, 19). In the only instance of transgression recorded later in the J epic it is described as a rejection of Yahweh that is punishable by physical blows (Num. 14.11 *n'ṣ*, *nkh*) and by the disbanding of the people and the creation of another nation in its place (Num. 14.11-12 *'ām*, *gôy*). In Isaiah's version the culprits are the people and the nation (1.4 *gôy*, *'am*), and their rejection of Yahweh has actually resulted in physical blows (1.4-5, *n'ṣ*, *nkh*). In the J epic the covenant expresses Yahweh's benign commitment to his people, and the story of rebellion

the J preamble (Deut. 1.1a; 5.1-4, 6-7, 9-11, 23a, 24a, 25, 27; cp. Exod. 34.6-7, 27) and outlines the agreement (Deut. 6.4-13, 15a; 7.1-2abβ, 17-18, 21, 23-24; 8.1, 7-10, 11-14, 17, 19-20; cp. Exod. 34.11-12, 14); it repeats the second part of the J preamble (Deut. 9.1-3; 10.12-15, 17-18, 20-21; 11.8-25; cp. Exod. 34.10) and then presents its revised version of the covenant obligations (Deut. 12.13-14, 17, 18aαb, 20, 26; 14.4-5, 9-10, 11-12, 22, 25-26; 15.19-20; 16.1-2a, 3aα, 7, 16aαb; cp. Exod. 34.19, 20b, 22, 24); it ends with reflection on the covenant and with the appointment of Joshua to ensure its ratification (Deut. 29.1a, 9a, 11, 13-14; 31.1, 2a, 3a, 6).

in the wilderness emphasizes its durability. In Isaiah's version this commitment is presupposed, but the covenant has just a destructive force.

Isaiah's text continues abruptly with the song of the vineyard (5.1-2, 4-5) and the vision of approaching hordes (5.26-29) which also have no adequate parallel but which, like the first lesson, are supplied with an explanatory context, this time not a framework but soliloquies infixed between the allegory and the image (5.11-12, 18-19). The song of the vineyard suggests drinking bouts where everyone is too involved to realize what Yahweh has accomplished or to notice what he is about to do (5.11-12); the vision of the relentless hordes pressing forward their attack is introduced by the image of a desultory people dragging cartloads of sin and wrongdoing and doubting that Yahweh will act (5.18-19). The commentary is imaginative but it insists on the nation's inability to perceive what Yahweh is doing (*r'h*, *nbṭ*, *'śh*, *p'l*). This is a parody of the J covenant (Exod. 34.10) in which Yahweh declares that he is about to perform wonders (*'śh*) in driving out the foreigners who inhabit the land and that everybody will see the marvellous things that he does (*r'h*, *'śh*). This appreciation of Yahweh's involvement in the destiny of the nation is crucial for J and is repeated again at the end of the epic when the prophet Balaam sees (*r'h*, *nbṭ*, Num. 23.9, 21) the people settled in the land, recalls Yahweh's promise to intervene (*dbr*, *'śh*, Num. 23.19), and marvels at what Yahweh has done for them (*p'l*, Num. 23.19, 23). Isaiah's quotations are slight but unmistakable as they use the words of the source in an opposite sense—to describe not the beneficence of Yahweh witnessed by the people, but a punishment that they do not understand.

The third lesson (10.5-7, 13-14, 28-32) resumes the first two: the punishment for sin is invasion; the invading hordes are Assyria; the invasion has begun and the enemy is at the gates of Sion. The previous point taken from J—that it is God who acts (*'śh*)—is repeated in the central soliloquy (10.13-14). The only new element is Yahweh's indignation (10.5 *za'mî*). This is unique and anomalous in Isaiah, but it is familiar from the oracles of Balaam where it is the opposite of divine blessing and epitomizes the curse that a seer might invoke (Num. 23.7-8). In the epic's perception it did not apply to the nation that Yahweh had blessed; in Isaiah's version it explains contemporary events.

It is only in the second part of his prophecy that Isaiah explicitly mentions the covenant, and then only in order to reject it.

In the fourth lesson he points out, in the image of foreigners learning the alphabet, that the people who refused to listen to God's advice will have to listen to the babbling of the Assyrians (28.9-13). In the explanation that follows, Isaiah attributes this unwillingness to their reliance on the covenant (28.14-15); therefore, in his concluding cornerstone allegory, he rejects the covenant and replaces it with faith and the requirements of ordinary justice (28.16-19). He talks about the covenant that their leaders made (*kāratnû b^{e}rît*, 28.15), rather than in epic terms about the exclusive covenant that Yahweh made with them (Exod. 34.10, 12). He calls it a covenant with Death and Sheol (28.15) when, on the contrary, the J epic thought of Death and Sheol as the punishment for disavowing the covenant (Num. 16.27b-32a, 33a). He thinks of it as a trap (28.13 *yqš*) as the epic had thought of alliances with the inabitants of the land (Exod. 34.12 *yqš*). He opposes the ideal of covenant with the realities of common law that have no basis in the covenant, and he confronts the city's reliance on the covenant with the faith that the epic thought was supposed to motivate it (28.16 *'mn*; cf. Exod. 14.31; Num. 14.11).

In the next lesson Isaiah begins with the allegory of Ariel (29.1-4), continues with the image of terror besetting the city like night falling on the prophets (29.9-12), and ends with an explanation that ascribes the city's present predicament to its reliance on the covenant (29.13-14). He admits that the people have been faithful to the covenant but insists that the covenant is wrong. They think of it as worship of God, but it is just obedience to arbitrary human commandments (29.13). These are the commandments of the epic covenant (*ṣwh*, 29.13; Exod. 34.11); they have nothing to do with justice or with common decency, but just prescribe the annual festivals (29.1 *s^{e}pû šānāh 'al šānāh* / *ḥaggîm yinqopû*; Exod. 34.22, 25 *ḥag...w^{e}ḥag...t^{e}qûpat haššānāh* / *šālôš p^{e}'āmîm baššānāh*) that the people observe while ignoring God. But, Isaiah insists, the time for ignorance is over and the wonderful things that the people keep expecting from the covenant are now the wonderful things that Yahweh will do to punish them (29.14 *lākēn hin^{e}nî yosēp l^{e}haplî'* / *'et hā'ām hazzeh haplē' wāpele'*; Exod. 34.10 *neged kol 'amm^{e}kā 'e'^{e}śeh niplā'ôt*).

In the last lesson Isaiah describes Judah's alliance with Egypt in the image of ambassadors sprawled under the pitiful shade of the Pharaoh

(30.1-5), and depicts the fate of Jerusalem in the allegory of a bulging wall that suddenly collapses (30.12-14). The allegory is preceded by its interpretation (30.9-11) and the image is explained at the end of the lesson (30.15-17). The interpretation is that the covenant has been a false support, a perversion of fundamental justice, and a source of wrongdoing (30.12b-13a), and that it is to be replaced by the teaching of Yahweh (30.9) that Isaiah has announced and, in imitation of the Sinai covenant, is committing to writing (30.8, 10-11; cf. Exod. 34.27). The explanation is that Jerusalem could have relied on Yahweh instead of establishing a military alliance with Egypt, but since it did not it will be defeated in battle and left, as it was in the beginning, like a flag on a mountain or a signal on a hill.

It is evident, therefore, that Isaiah knew the epic version of the covenant at Sinai and rejected it. The magic of his prophecy is his imagination, but his lessons are conceptual and cold. The two parts of his prophecy correspond: the first and last lessons concern the stubborness of God's children (1.2-3; 30.9) who were bent on war and refused to listen; the second and fifth describe the festivals celebrated in Jerusalem by an insouciant populace unaware of what Yahweh was doing; the third and fourth explain that the Assyrian invasion is Yahweh's doing and that the covenant is no defence against it. Elements of the epic covenant are consistently quoted in a contradictory sense: the children are the heirs to the covenant but far from enjoying its benefits they are being punished for their transgressions; the festivals are supposed to be a celebration of what Yahweh has done for them, but in fact they are celebrations that dull them to what Yahweh is actually doing; what he is doing is turning the covenant against them, using the Assyrians, like a stick is used to beat animals to punish his children. That is, since they have refused to listen to Yahweh's advice (30.9 *tôrāh*), they will learn from the Assyrians that the covenant is debilitating and that, far from saving them, condemns them to death; specifically, that their festivals are useless and do not reflect the wonders that Yahweh is about to perform. In the end, they are left with only the teaching of Yahweh that they or their children will have to listen to some day.

The covenant is opposed on the most general grounds that it does not work: the pact that was supposed to save them obviously has not. From this fact Isaiah simply argues that the things it was supposed to enshrine have fallen into disrepute; that is, that confidence in the God who acted on their behalf has been replaced by confidence in the covenant itself, in the vast fidelity of God that overrides every transgression. The evidence that this confidence is misplaced is the perversion of justice, extortion (*'šq*), failure to protect the innocent (*mišpāṭ* and *ṣᵉdāqāh),* and therefore Isaiah simply proclaims the end of the covenant and the rebuilding of Jerusalem on the firm foundation of faith and justice.

Such overwhelming reliance on the epic source is just slightly less surprising than the deliberate rejection of its basic tenets. Both are corroborated, however, in the witty response to Isaiah by the contemporary Deuteronomistic historian.

III. *Isaiah and the Deuteronomist* (*Dtr 1*)[1]

The history of the reign of Hezekiah (2 Kgs 18–20) is a well-defined segment in the second to last part (2 Kgs 14–20) of the Deuteronomistic History (Dtr 2). It brings to an end the era of Assyrian domination that began with a series of bitter conflicts between Israel and Judah (2 Kgs 14–16) and culminated in the fall of Samaria (2 Kgs 17). It has the usual opening and closing regnal formulae (2 Kgs 18.1-4; 20.20-21) and is composed of three symmetrically arranged chapters that contrast Hezekiah's revolt against Assyria (A = 2 Kgs 18) with his submission to the Babylonians (A′ = 2 Kgs 20) and revolve around consultation with Isaiah (B = 2 Kgs 19; cf. Ackroyd 1974, 1981, 1984; Gonçalves 1986).

A. The three chapters deal with different topics, are distinguished

1. The extra fifteen years would allow either chronology to be transposed to an absolute scale. In the Deuteronomist's (Dtr1) reckoning Hezekiah reigned 29 years (2 Kgs 18.2), his 14th year was 701 BCE (2 Kgs 18.13) and, consequently, his reign lasted until 686 BC: this extra fifteen years would be the difference between his actual accession (701 + 14 = 715 BCE) and his supposed accession six years before the fall of Samaria (2 Kgs 18.10: 723 + 6 = approximately 715 + 15). In the Deuteronomistic Historian's (Dtr2) calculation Hezekiah's sixth year was the ninth year of Hosea which was the date of the fall of Samaria in 723 BCE; therefore, Hezekiah's first year would have been about 729 BCE, his last year would have been c. 700 BCE, and the extra fifteen years allowed him to reign until c. 686 BCE—depending on the exact regnal system being used. At any rate, the chronological discrepancies are due to the different interests of the two writers, and the Dtr2 solution is cunning and artificial and not simply mistaken as Cogan and Tadmor suppose (1988:228).

from each other by their separate organization, and are related to each other by overt cross-references.

The first chapter (2 Kgs 18) deals with Hezekiah's trust in God and rebellion against Assyria. It is composed of twelve paragraphs in matching pairs that record (1) Hezekiah's reforms and confidence in God (a = 18.1-4; a′ = 18.5-6); (2) his rebellion against Assyria and the Assyrian capture of Samaria (b = 18.7-8; b′ = 18.9-12); (3) the Assyrian invasion of Judah and their legation to Jerusalem (c = 18.13-15; c′ = 18.16-19a); (4) their ridicule of the rebellion that they knew had to be based either on help from Egypt or on trust in Yahweh (d = 18.19b-22) matched with their contempt for Egypt and their confidence that it was Yahweh who had sent them against the land (d′ = 18.23-25); (5) their refusal to speak Aramaic instead of Hebrew and their insistence on speaking Hebrew so that the people would understand (e = 18.26-27; e′ = 18.28-32a); and (6) their final warning not to believe Hezekiah when he says that God will save them, countered by Hezekiah's quiet confidence (f = 18.32b-36; f′ = 18.37).

The second chapter (2 Kings 19) has four sets of matching paragraphs that record (1) Hezekiah's consultation with Isaiah (a–a′ = 19.1-4, 5-7), (2) another Assyrian embassy and the prayer of Hezekiah (b–b′ = 19.8-13, 14-19), (3) Isaiah's response to Hezekiah and the Assyrians (c–c′ = 19.20-28, 29-31), and (4) the deliverance of Jerusalem and the death of Sennacherib (d–d′ = 19.32-34, 35-37). It is linked to the first by a series of repetitions and cross-references: the first set of paragraphs begins by repeating in inverse order all the persons and actions mentioned at the end of the first chapter (19.1-2 = 18.37); the second set refers to the original legation sent from Lachish (cf. 18.14; 19.8) and repeats the argument from their final warning (cf. 18.32b-35; 19.10-13); the third set includes an assurance of survival and prosperity in their own land that mimics the offer made by the Assyrians (cf. 18.31b; 19.29); the last set records Sennacherib's inability to take the city and his ignominous death in his own land (cf. 18.13; 19.36).

The third chapter is composed of four paragraphs that relate the events surrounding Hezekiah's illness from two related points of view. The first set observes that he was sick enough to die but miraculously survived and lived for fifteen more years (a–b = 20.1-3, 4-11). The second records that when he was sick the king of Babylon sent a delegation to enlist his support, and then he died (a′–b′ = 20.12-19, 20-

21). The first set refers to Hezekiah's Davidic ancestry and goodness that were mentioned at the beginning of the segment (20.3, 5; 18.5) and repeats that the city will be, although in fact it has been, delivered out of the hands of the Assyrians (20.6 = 18.35 + 19.34). The second set mentions another diplomatic exchange (20.13 [*s^e^pārîm*]; cf. 19.14) and refers once more to the reservoirs and aqueducts built by Hezekiah (20.20 = 18.17bβ).

B. This sort of cross-reference is a familiar editorial feature and suggests that the segment is composed of text and commentary. This suspicion is confirmed by similar patterns of repetition and cross-reference within the first two chapters, some of them internal to the chapters, others relating the chapters to larger issues in the Deuteronomistic History.

The synchronism at the beginning of the first chapter is a standard feature of regnal formulae, but it also supposes, and repeats in inverse order, elements from the preceding two chapters: the fact that Hezekiah was the son of Ahaz was stated in the penultimate chapter (18.1b = 2 Kgs 16.20); the mention of Hoshea, King of Israel, recalls the beginning of the preceding chapter (18.1a = 2 Kgs 17.1). Excluding this cross-reference, the original introduction to the chapter would have comprised the rest of the regnal formula, including the age of Hezekiah at his accession, the length of his reign, and the name of his mother (18.2). The synchronism, then, would have been added in the usual way by repeating a key word from the original text in a different context (*mlk*, 18.1, 2).

The evaluation of Hezekiah (18.3-4) contains standard elements (18.3), a summary list of cult installations and objects that were prohibited by the law of centralization (18.4a = Deut. 12.1-3; 16.21-22) and excoriated in the preceding chapter (2 Kgs 17.9-10), and a reference to one of the Deuteronomistic stories told in the Pentateuch (18.4b = Num. 21.4-9).

The special pleading for Hezekiah that follows (18.5-6) continues the revised version's general interest in synchronism by situating him in the total sequence of Judaean kings (18.5b). It attributes to him in particular the trust in God that is the point of the following story (18.5 *bāṭaḥ*, cf. 18.19-24, etc.), and combines this simple repetition with Deuteronomistic clichés that make him the paragon of observance of the law (18.5-6; cf. Deut. 11.22; 1 Sam. 12.20). But the revision also takes the following text in an opposite sense by referring, not to the commands issued by Moses (18.12), but to the law that Yahweh commanded Moses to teach the people (18.6; cf. Deut. 1.3; 4.14; 6.1; 28.69; 34.9; Josh. 9.24).

The subsequent reference to Hezekiah's defeat of the Philistines (18.8) is included in the paragraph that mentions his rebellion against Assyria and seems strategically plausible (Cogan and Tadmor 1988: 221). But it is actually constructed of cliches and cross-references that betray the interests of the revised version: the emphatic pronoun that introduces it (18.8a *hû' hikkāh*) brings the statement into line with the earlier account of Hezekiah's cultic reforms (18.4 *hû' hēsîr*); the reference to Gaza and its dependencies (18.8 *'ad 'azzāh w^{e}'et g^{e}bulêhā*) is standard in the political geography of the Deuteronomistic Historian (cf. Judg. 1.18; 1 Sam. 5.6 etc.); but its further specification that Gaza was completely overrun 'from outpost to fortified city' is an explicit cross-reference to the geographical description in the preceding chapter (18.8b = 2 Kgs 17.9bβ).

The fall of Samaria (18.9-11) is dated by synchronizing the reigns of Hezekiah and Hoshea. The synchronism is calculated for the occasion and repeats in parentheses the correct dates established in the preceding chapter (18.10b = 17.6aα; 18.9aβ = 18.1 + 18.9aα). The parentheses begin with the characteristic emphatic pronoun (19.9aβ, 10b *hî'*) and are inserted according to the usual principles of verbatim repetition (18.9aβ *haššānāh* = 18.9aα *baššānāh*; 18.10bα *š^{e}nat* = 18.10aβ *bišnat*; 18.10bβ *nilk^{e}dāh šomrôn* = 18.9b-10aα *'al šomrôn . . . wayyilk^{e}dûhā*). The rest of the account, except for the inclusion of Hezekiah, is substantially the same in both chapters (18.9aαb, 10a = 2 Kgs 17.5-6).

The submission of Hezekiah (18.14-16) displays the same uses of repetition and cross-reference. The first words of this intrusive account (18.14 *wayyišlaḥ ḥizqîyāh melek y^{e}hûdāh 'el melek 'aššûr lākîšāh*) repeat in opposite order the first words of the paragraph that it displaced (18.17a *wayyišlaḥ melek 'aššûr...min lakîš 'el hammelek ḥizqîyāhû*). The account itself keeps repeating the names and titles from this heading (the king of Assyria, 18.14b, 16b; Hezekiah, king of Judah, 18.14b, 15, 16a), and illustrates the Deuteronomistic Historian's prevailing interest in wealth (cf. 1 Kgs 9.14; 10.10; 20.39; 2 Kgs 5.22; 15.19) and in the money that was kept in the temple and palace treasuries (18.15; cf. 2 Kgs 12.11, 19; 16.8; 22.9).

The building activities of the king which are mentioned obliquely in this account (18.16) are referred to again in the next paragraph. In the original account the Assyrian ambassadors went up to Jerusalem (18.17bα *wayya'ᵃlû wayyābo'û yᵉrûšālāyim*) and read their proclamation to the king from outside the walls (cf. 18.18 *wayyēṣē'*; 18.27). The revised version specifies that they stood by the aqueduct of the upper reservoir—a feat of royal engineering that is mentioned again in the final assessment of Hezekiah's reign (2 Kgs 20.20)—and it manages the insertion by simply repeating that the Assyrian ambassadors went up to the city (18.17bβ *wayya'ᵃlû wayyābo'û...*).

The proclamation explains that Hezekiah's rebellion is hopeless because neither Yahweh nor Egypt will be of any help, and it calls on the city to submit to Assyria. The revised version adds some closing remarks that propel its argument from the realm of political ridicule to sheer blasphemy (18.32b-35, 37). As usual, the addition is made by repeating the immediate context, and is justified by cross-references to proof texts. The suture consists of the repetition of the exhortation not to listen to Hezekiah (18.32bα = 18.31a), in restating his argument in the opposite order (18.32bβ *yhwh yaṣṣilēnû* = 18.30aβ *haṣṣēl yaṣṣilēnû yhwh*), and in insisting against the original version that nothing could save the city from the hand of the Assyrian king (*miyyad* / *miyyadî*, 18.33-35, cf. 18.29, 30). The cross-references are to the preceding chapter where it has already been proved that the Gods of Samaria and the other nations could not save them from the hand of the Assyrian king (18.34; cf. 2 Kgs 17.24, 29-31) and to the earlier part of this chapter listing the members of the Judaean delegation (18.37; cf. 18.18).

The beginning of the next chapter repeats the list but, as usual in the Deuteronomistic history, includes the priests among the important government officials (19.1-2 = 18.37), and then begins the second version's argument that the city was not spared because of Hezekiah's trust in God but because of Yahweh's promise to David (cf. 19.34). The point is made by having the Assyrians repeat their blasphemy (19.9b-13 = 18.33-34) so that Hezekiah, Isaiah and God might reply (19.14-19, 20-28, 29-31, 32-34). The only really intrusive element in this account is the original sequel to Sennacherib's proclamation (19.8-9a, 36-37): when the people ignore the proclamation, the

Assyrian delegation returns to Libnah to report to Sennacherib; when the king hears that an Egyptian army is advancing against him, he leaves and returns home safely to Nineveh, but there he is killed by two of his sons and succeeded by another. The intrusion means that the delegation has to return to Jerusalem to repeat its blasphemy, but this is easily done by deploying the usual editorial devices. It returns by the mere repetition of the original verbs (19.9bα *wayyāšāb* = 19.8a, 36aβ *wayyāšāb*) and the original orders (19.9bα *wayyišlaḥ mal'ākîm* = 18.17 *wayyišlaḥ*...); the second story seems plausible because it merely repeats what has already been said (19.10-13; cf. 18.30b, 35a, 34a) with some modification (19.10aβ; cf. 18.29) and amplification (19.12).

The third chapter draws the moral of this story for succeeding generations and attempts to deal with the principal chronological issues that it has raised. It is mostly concerned with the length of Hezekiah's reign (20.1-3, 4-11, 20-21) and the fate of the Davidic dynasty (20.5-6, 16-19). This is consistent with its interests in the first two chapters where it alluded to the dynastic promise to David (18.5-6; 19.32-34) and corrected the dates of Hezekiah's reign (18.1, 9aβ, 10b). This correction consisted in adding a synchronism with the reign of Hoshea of Israel in order to get the right date for the fall of Samaria as this was established in the preceding chapter (2 Kgs 17.5-6). But this resulted in the wrong dates for the reign of Hezekiah, and in order to restore the correct chronology of the Babylonian exile (20.16-19), it was necessary to add fifteen years to his reign (20.4-11).[1] The sickness and piety that occasioned this miraculous respite might have been fanciful or fictitious, but they acquired the aura of historicity from their association with the Babylonian uprising under Merodach Baladan II[2] and from the references they contain to the actual words of Isaiah (19.3; cf. Isa. 1.5, 18) and Hosea (19.3; cf. Hos. 13.13; 20.5; cf. Hos. 6.1-3).

1. Brinkman 1964. Babylonia revolted c. 722 BCE, took the offensive against Assyria in 720, and was defeated by Sargon II in 710. Merodach-Baladan II became king again in 703, and was finally defeated by Sennacherib in 700 BCE.

2. The contradictions and the retelling of the story are often resolved by supposing that Sennacherib made two campaigns against the city, one in which it succumbed (2 Kgs 18.14-16), the other from which it was saved (2 Kgs 18.17–19.37, including the duplicates 18.17–19.9a, 36-37 and 19.9b-35): cf. Childs 1967; Na'aman 1974; Shea 1985.

C. The two versions of the reign of Hezekiah have their peculiar sense and background. The revised version, as is obvious from its insistent cross-references, is the immediate sequel to the preceding chapter that explains the fall of Samaria and its implications for Judah and Jerusalem (2 Kgs 17). The original version, consequently, is the sequel to the penultimate chapter that records Judah's submission to Assyria in the reign of Ahaz (2 Kgs 16.5, 7, 9) and the non-synchronic accession of Hezekiah (2 Kgs 16.20). This version tells the amazing story of Jerusalem's deliverance in the time of Hezekiah, a story all the more amazing by comparison with the sorry fate of Samaria. The revised version emphasizes the comparison by constantly referring to the preceding story of Samaria's fall but insists that the same fate awaits Jerusalem.

The original version (18.2, 7, 9aαb, 10a, 11-13, 17abα, 18-32a, 36; 19.8-9a, 36aβb, 37) tells the story of the Assyrian invasion by describing the threat (A–B–C–D), and explaining the details of its resolution (D′–C′–B′–A′). Hezekiah, apparently at the very beginning of his reign, disregarded the treaty made by his father and rebelled against Assyria and, because Yahweh was with him, the revolt was a complete success (A = 18.2, 7). But in his fourth year Samaria was besieged by Shalmaneser and in his sixth year it was taken because it had not obeyed Yahweh but had abandoned his covenant and failed to observe the commandments of Moses (B = 18.9aαb, 10a, 11-12). However, in his fourteenth year Sennacherib captured all the fortified cities of Judah and sent an embassy to the city demanding its capitulation (C = 18.13, 17abα, 18-19a). The Assyrian ambassadors questioned the reasons for Hezekiah's revolt and, in anticipation of the reply that he was in alliance with Egypt or that he relied on Yahweh, retorted that Egypt was too weak to be trusted and that Yahweh had been offended by the removal of his altars and high places and the centralization of worship in Jerusalem (D = 18.19b-22). They gave the argument an ironic twist by taunting Hezekiah that Judah and Egypt together, even with help from Assyria, would be too weak to resist the Assyrian army that Yahweh had sent against the city (D′ = 18.23-25). But the Judaean legation did not reply to the argument or the taunt, and when they professed to know Aramaic as well as Hebrew they were told that the proclamation was not addressed to them but to the entire populace (C′ = 18.26-27). The Assyrian delegation then addressed the people directly, urging them to resist

Hezekiah's unfounded trust in Yahweh, and offering them a covenant with a guarantee of safe conduct into exile (B′ = 18.28-32a). The people did not reply either and the delegation returned to the camp at Libnah. But intelligence reported that the Egyptian army under Tirhaqah was advancing and Sennacherib returned to Nineveh where he was murdered by two of his sons and succeeded by another son Esarhaddon (A′ = 18.36; 19.8-9a, 36aβb-37).

The revised version follows the story but traces the revolt to Hezekiah's pious renovation of the cult and faithful observance of the law (18.1-4, 5-6). It is more specific in its chronology, both by relating his revolt to his interference in Philistine affairs, and by predating the fall of Samaria to the reign of Hoshea (18.7-8, 9-12). It is aware of Hezekiah's trust in Yahweh and refers obliquely to his building activities but it simply contradicts the original version by noting that Hezekiah submitted to Assyria and paid tribute to Sennacherib (18.14-15, 16-19a). It follows the Assyrian argument and its lack of effect on the populace but changes it into a blasphemy that God cannot ignore (18.32b-35, 36-37). Then it simply retells the same story, not in praise of Hezekiah or his reforms but from the totally different perspective of God who has been blasphemed. In this version Hezekiah is completely shaken by the Assyrian embassy, and sends the Judaean delegation to report their blasphemy to Isaiah, who replies by simply retelling how the original story ended (19.1-4, 5-7); the Assyrians then return to Jerusalem and repeat their blasphemy, and Hezekiah responds by composing prayers of praise and petition (19.8-13, 14-19); Isaiah intervenes with an oracle predicting the downfall of the Assyrian empire, and with further assurance that a remnant will survive the invasion (19.20-28, 29-31), and the chapter ends with Yahweh's miraculous intervention against the Assyrian army and with the death of Sennacherib (19.32-34, 35-37). The eclipse of Hezekiah effected by this retelling continues in the third chapter, where the Babylonian exile and the fate of the Davidic dynasty take precedence over contemporary affairs, and where Hezekiah himself is portrayed as vain and rather stupid.[1]

D. The two versions are obviously different and, in matters of

1. Xella 1980. The Assyrian claim that the people of Jerusalem are doomed to eat their own excrement and drink their own urine alludes to the fate of the dead and damned rather than to the effects of famine.

historical reconstruction, it is the revised version that is more literally correct. It is wrong to conclude from the original presentation that only seven or eight years separated the fall of Samaria from the Assyrian invasion of Jerusalem (cf. 18.9aα, 10a, 13), and it is not true that Sennacherib was a contemporary of Tirhaqah, King of Egypt (19.9a; Kitchen 1973. 383-393). It is right, on the other hand, that Samaria fell in the reign of Hoshea of Israel, and that Hezekiah was involved in the revolt of Philistia and paid tribute to Assyria. But it would be presumptuous to suppose that the author of the original version was simply ignorant or mistaken, since it is this version that correctly attributes the siege of Samaria to Shalmaneser (2 Kgs 18.9b), that is familiar with Assyrian protocol (Cohen 1979), and that knows the names of the individuals who killed Sennacherib (2 Kgs 19.37; Parpola 1980). And, conversely, it would be naive to think that the author of the second version was intent on writing a merely factual history since it is this version that first constructs a false synchronism between Hezekiah and Hoshea and then invents a marvelous cure to correct the chronology. It is more useful to suppose that both writers were historians with their particular interpretations of the reign of Hezekiah, and that the problems that these create for a contemporary reconstruction of history are important clues to the sources and principles on which their interpretations were based.

The original version is a reply to Isaiah's criticism of the epic covenant. Its theoretical underpinning is expressed in the narrative framework to the story (18.2, 7, 9aαb, 10a, 11-13, 17abα, 18-19a, 36; 19.8-9a, 36aβb-37), and its response to Isaiah's criticism is presented in its reaction to the argument of the Assyrian delegation (18.19b-32a). All the issues are covered and its critique of Isaiah's position is unrelenting.

The theoretical underpinning of the narrative is the covenant that this writer explained in the book of Deuteronomy, traced through the history of the Davidic monarchy, and quoted in his preamble to the Assyrian embassy. The fact that Yahweh was with Hezekiah and made him victorious in all his battles (18.7a) puts him in the company of Moses, Joshua and David (cf. Josh. 1.5; 1 Sam. 17.37; 18.5). Ahaz's submission to Tiglath-Pileser III explicitly violated Yahweh's covenant with the Davidic dynasty (2 Sam. 7.14a; 2 Kings 16.7a) and therefore Hezekiah's revolt was a deliberate abrogation of that alliance (2 Kgs 18.7b *w^{e}lo' '^{a}bādô*; cf. 2 Kgs 16.7a *'abd^{e}kā . . . ' ^{a}nî*). Jerusalem survived because of Hezekiah but Samaria fell because it broke the covenant that Yahweh made with Israel on Horeb. This is the covenant that Moses recalls and summarizes and that Samaria has violated (18.12aβ; Deut. 5.2-3); it was on the occasion of this covenant that the people heard the voice of Yahweh to which Samaria did not pay attention (18.12aα; Deut. 5.23aα, 24a, 25b); it was in conjunction with this covenant that Moses, the servant of Yahweh (18.12aγ; Exod. 14.31; Josh. 1.2), gave them the command to worship only in the place that Yahweh might choose (18.12aγ; Deut. 12.14; cf. Deut. 6.6; 8.1; 11.8); it was on hearing the voice of Yahweh declaring the covenant on Horeb that the people agreed to listen and do as they were told (Deut. 5.27 *w*^{e}*šāma‘nû w*^{e}*‘āśînû* = 18.12b *w*^{e}*lo’ šām*^{e}*‘û w*^{e}*lo’ ‘āśû*). The siege and capture of Samaria is a foil for the deliverance of Jerusalem, and it suits the Deuteronomist's narrative purpose that they both should occur in the reign of Hezekiah. Samaria had violated the covenant by worshipping at Bethel and Dan instead of in Jerusalem (1 Kgs 12.28-29), and therefore the people of Israel were driven out of the land that Yahweh had given them (Deut. 11.17); Hezekiah observed the covenant by abolishing all the other cult places and centralizing worship in Jerusalem (18.22), and so could rely on the covenant assurance that no one would be able to withstand him (Deut. 11.22-25).

The centralization of the cult is the culmination of the covenant, and the deliverance of Jerusalem is a confirmation of the promise to David, and the original version of the history comes to a happy close. The ending is especially strange in its use of historical fact and disregard for chronology: Hezekiah's death is not recorded; Sennacherib's death at the hands of his sons Adrammelek and Sharezer seems to follow right after his retreat from Jerusalem; the end of the history is marked by the usual formula for the end of a king's reign (19.37b 'and his son...ruled in his stead') but the formula concerns the accession of Esarhaddon in Assyria instead of the accession of Hezekiah's son in Judah; Tirhaqah was the king of Egypt in the time of Esarhaddon, but was not a contemporary of Sennacherib. The history ends, obviously and abruptly, at the time of writing.

The debate with Isaiah deals especially with the issues that he raises in the second part of his prophecy, and attempts to refute his critique of the covenant. Each element in the speech of the ambassadors contains a quotation or allusion to his words and some other information that proves them wrong. In the end, of course, the Deuteronomist is right and the ambassadors go away empty handed.

The first segment of their speech concerns alliance with Egypt and reliance on Yahweh. It begins by questioning whether Hezekiah thinks that words are sufficient planning and preparation for war (18.20a *'āmartā 'ak d^ebar ś^epātāyim 'ēṣāh ûg^ebûrāh lammilḥāmāh*). Their argument is taken in an opposite sense from Isaiah who had accused those who relied on the covenant of flattering Yahweh with words (Isa. 29.13aβ *b^epîw ûbiśpātāyw kibb^edûnî*), of making plans and relying on Egypt without consulting Yahweh (Isa. 30.1aβ *la^{'a}śôt 'ēṣāh w^elo' minnî*), and of rejecting the trust in Yahweh that would have been the right preparation for war (Isa. 30.15aβ *b^ehašqēṭ ûbibṭ^eḥāh tihyeh g^ebûrātêkem*). It uses the language of Isaiah to ridicule Hezekiah for trusting in Egypt and relying on their help (18.21 *'attāh hinnēh bāṭaḥtā l^ekā 'al miš'enet haqqāneh... 'al miṣrāyim*; Isa. 30.12b *wattibṭ^eḥû b^e'ošeq w^enālôz wattišša^{'a}nû 'alāyw*). It follows Isaiah in referring explicitly to the Pharaoh (18.21bα *par'oh melek miṣrāyim* [cp.19.9 *tirḥāqāh melek kûš*]; Isa. 30.2-3 *mā'ôz par'oh // ṣēl miṣrayim*). But the segment also insists on the fact that Hezekiah did trust (18.19b[bis], 20b, 21bis, 22), and includes information that explicitly refutes Isaiah's charge that he did not (Isa. 30.15): the ambassadors suddenly turn from their ridicule of Egypt to anticipate the Judaean reply and quote them as saying that they do trust in Yahweh (18.22a *w^ekî to'merûn 'ēlay '^el yhwh 'elohēnû bāṭaḥnû*) and that they have been faithful to the covenant with Yahweh by centralizing worship in Jerusalem (18.22b).

The second segment (18.23-25) continues to present Isaiah's arguments in the words of the ambassadors, and at the same time to subtly suggest their refutation. The argument is that the Assyrian invasion is Yahweh's doing and it includes both points that Isaiah makes: Isaiah says that Yahweh has sent the Assyrians against his own people, and the ambassadors quote the command that Yahweh supposedly gave the king of Assyria (Isa. 10.5-6; 2 Kgs 18.25 *yhwh 'āmar 'ēlay ^{'a}leh 'al hā'āreṣ hazzo't*); but Isaiah also notes that the Assyrians do not realize that Yahweh has sent them and are actually intent on destroying the world (Isa. 10.7, 13-14 *l^ehašmîd, l^ehakrît, 'āsaptî*), and the ambassadors misquote Yahweh's command in the same sense to suggest that Yahweh has sent them to destroy both the city and the whole land (2 Kgs 18.25 *l^ehašḥitô...l^ehašḥîtāh*). The argument, however, is prefaced by its own refutation. Isaiah said that the people refused to be quiet and trust in Yahweh but insisted on riding their horses and chariots and therefore they would ride them to defeat, a thousand fleeing before a single foe, all of them fleeing before five of their enemies (Isa. 30.15-17). The ambassadors, on the contrary, say that Hezekiah relies on the Egyptians and does not have his own army, and they bet that if Sennacherib gave him two thousand horses, he would not be able to find riders for them—and even if he could, that they would not be able to repulse even one measly lieutenant in the Assyrian army (2 Kgs 18.23-24). In Isaiah's prophecy Yahweh has turned against his own people because they refuse to trust in him. The Deuteronomist thinks that this is Assyrian boasting because, obviously, Jerusalem does not have anyone else to trust.

The third segment (2 Kgs 18.26-27) deals specifically with Isaiah's charge that the people have been deceived by their leaders. Isaiah castigates the leaders in Jerusalem who rely on their covenant and refuse to listen to Yahweh, and he warns them that Yahweh will speak to the people through aliens stammering in a foreign tongue and that it will be sheer terror to hear what they have to say (Isa. 28.9-19). This is refuted diplomatically in the Deuteronomistic version where the aliens speak Judaean Hebrew, and the leaders of Jerusalem hear them without fear and merely suggest that they speak Aramaic so that the people will not have to listen (2 Kgs 18.26). Isaiah also blamed the people for not wanting to listen to the hard words spoken by the prophets, and he compared their fate to the sudden collapse of a bulging wall (Isa. 30.8-14). But in the Deuteronomistic version, the people sit quietly on the wall listening to every word, including the crude description of their fate,[1] spoken by the Assyrians (2 Kgs 18.27).

1. The legal principles endorsed by the Deuteronomist Historian are contained in the Book of Deuteronomy. This is a revision of the original Deuteronomist version that consists essentially of reinterpreting the covenant as a set of basic legal obligations (the Decalogue) rather than as a mutual fidelity to an agreement, in extending the obligations of the covenant to include a revised and rationalized version of the E laws, and in giving the new version a narrative context that combines earlier historiographic sources with prophetic criticisms of the covenant. It was a grand synthesis of tradition and became the standard interpretation of law, history and prophecy. History was rewritten with it in mind. The E legislation was revised to agree with its system (Hanson 1977) and , in this revised version, was thought to have influenced the actual course of events (2 Kgs 22–23).

The fourth segment (2 Kgs 18.28-32a) deals with Isaiah's rejection of the covenant. In his address to the leaders, Isaiah introduced what he was about to say as the word of God (Isa. 28.14a, 16a *lākēn šim'û d^ebar yhwh...lākēn koh 'āmar '^adonāy yhwh*), quoted their own words as a proof of their arrogance, and ridiculed the covenant as a covenant with death and Sheol (Isa. 28.14-15). In the same way the ambassadors begin their address to the people by introducing it as the word of the king of Assyria (2 Kgs 18.28-29 *šim'û d^ebar hammelek haggādôl melek 'aššûr koh 'āmar hammelek*), and they quote what Hezekiah had said (2 Kgs 18.30), but, instead of just rejecting the covenant with Yahweh, offer the people another covenant just like it (2 Kgs 18.31-32a): the king of Assyria invites them to make a treaty and surrender (2 Kgs 18.31bα); it is called a blessing (2 Kgs 18.31bα *b^erākāh*) because instead of proposing the terms of the treaty, the king simply describes its benefits; the benefits, however, are precisely those that Judah now enjoys under its covenant with Yahweh described in Deuteronomy—vineyards and olive trees and cisterns (2 Kgs 18.31bβ *gapnô...t^e'ēnātô...borô*; cf. Deut. 6.11 *borot...k^erāmîm w^ezētîm*; cf. Deut. 8.8 *w^egepen û^et^e'ēnāh*), a land in fact just like their own (2 Kgs 18.32a; Deut. 11.10), a land of grain and wine, of cereal and vineyards, a land of olive orchards, oil and honey (2 Kgs 18.32a = Deut. 8.8-9; 11.9, 14), a land where they can live (2 Kings 18.32a = Deut. 8.1); it is a treaty, consequently, that is of no interest to the people, and they ignore it and remain completely silent as Hezekiah has advised them (2 Kgs 18.36). This version refutes all three aspects of Isaiah's accusation: according to the Deuteronomist, the words that he proclaims are not the words of Yahweh but the words of the Assyrians; the leaders and the people are not arrogant and, in fact, do not say a word; their covenant, as even the Assyrians admit, is not a covenant with death but a covenant with life.

It is evident that Isaiah and the Deuteronomist had different interests and different interpretations of contemporary events. Isaiah was sure that reliance on political and military means would have the same disastrous consequences for Judah that they had had for the North. In the place of treaty and covenant and the lavish festivals they entailed, he urged faith and trust in Yahweh and ordinary decency among themselves. The Deuteronomist thought that Judah was different because it had been completely faithful to the covenant that Yahweh had made with Moses and the people. But this fidelity did not exclude alliances with other nations, and the arrival of Tirhaqah, though opportune, certainly did not undermine their confidence in Yahweh. The viewpoints were irreconcilable. Isaiah wrote in the reign of Hezekiah and had old time religion on his side; the Deuteronomist wrote in the reigns of Manasseh and Esarhaddon, and had to contend with the realities of Assyrian domination and hope, with the help of Tirhaqah, that it would not last (Kitchen 1983; Rainey 1976; Spalinger 1974).

IV. *II Isaiah and the Deuteronomistic Historian (Dtr2)*

The conflict between Isaiah and the Deuteronomist was resolved in different and unexpected ways by II Isaiah and the Deuteronomistic Historian (Dtr2). The Historian agreed with Isaiah but replaced his simple faith with an elaborate theory of sin and divine retribution. II Isaiah agreed with the Deuteronomist (Dtr1) but downplayed the national covenant, concentrating on the crucial role that the Davidic dynasty and the likes of Hezekiah would play in the postexilic restoration.

A. *The Deuteronomistic Historian (Dtr2)*

The Deuteronomistic Historian (Dtr2) lacked his predecessor's confidence in the epic covenant, identified the principles of fundamental justice to which Isaiah referred (Isa. 28.17 *mišpāṭ*, *ṣ*^{e}*dāqāh*) with the Deuteronomic law promulgated in Transjordan and, although Jerusalem had escaped unscathed, added the story of Merodach Baladan II to show that Isaiah's vision would come true in Babylonian times. The immediate and most evident results of this perspective were to introduce Isaiah as the protagonist, to diminish Hezekiah's heroic status, and to magnify God.

Hezekiah's submission to Assyria in this version (2 Kgs 18.14-16) negates his purported confidence in the covenant, and the terms of his submission (2 Kgs 18.14a 'I have sinned' [*ḥāṭā'tî*]) suggest that Isaiah was correct in his evaluation of the city's predicament (*ḥṭ'*, Isa. 1.4, 18; 5.18). Hezekiah's prayers do not appeal to the covenant but to prophetic tradition (2 Kgs 19.1-4; 20.4-6; cf. Nah. 1.7; Hab. 3.16; Zeph. 1.15; Isa. 1.5, 18; 30.5; Hos. 6.1-3; 13.13), to the uniqueness and transcendence of God (2 Kgs 19.14-19, 20-28, 29-31), and to the fidelity of the Davidic dynasty (20.1-3, 4-6). The earlier Deuteronomist's position is not explicitly refuted, just overwhelmed with facts and contrary opinion.

Isaiah thought that the observance of the principles of fundamental justice was more important than careless fidelity to the covenant, and the Deuteronomistic Historian agreed, but thought that these principles were enshrined in the law that was promulgated in Deuteronomy and illustrated in his history. This law included cultic stipulations (2 Kgs 18.4; cf. 2 Kgs 17.9-11), frequent exhortations to obedience (2 Kgs 18.5-6; cf. 1 Kgs 2.1-4; 9.1-9), warnings against worshipping the Gods of the nations (2 Kgs 18.32b-35; Deut. 7.1-5; 12.1-7; 29.15-27), and arguments for the transcendence of the God of Israel (2 Kgs 19.14-19; Deut. 4.32-40; 2 Sam. 7.18-29). Consequently, the Deuteronomistic Historian thought that it was for his observance of the law, and not for defence of the covenant, that Hezekiah was famous (2 Kgs 18.5-6; 20.1-3).

Isaiah's prophecy was written and preserved for some later time when suddenly it would be fulfilled (Isa. 30.8, 13), and the Deuteronomistic Historian did not hesitate to identify this time with the Babylonian exile (2 Kgs 20.17-19). By duplicating the Assyrian embassy and giving Isaiah a major role in responding to their threats (2 Kgs 19.1-7, 9b-35), the revised version lets Isaiah bring his own prophecy up to date.

II Isaiah. II Isaiah reconciled these three interpretations in three separate texts. He made Isaiah and the Deuteronomist both seem right by composing a biography of the prophet that predated Isaiah's antagonism toward the monarchy to the reign of Ahaz (Isa. 7.1-16; 8.1-15; 8.23–9.6). Among his oracles to the nations he had a vision of the fall of Jerusalem that subtly exonerated the king by blaming Shebna for the official arrogance condemned by Isaiah (Isa. 22.1-25; Clements 1980a: 182-91; Vermeylen 1977: 335-42). He quoted the later Deuteronomistic Historian's version of the Assyrian invasion but eased its conflict with the original version by omitting its synchronisms, its exaltation of the law, its story of Hezekiah's capitulation, and anything that might mar the image of Hezekiah as the most faithful king in the line of David (Isa. 36–39; Sweeney 1988: 13-16). This process of reconciliation allowed II Isaiah to praise Hezekiah and express continued confidence in the Davidic dynasty as the guarantors of fundamental justice, without neglecting either Isaiah's original vision or the recent promulgation of the Law by the Deuteronomistic Historian.

The temple vision composed by II Isaiah (Isa. 6) corroborates Isaiah's perception that the people of his own day would not listen to him. The ensuing debate with Ahaz proves the point, and begins by combining a quotation from the earlier Deuteronomist concerning the reign of Ahaz (Isa. 7.1 = 2 Kgs 16.1b, 5) with another from the later Deuteronomistic Historian concerning the Assyrian embassy in the reign of Hezekiah (Isa. 7.3b = 2 Kgs 18.17bβ). II Isaiah's words of comfort to the house of David are taken from Isaiah's address to the leaders of Jerusalem (Isa. 7.4aα *hiššāmēr w^{e}hašqēṭ*; cf. Isa. 30.15 *b^{e}hašqēṭ...tihyeh g^{e}bûrāt^{e}kem*) and are combined with the war oracle prescribed in Deuteronomy (Deut. 20.3 *'al yērak l^{e}bab^{e}kem 'al tir^{e}'û* = Isa. 7.4a *'al tîrā' ûl^{e}bāb^{e}kā 'al yērak*) and with another paraphrase of the Deuteronomistic sources (Isa. 7.5-6; cf. 2 Kgs 15.37; 16.5). The assurance that the Syro-Ephraimite conspiracy would not succeed repeats the key words that Isaiah used to condemn Hezekiah's confidence in the covenant (Isa. 7.7b, 9b *lo' tāqûm w^{e}lo' tihyeh / 'im lo' ta'^{a}mînû kî lo' t^{e}'āmēnû* = Isa. 28.16bβ, 18aβ *hama'^{a}mîn lo' yāḥîš / w^{e}ḥ^{a}zutkem 'et š^{e}'ol lo' tāqûm*), and the invitation to Ahaz to ask for something as deep as Sheol may allude to the same text (cf. Isa. 7.11b *ha'mēq še'ôlāh*; Isa. 28.15, 18). Ahaz's refusal to put God to the test would make him a faithful adherent of the Deuteronomic law (Isa. 7.12b; cf. Deut. 6.16a), just as the child called Immanuel would be identified with Hezekiah who had God on his side (2 Kgs 18.7 *w^{e}hāyāh yhwh 'immô*). The total effect of the debate is to identify Ahaz as the antagonist in Isaiah's time, to demean his stubborn self-righteousness, and to look forward to the reign of his successor Immanuel, presumably Hezekiah (* *'immô yhwh*).

The second child is supposedly Isaiah's, and its name (Isa. 8.1, 3 *māhēr šālāl ḥāš bāz*) actually sums up Isaiah's message that Assyria is advancing quickly and has been sent by Yahweh to loot and pillage (Isa. 5.26b *w^{e}hinnēh m^{e}hērāh qāl yābô'*; Isa. 10.6 *lišlol šālāl w^{e}lāboz baz*; Isa. 28.16 *hama'^{a}mîn lo' yaḥîš*). The point is immediately repeated, combined with another of Isaiah's oracles (Isa. 8.8 *šāṭap w^{e}'ābar* = Isa. 28.15b, 18b *šoṭ šoṭēp kî ya'^{a}bor*), and applied to Immanuel in whose reign Assyria will overrun the country. But despite overt dependence on Isaiah, II Isaiah disagrees with him and agrees instead with the earlier Deuteronomist that it was because of Immanuel—Hezekiah—that the invasion failed (Isa. 8.9-10 *kî* *'immānû'ēl*). In the end, however, II Isaiah comes back to what was said in the beginning (Isa. 8.12b-13 = 7.4), and quotes from the same text of Isaiah (Isa. 8.14b-15 = Isa. 28.13b + 16) to confirm Isaiah's idea that it was Yahweh and not the Assyrians who punished both kingdoms of Israel. The effect of the revision is to restate Isaiah's position without accepting or reaffirming his criticism of the monarchy.

The last part of the biography, after the interlude on Isaiah's child, returns to the birth of Immanuel and is explicit in its praise of the king. It begins with an another allusion to Pekah and the Syro–Ephraimite war (Isa. 8.23; 2 Kgs 15.29) and, by repeating key words from Isaiah's oracle about Assyria, describes how the Assyrian siege was lifted in the time of Hezekiah (Isa. 9.2-3 *šālāl*, *maṭṭeh*, *šēbeṭ* = Isa. 10.5-6 *šēbeṭ*, *maṭṭeh*, *šālāl*). The names of the child attribute to the king some of the qualities that Isaiah considered characteristic of Yahweh (Isa. 9.5b *pēlē' yô'ēṣ*; cf. Isa. 29.14 + 30.1), and the oracle at his birth predicts that he will achieve what Yahweh meant to accomplish (Isa. 9.6aβ *l^ehākîn 'otāh ûl^eṣa'ădāh / b^emišpāṭ ûbiṣdāqāh* = Isa. 28.17a *w^eśamtî mišpāt l^eqāw / ûṣ^edāqāh l^emišqālet*). The boldness of this interpretation of Isaiah's words is confirmed by quoting a slogan from the Deuteronomistic Historian's version of the siege in which Jerusalem is preserved for the sake of David and through Yahweh's personal initiative (Isa. 9.6bβ *qin'at yhwh ṣ^ebā'ôt ta'^aśeh zo't* = 2 Kings 19.31b).

The oracle on the valley of vision (Isa. 22) is directed against the Judaean delegates whom Hezekiah sent to negotiate with the Assyrian embassy, and its portrayal of their role is faithful to the Deuteronomistic Historian's perspective in combining the contemporary threat to Jerusalem with the later Babylonian siege of the city. The quotation of the Historian's version of the reign of Hezekiah (Isa. 36–39 = 2 Kgs 18–20) deals more realistically with the Assyrian invasion, and is especially apt, since it allows II Isaiah to end his commentary on Isaiah with the Babylonian exile (Isa. 39.5-8) before continuing with his own work on the restoration (Isa. 40.1-11, etc).

The debate continued in the writings of III Isaiah and the Chronicler but it concerned the relative merits of Hezekiah in the line of David rather than the conflict between prophets and historians. Every time that II Isaiah wrote in favour of the Davidic monarchy, III Isaiah included an obscure text to cloud the issue and argue instead for the survival of a holy remnant (Isa. 6.12-13; 7.17-25; 8.16-22; 9.7-20). The Chronicler (2 Chron. 29–32) tried to combine the best of both historians, recording Hezekiah's building projects and cultic reforms as the later version had done, but still insisting on the covenant and its festivals, ignoring his capitulation to Assyria, and omitting his confrontation with Isaiah (Begg 1988), as the earlier Deuteronomist had done. The Law had been promulgated, prophecy had become a ritual function, and the principles of fundamental justice were no longer at stake.

Prophecy and history did not have much in common, and in their conflicts, history always seemed to have the upper hand. The epic history culminated in the covenant at Sinai in which Yahweh gave Israel the possession of the land in return for their total devotion. This devotion was manifested in exclusion of alliances with the local inhabitants and in the celebration of the annual festivals, and did not entail any other obligations. Against it, Isaiah argued that it should have included the principles of common law, and that recent events, in which Jerusalem was saved by Egypt and not by God, had proved it wanting. The early Deuteronomist tried to show that Egyptian help was accidental and that recent events, in which Jerusalem was saved because Hezekiah had trusted in Yahweh and had reorganized his worship in Jerusalem, proved the validity of the covenant that had inspired him. The Deuteronomistic Historian realized that the premise was false—in fact Hezekiah had capitulated to the Assyrians—and that Isaiah's long-range predictions were correct—in fact Jerusalem had fallen to the Babylonians—and he modified the covenant to include the Decalogue and all the legislation that it resumed. II Isaiah salvaged the early Deuteronomist idea that Hezekiah had been faithful to the covenant, and made him the model Davidic king, but, in agreement with Isaiah's concern for the principles of law, he made the king the arbiter and dispenser of justice. III Isaiah had little interest in the line of David, but agreed with the Deuteronomistic Historian on the importance of a purified remnant worshipping Yahweh in Jerusalem in accordance with all the rituals prescribed by the Law. The Chronicler was eclectic and the restoration made him slightly more irenic. All contributed in their own way to the rationalization of the law, arguing for the rule of precedent and judicial procedure, or simplifying the laws and customs in a comprehensive code, or subordinating law and justice to a prior constitutional covenant.

BIBLIOGRAPHY

Ackroyd, P.R.

1974 An Interpretation of the Babylonian Exile: A Study of 2 Kings 20, Isaiah 38-39. *Scottish Journal of Theology* 27: 329-352.

1977 Isaiah 1–12. Presentation of a Prophet. *Supplements to Vetus Testamentum* 29: 16-48.

1981 The Death of Hezekiah—a Pointer to the Future? In *De la Tôrah au Messie*, 219-26. Ed. M. Carrez, J. Doré, P. Grelot. Paris: Desclée.

1984 The Biblical Interpretation of the Reigns of Ahaz and Hezekiah. In *In the Shelter of Elyon. Essays on Ancient Palestinian Life and Literature in Honor of G.W. Ahlström*, 247-59. Ed. W.B. Barrick, J.R. Spencer. Sheffield: JSOT Press..

Albright, W.F.

1963 *The Biblical Period from Abraham to Ezra. An Historical Survey*. New York: Harper & Row.

Alter, R.

1981 *The Art of Biblical Narrative*. New York: Basic Books.

Barth, H.

1977 *Die Jesaja-Worte in der Josiazeit. Israel und Assur als Thema einer produktiven Neuinterpretation der Jesajaüberlieferung*. Neukirchen–Vluyn: Neukirchener Verlag.

Beentjes, P.C.

1982 Inverted Quotations in the Bible. A Neglected Stylistic Pattern. *Bib* 63: 506-23.

Begg, C.T.

1988 The Classical Prophets in the Chronistic History. *BZ* 32: 100-107.

Bickert, R.

1987 König Ahas und der Prophet Jesaja. Ein Beitrag zum Problem des syrisch-ephraimitischen Krieges. *ZAW* 99: 361-84.

Brinkman, J.A.

1964 Merodach Baladan II. In *Studies Presented to A. Leo Oppenheim*, 6-53. Ed. R.A. Biggs, J.A. Brinkman. Chicago: Oriental Institute.

Carmichael, C.M.

1974 *The Laws of Deuteronomy*. Ithaca: Cornell University.

1985 *Law and Narrative in the Bible: The Evidence of the Deuteronomic Law and the Decalogue*. Ithaca: Cornell University.

Chambers, H.E.

1983 Ancient Amphictyonies, Sic et Non. In *Scripture in Contex*. II. *More Essays on the Comparative Method*, 39-59. Ed. W.W. Hallo, J.C. Moyer, L.G. Perdue. Winona Lake, IN: Eisenbrauns.

Childs, B.S.

1967 *Isaiah and the Assyrian Crisis*. London: SCM Press.

1979 *Introduction to the Old Testament as Scripture*. Philadelphia: Fortress Press.

Christensen, D.L.
1976 The March of Conquest in Isaiah 10:27c-34. *VT* 26: 385-99.

Clements, R.E.
1965 *Prophecy and Covenant*. London: SCM Press.
1975 *Prophecy and Tradition*. Oxford: Basil Blackwell.
1980a *Isaiah 1–39*. Grand Rapids: W.B. Eerdmans.
1980b *Isaiah and the Deliverance of Jerusalem. A Study of the Interpretation of Prophecy in the Old Testament*. Sheffield: JSOT Press.
1980c The Prophecies of Isaiah and the Fall of Jerusalem in 587 BC. *VT* 30: 421-36.
1985 Beyond Tradition-History. Deutero-Isaianic Development of First Isaiah's Themes. *JSOT* 31: 95-113.

Coats, G.W.
1983 *Genesis, with an Introduction to Narrative Literature* (The Forms of the Old Testament Literature, 1). Grand Rapids: Eerdmans.

Cogan, M., and H. Tadmor
1988 *II Kings*. AB, 11. Garden City, NY: Doubleday.

Cohen, C.
1979 Neo-Assyrian Elements in the First Speech of the Biblical Rab-Šāqê. *Israel Oriental Studies* 9: 32-48.

Dentan, R.C.
1963 The Literary Affinities of Exodus 34.6f. *VT* 13: 34-51.

Exum, J.C.
1982 'Whom Will he Teach Knowledge?' A Literary Approach to Isaiah 28. In *Art and Meaning. Rhetoric in Biblical Literature*, 108-39. Ed. D.J.A. Clines, D.M. Gunn, A.J. Hauser. Sheffield: JSOT Press.

Fohrer, G.
1962 Jesaja 1 als Zusammenfassung der Verkündigung Jesajas. *ZAW* 7: 251-68.

Fornara, C.W.
1983 *The Nature of History in Ancient Greece and Rome*. Berkeley: University of California Press.

Gonçalves, F.J.
1986 *L'expédition de Sennachérib en Palestine dans la littérature hébraïque ancienne*. Louvain: Institut Orientaliste.

Halbe, J.
1975 *Das Privilegrecht Jahwes, Ex 34, 10–26. Gestalt und Wesen, Herkunft und Wirken in vordeuteronomischer Zeit*. Göttingen: Vandenhoeck & Ruprecht.

Halpern, B.
1986 The Excremental Vision: The Doomed Priests of Doom in Isaiah 28. *Hebrew Annual Review* 10: 109-21.

Hanson, P.D.
1977 The Theological Significance of Contradiction within the Book of the Covenant. In *Canon and Authority. Essays in Old Testament Religion and Theology*, 101-31. Ed. G.W. Coats, B.O. Long. Philadelphia: Fortress Press.

Kitchen, K.A.
1973 *The Third Intermediate Period in Egypt (1100–650 BC)*. Warminster: Aris & Phillips.
1983 Egypt, the Levant and Assyria in 701 BC. In *Aegypten und Altes Testament, 5: Fontes atque Pontes. Eine Festgabe für Helmut Brunner*. Ed. M. Görg. Weisbaden: Otto Harrassowitz.

Kuhl, C.
1952 Die 'Wiederaufnahme'—eine literarkritisches Prinzip? *ZAW* 64: 1-11.

Lang, B.
1984 Max Weber und Israels Propheten. *ZRGG* 36: 156-65.

Levenson, J.D.
1979 Who Inserted the Book of the Torah? *HTR* 68: 203-33.

L'Hereux, C.
1984 The Redactional History of Isaiah 5:1–10:4. In *In the Shelter of Elyon. Essays on Ancient Palestinian Life and Literature in Honor of G.W. Ahlström*, 99-119. Ed. W.B. Barrick, J.R. Spencer. Sheffield: JSOT Press.

Machinist, P.
1983 Assyria and its Image in the First Isaiah. *JAOS* 103: 719-37.

McKane, W.
1979 Prophecy and the Prophetic Literature. In *Tradition and Interpretation*, 163-88. Ed. G.W. Anderson. Oxford: Clarendon Press.
1982 Prophet and Institution. *ZAW* 94: 251-266.

Na'aman, N.
1974 Sennacherib's 'Letter to God' and his Campaign to Judah. *BASOR* 214: 35-39.

Nicholson, E.W.
1986 Covenant in a Century of Study since Wellhausen. *OTS* 24: 54-69.

Niditch, S.
1980 The Composition of Isaiah 1. *Bib* 61: 509-29.

Niehr, H.
1986 Zur Gattung von Jes 5, 1-7. *BZ* 30: 99-104.

Nielsen, K.
1986 Is. 6.1-8,18 as Dramatic Writing. *ST* 40: 1-16.

Noth, M.
1943 *Überlieferungsgeschichtliche Studien*. Halle (Saale): Max Niemeyer.
1948 *Überlieferungsgeschichte des Pantateuch*. Stuttgart: W. Kohlhammer.
1962 *Exodus—A Commentary*. Trans. J.S. Bowden. Philadelphia: Westminster Press.

Oden, R.A., Jr.
1987 The Place of Covenant in the Religion of Israel. In *Ancient Israelite Religion. Essays in Honor of Frank Moore Cross*, 429-47. Ed. P.D. Miller, Jr, P.D. Hanson, S.D. McBride. Philadelphia: Fortress Press.

Parpola, S.
1980 The Murderer of Sennacherib. In *Death in Mesoptamia*, 171-82. Ed. B. Alster. Copenhagen: Akademisk Forlag.

Paul, S.M.
1970 *Studies in the Book of the Covenant in the Light of Cuneiform and Biblical Law*. Leiden: Brill.

Peckham, B.
1985 *The Composition of the Deuteronomistic History*. Atlanta, GA: Scholars Press.

Perlitt, L.
1969 *Die Bundestheologie im Alten Testament*. Neukirchen-Vluyn: Neukirchener Verlag.

Phillips, A.
1982 Prophecy and Law. In *Israel's Prophetic Tradition. Essays in Honor of Peter R. Ackroyd*, 217-32. Ed. R. Coggins, A. Phillips, M. Knibb. Cambridge: Cambridge University Press.

Rad, G. von
1938 *Das formgeschichtliche Problem des Hexateuch*. Stuttgart: W. Kohlhammer.
1965 *Old Testament Theology. II. The Theology of Israel's Prophetic Traditions*. Trans. D.M.G. Stalker. New York: Harper & Row.

Rainey, A.F.
1976 Taharqa and Syntax. *Tel Aviv* 3: 38-41.

Rendtorff, R.
1984 Zur Komposition des Buches Jesaja. *VT* 34: 295-320.

Roberts, J.J.M.
1985 Isaiah and his Children. In *Biblical and Related Studies Presented to Samuel Iwry*, 193-203. Ed. A. Kort, S. Morschauer. Winona Lake: Eisenbrauns.

Shea, W.H.
1985 Sennacherib's Second Palestinian Campaign. *JBL* 104: 401-18.

Spalinger, A.
1974 Esarhaddon and Egypt: An Analysis of the First Invasion of Egypt. *Or* 43: 295-326.

Sweeney, M.A.
1988 *Isaiah 1–4 and the Post-Exilic Understanding of the Isaianic Tradition*. Berlin: de Gruyter.

Van Seters, J.
1983 *In Search of History. Historiography in the Ancient World and the Origins of Biblical History*. New Haven: Yale University Press.

Vermeylen, J.
1977 *Du Prophète Isaïe à l'apocalyptique. Isaïe 1–35, miroir d'un demi-millénaire d'expérience religieuse en Israël*. Paris: J. Gabalda.

Weinfeld, M.
1987 The Tribal League at Sinai. In *Ancient Israelite Religion: Essays in Honor of Frank Moore Cross*, 303-14. Ed. P.D. Miller, Jr, P.D. Hanson, S.D. McBride. Philadelphia: Fortress Press.

Wellhausen, J.
1878 *Prolegomena zur Geschichte Israels*. Leipzig: de Gruyter.

Werner, W.
1985 Vom Prophetenwort zur Prophetentheologie. Ein redaktionskritischer Ver such zu Jes 6, 1-8, 18. *BZ* 29: 1-30.

Willis, J.T.
1984 The First Pericope in the Book of Isaiah. *VT* 34: 63-77.
1985 Lament Reversed—Isaiah 1:21ff. *ZAW* 98: 236-48.

Wilson, R.R.
1979 Prophecy and Ecstasy: A Re-examination. *JBL* 98: 321-37.
1980 *Prophecy and Society in Ancient Israel*. Philadelphia: Fortress Press.

Xella, P.
1980 Sur la nourriture des morts. Un aspect de l'eschatologie mésopotamienne. In *Death in Mesoptamia*, 151-60. Ed. B. Alster. Copenhagen: Akademisk Forlag.

DEUTERONOMY 13:
THE SUPPRESSION OF ALIEN RELIGIOUS PROPAGANDA IN ISRAEL DURING THE LATE MONARCHICAL ERA*

Paul E. Dion

In three unrelenting paragraphs (vv. 2-6, 7-12, 13-18) Deuteronomy 13 prescribes the execution of any prophet inciting Israel to worship other deities instead of YHWH, the denunciation and stoning of any relative or friend giving the same advice, and the utter destruction of any community welcoming such propaganda.

This is a very special law, unparalleled in the Hebrew Scriptures. From the long fight between the 'YHWH alone' party and promoters of other religious attitudes, the Bible preserves many tales of bloody confrontation, some projected into the hoary past (Levites versus golden calf worshippers, Exod. 32.25-29; Phinehas versus worshippers of Baal Peor, Num. 25), others from the better known monarchical era (Jezebel versus prophets of YHWH, and Elijah versus prophets of Baal, 1 Kgs 18; Jehu versus worshippers of Baal, 2 Kgs 10.18-28; the people of Judah versus Mattan, the priest of Baal, 2 Kgs 11.18; Josiah versus the priests of the northern shrines, 2 Kgs 23.20). Deuteronomy 13 is also foreshadowed by older laws, forbidding the worship of other gods than YHWH (Exod. 20.3), and threatening with the *ḥrm* whoever offers sacrifice to them (Exod. 22.19). And yet this remarkable document has its own, very specific object; it is the only biblical law aimed at those who might *proselytize* for other deities.

This emphatic exhortation to denounce and to kill dissenters so as to win back YHWH's mercy has been branded as the prototype of the mediaeval Inquisition (Renan 1891: 216, 218; Budde 1916: 187,

* Professor N. Lohfink is to be thanked for his careful scrutiny of this monograph and for his invaluable suggestions. However the writer alone must bear the responsibility for his conclusions.

194-95; Lang 1984: 23 n. 9, 34-35),[1] and historians have been much exercised with its severity.

Ernest Renan (1891: 218) interpreted the harshness of Deuteronomy 13 as sheer rhetoric,[2] and Gustav Hölscher (1922: 192-93) stressed its lack of realism. In keeping with his thesis about the exilic origin of the book, Hölscher described Deuteronomy 13 as purely theoretical speculation that could only emerge once there was no more Israelite nationhood, and no king to be confronted with the nightmare of sacrificing entire cities and eventually Jerusalem itself, should they fall into idolatry. Only in very late legends such as Judges 20, he argued, do we find Israel waging a religious war on one of its own towns, as prescribed in the third part of Deuteronomy 13. Pre-exilic prophets, even those considered pseudo-prophets, are not known to have incited the people to defect from YHWH as the prophet or 'dreamer' in the first paragraph of this law. Neither was it necessary, before the exile, to keep any secrecy when proselytizing for other deities, as the private individuals envisioned in v. 7 are imagined as doing.

Hugo Gressmann (1924: 332-33) rejected the postexilic dating of Deuteronomy, and noted against Hölscher the devastating zeal of pre-exilic extremists like Jehu.[3] Taking a complementary approach, Max Löhr (1925: 175) contrasted the leniency of *Mekilta* and *Sifre* to the

1. According to Renan (1891: 219), 'Le terrible *Directorium Inquisitorum* de Nicolas Eymeric est calqué sur le Deutéronome'. However, this book never quotes Deut. 13. This was first brought to my attention in December 1980 by Fr R. Boyle, OP, now Director of the Vatican Library. My own search through a modern edition of the *Directorium* (Sala-Molins 1973), did not uncover any reference to Deut. 13. The only possible allusion is the injunction to admit spouses, sons or closely related people as witnesses for the prosecution; cf. perhaps Deut. 13.7.

2. 'Notre Occident, avec sa lourde bonhomie [sic], n'a pu comprendre que, par simple figure de style et par hyperbole, on ait écrit de telles horreurs, avec l'arrière-pensée qu'il n'y aurait personne pour les appliquer et les prendre au sérieux.'

3. The rest of Gressmann's argumention is less convincing. He quotes Ezek. 8.7-12 as evidence for the necessity of secrecy for pre-exilic idolators, but other examples in this same context do not agree with the point he makes, and in any case Ezek. 8 refers to a period after Josiah's reform. To demonstrate the possibility for pre-exilic Israelite prophets to preach Baal, Gressmann refers to Jer. 2.8, 11; 23.10, 14, 27; 29.23; but these examples either are not clearly independent from Deuteronomy, or do not point clearly to a defection as radical as that condemned in Deut. 13.2-6.

'fanaticism' of Deuteronomy 13, which he associated with 'very early' times. A year later, Karl Budde (1926: 180-82, 206-13), who also believed in the pre-exilic origin of Deuteronomy, emphasized its programmatic character. In his opinion, this was not a law code drawn up by authorities responsible for its enforcement, but the manifesto of a limited circle seeking to impart a new spirit to the nation. In 1930, Friedrich Horst (1961: 41) admitted the 'theoretical' character of Deuteronomy 13, while assuming, somewhat too easily, that a law which took for granted the state's willingness and ability to intervene against religious defection had to be genuinely pre-exilic.

This old debate is still echoing through contemporary scholarship (Patrick 1985: 108). Its solution may well lie in the Near Eastern political background pointed out by Moshe Weinfeld (1972: 91-100), but a comparative approach like his needs the support of a systematic analysis of the whole text. Accordingly, my historical discussion will be introduced by (1) text-critical and philological notes; (2) studies on the relationship of Deuteronomy 13 to its immediate context and to its parallel in Deut. 17.2-7; (3) a formal description of vv. 2-18; (4) a source-critical analysis aimed at isolating the original nucleus of the chapter; and finally (5) a discussion of its possible *Sitz im Leben*.

1. PRELIMINARY ANALYSES

1.1. *Text-critical and Philological Notes*

1.1.1. *General Remarks*

In addition to the usual and long-known witnesses, the text of Deuteronomy 13 is documented by 11QTemple 54.5–55.14 (Yadin 1977: 2.171-175; 3, pls. 69-70), and (fragmentarily) by 1Q4 7-8; 9; 10 (Barthélemy and Milik 1955: 55). In 11QTemple, Deut. 13.8-12 are missing due to the general loss of the upper part of this manuscript. 11QTemple 55.15-21 attaches a related law, Deut. 17.2-7 (only vv. 2-5 are preserved) to the end of Deuteronomy 13.

Several variants testify to a distinctive textual tradition, common to Qumran, the Septuagint and, to a lesser extent, the Samaritan Pentateuch. At vv. 3, 14, 16 and probably also 5 (see below), 11QTemple shares special readings with LXX. At vv. 6, 7 and 19, this witness agrees with the Samaritan Pentateuch as well as with LXX. Almost every variant carried by this textual tradition can be explained away as a scribal mistake or exegetical modification; but at the beginning of 10a, LXX preserves an important superior reading (see below).

The oscillation between singular and plural address was noticed by ancient scribes and translators, and, to varying extents, they ironed it out. LXX harmonizes locally (v. 1 singular, with 11QTemple, Vulgate, Peshitta; v. 4 plural; v. 6, singular but for its formulaic end, with 11QTemple, Samaritan Pentateuch). The Palestinian Targums put everything in the plural, except v. 7 where an individual is too obviously being addressed. This curious you/thou alternation, which the Ancients thought necessary to deal with in their own rather heavy-handed way, might turn out to be of real significance in analysing Deuteronomy 13.[1]

1.1.2. *Selected Problems*

Verses 2-3a. This sentence is loosely built. *l'mr* should introduce a quotation corresponding to the last verb of speaking, *dbr*, and LXX understands it this way. However this verb is a mere resumption of *ntn,* and it refers therefore to the 'giving' of a sign, not to the exhortation which *l'mr* really opens (v. 3b). In other words, vv. 2b-3a are parenthetical, and v. 2a finds its direct continuation in v. 3b. Vulgate and Peshitta correctly avoid subordinating the exhortation in v. 3b to *dbr*, but their translations are not entirely satisfactory. These versions suggest that the prophet makes his propaganda pitch after the fulfillment of his predictions; but more probably, the meaning is that he first delivers his message and then supports it by a sign, which in turn gets fulfilled; cf. Samuel in 1 Samuel 10, or Isaiah in 2 Kings 20.

Verse 3b.

MT	11QTemple, LXX
nlkh	*nlkh*
	wn'bwdh
'ḥry 'lhym 'ḥrym	*'lwhym 'ḥrym*
'šr l' yᵉda'tām	*'šr lw' yd'tmh*
wn'bdm	

The tradition represented by LXX and 11QTemple harmonized 3b

1. See my remarks on the frequent coincidence of ancient and modern preoccupations, on the basis of Deut. 21.1-9 (Dion 1984).

with 7b and 14b, perhaps because such a reading removes some of the awkwardness of having the lawgiver's disparaging remark 'that you do not know' inserted within the prophet's speech; but the MT reading is superior, since it is reflected by the beginning of v. 5, *'ḥry yhwh 'lhykm tlkw*, obviously intended to be a reverse image of 3b.

In vv. 3 and 7, the main textual witnesses disagree superficially in their treatment of *yd't(m)*, but all seem to have considered 'that thou hast not known'[1] as forming part of the proselytizer's speech.[2]

In v. 3, the MT puts the verb in the singular and construes the final *-m* as an object suffix referring to the gods; in so doing it quotes the prophet or 'dreamer' as addressing his audience as a single individual, as the deuteronomic writers themselves so often do. In v. 7, where an individual—well-provided with brothers, sons, wives, and so on—is being addressed, the verb is in the singular again; but in v. 14, the assumption is that the 'worthless fellows' have approached 'the inhabitants of their town' severally.

The Greek translator looks upon the audience of the prophet (v. 3) as a crowd, and reads *yd'tm* as a second person plural. In v. 7, it is clearly an individual who is being tempted, and the translator uses the singular; it is impossible to determine whether his *Vorlage* had *yd't* (as the MT), or if he read **yĕda'tām* from a *Vorlage *yd'tm* (cf. 11QTemple).

Finally, 11QTemple has the unequivocal second person plural *yd'tmh* at all three places. At an earlier stage in this textual tradition, *yd'tm* was probably read *yĕda'tem* in v. 3 (cf. LXX); and in v. 7, **yd't* was changed to **yd'tm* for better congruence with a double subject (*'th w'btyk*), as noted by Yadin (1977: 2.172).

Verse 5. The hypothetical restorations suggested below bring order into the apparent chaos of these three different arrangements of the loyalty phrases.

1. Readers will kindly forgive this archaic second person singular, here and in translations given below. Since the oscillation between 'you' and 'thou' seems to point to a plurality of hands in the text of Deut. 13, I have to reflect it in English in my discussions.

2. It may seem strange to find this disparaging deuteronomistic expression on the very lips of the seducer, but as we shall see later (1.4.1.), this is by no means impossible.

The Internal Arrangement of Verse 5

MT, Vg, Syr, Tgs	11QTemple	LXX
'ḥry yhwh 'lhykm tlkw	*'ḥry yhwh 'lwhykmh tlkwn*	*opisō kyriou tou theou hymōn poreuesthe*
....	*w'wtw t'bwdwn*	⟨kai autō douleuesthe⟩
w'tw tyr'w	*w'wtw tyr'w*	*kai auton phobēthēsesthe*
w't mṣwtyw tšmrw	⟨w't mṣwtyw tšmrwn⟩	*kai tas entolas autou phylaxesthe*
wbqlw tšm'w	*wbqlw tšm'wn*	*kai tē phonēs autou akousesthe*
w'tw t'bdw	....	
		....
wbw tdbqwn	*wbw tdbqwn*	*kai autō prostethēsesthe*

It is assumed that, at some early stage, all six phrases were present in the common parent text of 11QTemple and LXX as well as in that of MT, but with *w'tw t'bdw* placed differently. Later, the Hebrew manuscript traditions behind LXX and 11QTemple, independently from each other, lost two different items by the mechanical operation of *homeoarkton* or *homeoteleuton*.

1Q4.9 (Barthélemy and Milik 1955: 55) represents an even later stage of the Qumran textual tradition. This MS agrees with 11QTemple in placing *w'wtw t'b*[*dw*] right after *tlkwn*, but it preserves the *resh* of *tšmrw* just before v. 6 (with the final -*w* lost by haplography). This may be due to a belated and misplaced restoration of *w't mṣwtyw tšmrw*, which had been lost previously and is still missing in 11QTemple.

One can discover in the MT a symmetrical organization, which may have been intended by the author of v. 5. The two clauses with an object other than YHWH himself form the center, and both of their verbs begin by *tišm*. On each side are the clauses with *'tw*, and the extremes are formed by clauses in which YHWH is represented by a prepositional phrase. In the LXX–Qumran text tradition too, there is an intelligent arrangement: the modifiers of the verbs are: YHWH, him, him, his..., to his..., to him. The order preserved in the MT is probably the original one, since the same order prevails at 6.13 and 10.20. The different slot filled by *w'tw t'bdw* in the rival text tradition cannot be explained as an ordinary scribal mistake; this phrase may have been moved deliberately to the second position in the row, in order to couple it with the other 'him' phrase, *w'tw tyr'w*.

Verse 6a. dbr srh, 'speak mendaciously'. The same expression occurs at Jer. 28.16; 29.32; cf. Isa. 59.13 (*dbr 'šq wsrh*). *srh* appears four other times in the OT: Deut. 19.16; Isa. 1.5; 14.6; 31.6. At Isa. 14.6, *srh* is clearly derived from the root *swr* and *blty srh* means 'unceasingly'. From the semantic standpoint, this example has nothing to do with the others, and it is probably not derived from the same root.

Semantically, the root *swr* could easily yield a noun meaning 'defection' (see the examples of *swr* in Hoffmann 1980: 332), and in Deuteronomy 13 such a meaning would match the context (v. 3b!). However, morphologically, *srh* is much more easily analysed on the basis of the root *srr* (cf., e.g., *mrh* from *mrr* and *ṣrh* from *ṣrr*), and, even semantically, at Isa. 1.5; 31.6 the context seems more suitable to a derivation from the root *srr* and a translation of *srh* by 'insubordination'. In light of accumulating Akkadian examples of the words *sartum* and *surrātum*, '(malicious) lie', also derived from the root *srr*, it now appears that this etymology can suit all the Hebrew examples of *srh* except Isa. 14.6. In Deut. 19.16, the *srh* statement made by the malevolent witness is reminiscent of the *šibūt sarrātim* ('false witness') condemned in para. 3 of Codex Hammurapi; and in Deut. 13.6 and similar contexts, as noted by Moses Schorr (1909: 432), *dbr srh* corresponds to *dabābu sarrātim/surrātim* ('speak mendaciously'), found in political contexts in the neo-Assyrian royal inscriptions. For a complete demonstration see Jenni (1981).

Verse 7a. 'ḥyk bn-'mk. The Samaritan Pentateuch, LXX and 11QTemple insert *bn-'byk 'w* after *'ḥyk. Tg. Ps.-J.* adds *kl dkn* ('and of course') after *'mk* and before *br 'byk*, thus showing the exegetical origin of the variant. MT, which reflects conditions prevailing in a polygamous family, is certainly correct; see König (1917: 123).

Verse 10a. ky hrg thrgnw: LXX *anangellōn anangeleis peri autou* i.e.: **ky hgd tgdnw*. 11Q Temple is missing. Beside the obvious graphic similarity in the Hebrew script, between *hgd* and *hrg*, which makes scribal confusions rather easy, K. Budde (1916: 187-88) notes in favour of LXX **hgd tgdnw* that the true correlative of 'not to cover up for' (end of v. 9) is 'to report' (*hgd*), not 'to kill' (*hrg*). Budde adds four exegetical arguments (see also Horst 1961: 54-55), and M. Weinfeld (1972: 92-94) quotes four ancient Near Eastern texts comparable to Deuteronomy 13, which contain phrases equivalent to 'you shall not cover up for him'.

Budde's stylistical argument can be sharpened even more by tabulating vv. 9-10:

9a	*l'-t'bh lw*	*wl'-tšm' 'lyw*
9b*	*wl'-tḥws 'nk 'lyw*	*wl'-tḥml*
9b*-10a*	*wl'-tksh 'lyw*	*ky *hgd tgdnw*
10a*-b	*ydk thyh-bw br'šnh lhmytw*	*wyd kl-h'm b'ḥrnh*

The phrases used in v. 9, down to 'not to cover up', form two synonymous pairs, and 10a[b] forms another pair with 10b; one would expect 'not to cover up' and the expression used at the beginning of 10a to form a pair also, and indeed a pair of opposites, since these phrases are linked by *kî* instead of *waw*.

Even apart from the stylistical and exegetical arguments, the matter should be decided by the fact that there is no other example of the verb *hrg* in Deuteronomy. At first sight, accepting this example of *hrg* as a legitimate exception (like Rose 1975: 23 n. 1) might seem a more objective attitude than sacrificing it to the LXX variant; but the conspicuous absence of *hrg* from a book that speaks so much about killing would be enough to cast doubt on its authenticity at 13.10 even without the witness of the Greek. At a later stage, the replacement of *hgd* in its relatively rare meaning of 'reporting' (Lev. 5.1; Jer. 20.10; Prov. 29.24; Qoh. 10.20; cf. Est. 2.22) by such a common Hebrew verb as *hrg* (×167 in the Bible) is more likely to have taken place than the reverse (Weinfeld 1972: 94). As a last confirmation, note *whgd lk* in Deut. 17.4, a passage which probably depends on this one (see below).

Verse 14a. wydyḥw 't-yšby 'yrm :: LXX, 11QTemple insert *kwl* before *yšby*. Yadin suggests an influence of Gen. 18.24 (Intercession of Abraham), and in mainstream Judaism a tendency to reduce the applicability of Deut. 13.13-19 as much as possible is well documented. *Sifre* para. 92 comments that authorities are not to go out of their way looking for cities fallen into paganism, and oversubtly notes that the law only applies to '*one* of your cities', not more, and to dwelling places, not to Jerusalem. *M. Sanh.* 10.4-5 and *Sifre* para. 93-4, in the same spirit, heap up pretexts for preventing the application of the biblical instruction. *T. Sanh.* 14.1 emphasizes that the fallen city to be put under the ban is only a theoretical model.

However one hesitates to attribute leniency to the Essenes, and the free addition or omission of *kol* is a common phenomenon in the transmission of the biblical text. In Deut. 13.16 *kol* is twice gratuitously inserted by 11QTemple, and the first addition is shared by LXX. The variant in v. 14 is most probably nothing more than this.

Verse 14b. wn'bdh 'lhym 'ḥrym :: 11QTemple omits *'ḥrym* The disparaging deuteronomistic phrase of the MT is emasculated in the variant, and the resulting expression is less surprising on the lips of the proselytizer; but if this change had been intended, it should have also appeared in vv. 3 and 7. The fall of *'ḥrym* is probably due to a banal homeoteleuton.

Verse 15a. wdršt wḥqrt wš'lt hyṭb :: LXX B omits the first verb. This is probably a mere internal variant of the LXX, simply due to a scribal parablepsis (Wevers 1978: 124); Horst (1961: 37-38) builds too much on this mechanical mistake.

Verse 17a. klyl lyhwh 'lhyk. All the versions give to *klyl* the adverbial value apparent in Isa. 2.18, Lev. 6.15, *et al.*: LXX *pandēmei*, Aquila *holotelōs*, Vulgate *universa*, Peshitta *lagmōr*, *Tgs. Onqelos, Pseudo-Jonathan, Neofiti* 1 *gmyr*. However, the old sacrificial meaning 'whole offering' (Loretz 1975), reflected in Egyptian (Dussaud 1921: 159-62), documented in Punic inscriptions (*KAI* 69; 74), and still evident in the Bible in Lev. 6.16; Deut. 33.10; 1 Sam. 7.9; Ps. 51.21, cannot be excluded.

Better than by an obscure passage of the Mesha inscription (*KAI* 181, lines 11-12), the plausibility of such a metaphor in a seventh-century context is supported by a text of Ashurbanipal. In his Annals, sixth campaign, this king of Assyria boasts of slaying people involved in the murder of his grandfather Sennacherib 'as a burial offering for him' (*ina kispišu*) (Rassam Cylinder, col. IV line 72; Streck 1916: 2.38; *ANET* 288). As noted by Zimmern (*apud* Streck 1916: 2.39 n. 7), this is undoubtedly a rhetorical metaphor.[1] In Deut. 13.17, a comparable meaning is certainly plausible.[2]

1.1.3. *Summary*

This brief look at the text and transmission of Deuteronomy 13 has confirmed the general trustworthiness of MT, except for the beginning of v. 10, where *hgd tgdnw* is to be read with LXX. Our attention has also been drawn to the solidarity between Deuteronomy 13 and Deut. 17.2-7 assumed by the author of 11QTemple, the oscillation between 'you' and 'thou', and the broken continuity within vv. 2-3a.

1.2. *Deuteronomy 13 and its Immediate Context*

In the finished state of Deuteronomy, the laws collected in chs. 12–26 are headed by two chapters concerned with different facets of religious unity; but several aspects of ch. 12 are picked up again by chs. 14–16, in contrast to ch. 13 which is an entirely self-contained unit. Its author does not waste one word about the geographical centralization of worship, while this topic, and various formulaic expressions associated with it, play a prominent part in chs. 14–16 as well as in ch. 12. This is true above all of the so-called *mqwm* formula, 'the place YHWH thy God will choose to set his name there',[3] of the designation of Israelite towns by 'your gates',[4] and of the lists of categories of people invited to eat together before YHWH.[5]

1. Cf., in earlier times, the boast of the 17th-century Hittite ruler Hattushili I in his Annals, 1.19: 'When the Great King Tabarna ruined the King of Hassi ⟨(and) Hassi⟩, the King of Hahhi (and) Hahhi, he did set (them, i.e. the towns) afire and the smoke he showed to the Sun God of Heaven and to the Storm God' (Houwink Ten Cate 1983: 54).

2. Even in ancient times the sacrificial metaphor was present to the Jewish tradition. A saying attributed to Rabbi Simeon runs like this: 'The Holy One, blessed is he, said, "When ye execute judgement against an Apostate City I will reckon it to you as if ye offered up before me a whole burnt offering"' (*m. Sanh.* 10.6).

3. ×6 in ch. 12; ×3 in ch. 14; ×1 in ch. 15; ×6 in ch. 16.

4. ×5 in ch. 12; ×4 in ch. 14; ×2 in ch. 15; ×4 in ch. 16.

5. Abridged in 12.7, full at 12.12, 18; 14.26; 16.11, 14.

Beside their common concern for religious unity, chs. 12–13 are linked by their external frame:[1]

Ch. 11		
31	*ky 'tm 'brym 't-hyrdn*	
	lb' lršt *'t-h'rṣ* ***'šr-yhwh 'lhykm ntn lkm***	cf. 12.1
	wyrštm 'th	cf. 12.29
	wyšbtm-bh	cf. 12.29
32	wšmrtm l'śwt 't kl-	cf. 12.1; 13.1
	hḥqym w't-hmšpṭym	cf. 12.1
	'šr 'nky *ntn lpnykm* hywm	cf. 12.28; 13.1, 19
Ch. 12		
1	***'lh hḥqym whmšpṭym***	cf. 12.1
	'šr tšmrwn l'śwt	cf. 11.32; 13.1
	b'rṣ 'šr ntn yhwh 'lhy *'btyk lk* ***lršth***	cf. 11.31
	kl-hymym 'šr-'tm ḥyym 'l-h'dmh	
28	šmr *wšm't* 't kl-hdbrym *h'lh* 'šr 'nky mṣwk	cf. 11.32 13.1, 19
	lm'n yyṭb lk wlbnyk 'ḥryk 'd-'wlm	
	*ky t'*śh *hṭwb* whyšr b'yny yhwh 'lhyk	cf. 13.19b
29	*ky-ykryt yhwh 'lhyk*	
	't-hgwym 'šr 'th b'-šmh lršt 'wtm	cf. 11.31; 12.1-2
	mpnyk	
	wyršt 'tm	cf. 11.31
	wyšbt b'rṣm	cf. 11.31
Ch. 13		
1	't kl-hdbr 'šr 'nky mṣwh 'tkm	cf. 12.28
	'tw tšmrw l'śwt	cf. 11.32; 12.1
	l'-tsp 'lyw	
	wl' tgr' mmnw	
19	*ky tšm' bqwl yhwh 'lhyk*	
	lšmr 't-kl-mṣwty*w*	cf. 12.28; 13.1
	'šr 'nky mṣwk hywm	cf. 12.28
	l'śwt hyšr b'yny yhwh 'lhyk	cf. 12.28

1. In the following chart of the framework around Deut. 12–13, expressions peculiar to 11.31-32; 12.1, 29 are in boldface italic; expressions characteristic of 12.28; 13.1, 19 are in roman.

Deuteronomy 12 is surrounded and bound to ch. 11 by a very strong frame: 11.31-32 and 12.1, 29 are linked by *ḥqym wmšpṭym*, *'rṣ*, and the root *yrš*, persistently repeated.

Deuteronomy 13, in turn, is surrounded and bound to ch. 12 by another frame: 12.28 and 13.1, 19. These verses are bound together by the persistently repeated root *ṣwh*, the designation of YHWH's commands as *dbr*[*ym*] and the phrase **'śh hyšr b'yny yhwh 'lhyk*.

Expressions shared by both frames are less numerous; they boil down to *šmr l'śwt 't-kl 'šr 'nky* + a participle of commanding, a second person pronoun, + *hywm*.

The frame attaching ch. 12 to ch. 11 is one piece with both 12.2-7 and 12.29-31, the two substantive parts of ch. 12 usually considered by critics as the latest accretions to this chapter. Both of these sections use the verb *yrš*, and the second one forms with 12.29 a hypothetical syntagmeme.

The situation is different with ch. 13 and its frame. 12.28 and 13.1, 19 are much less useful to their context than 11.31-32; 12.1. The interference of 12.28 separates 12.29-31 from the main bulk of ch. 12, in spite of the strong affinity of this paragraph for 12.2-7. The only serious link between ch. 13 and its frame is the association of *šmr* and *mṣwtyw*, which appears in 13.5 as well as in 13.19; but Deut. 13.5 is generally considered as secondary (Merendino 1969: 61, with references to earlier scholarship; Seitz 1971: 151; Mayes 1979: 232).

It would seem, therefore, that 12.28 and the rest of this frame were inserted in order to attach 12.29-31 to ch. 13, and to build a complex of instructions against religious contamination by Canaanites (cf. Seitz 1971: 153). The warning against imitating the dispossessed nations (v. 30) does have some affinity for the proscription of alien propaganda (Merendino 1969: 81); but the combination of 12.29-31 with ch. 13 is superficial and probably secondary. Deut. 13.2-18 is aimed against 'other deities' in general, not specifically against Canaanite religion; and the proselytism it condemns is portrayed as originating among the Israelites themselves, without reference to foreign influence. The recurrence of *'bd...'lhym* in 12.30, 13.3 and elsewhere, is but a tenuous link between these chapters. In 12.30, the question is *how* YHWH is to be worshipped (should he be worshipped as the gods of Canaan?); but ch. 13 bears directly on the exclusiveness of his claim on Israel; in any unified and logically ordered composition, this question should have been given priority over the other. The recurrence of *śrp b'š* at 12.31 (child sacrifice) and 13.17 (destruction of town and spoils; no sacrifice) is an even more tenuous link between ch. 13 and the end of ch. 12. Such catchwords may have eased out the insertion of ch. 13 and the setting of the framework we have discussed, but they cannot prove its original continuity with 12.29-31. In spite of redactional efforts to tie it to ch. 12, Deut. 13.2-18 remains an isolated composition.

1.3. *Deuteronomy 13 and 17.2-7*

Deuteronomy 13 is more closely related to 17.2-7 than to the end of ch. 12. Little wonder that the author of the Temple Scroll transcribed this part of ch. 17 at the end of Deuteronomy 13. Especially since Budde (1916: 193-96), many modern interpreters posit the original continuity of these two passages, but they usually place ch. 13 *after* 17.2-7, which embodies the simplest case of idolatry and the most general rules about its punishment.[1] According to Merendino (1969: 80-81), ch. 13 was moved to the end of ch. 12 by the dtr redactor who also wrote 12.29-31, while 17.2-7 remained in the judicial context where it truly belongs. Others (e.g. Rofé 1987: 228) believe 16.21–17.7 to have been misplaced, as a whole column of text, at an early stage of the manuscript tradition, from its original location after ch. 12, or more precisely, between 13.1 and 13.2.[2]

However, there is no consensus on the pristine unity of Deuteronomy 13 and 17.2-7. Among our contemporaries, the dissent of Richter (1964: 83), Seitz (1971: 153-55) and Carmichael (1974: 100-101) is worthy of notice. As König (1917: 29) and Hölscher (1922: 198) already objected, the aim of Deut. 17.2-7 differs from that of ch. 13. This instruction is focused on idolatrous propaganda, but in 17.2-7 the topic of idolatry is merely ancillary to the description of a trial, and the emphasis lies on matters of procedure. The choice of idolatry for an example shows the author's obsession

1. Horst (1961: 57 n. 86), an adversary of this view who wrote in 1930, lists among its supporters Wellhausen, Dillmann, Bertholet, Puukko, Budde, Steuernagel and Marti.

2. Already, Horst (1961: 58) reasonably raised against this hypothesis the inappropriateness of 17.1, the prohibition of tainted sacrificial victims, in a context (Deut. 12–13) supposedly focused on the elimination of *Canaanite* ritual practices.

with this topic, but his essential purpose is to provide an illustration for the functioning of the tribunals of 16.18.

Deuteronomy 17.2-7 leans heavily on ch. 13 and other materials from Deuteronomy. It falls into the same basic divisions as 13.2-18: a protasis describing the discovery of a case of idolatry in Israel (vv. 2-3; cf. 13. 2-3, 7-8, 13-14); an apodosis prescribing to ascertain the guilt of the suspect (v. 4; cf. 13.9b[end]-10a*[emended], 15) and to execute him (v. 5, 7a; cf. 13.6a, 10a* -11a, 16); and a motive clause (v. 7b; cf. 13.6b, 12, 18b). The only division of 17.2-7 without any counterpart in ch. 13 is the rule requiring two witnesses (v. 6), which is almost perfectly identical to 19.15b.

This similarity of structure in the anti-idolatry legislation is accompanied by a far-reaching identity of phraseology. The beginning of v. 2a is reminiscent of both 13.2a (*ky* + 3rd person imperfect + *bqrbk* and 13.13a (*b'ḥd* / *b'ḥt* + a word for 'thy towns'); v. $2a^{b}$ = another part of 13.13a; v. 3a changes into a narrative the speech found at 13.3b, 7b, 14b; vv. 4b, 7a and 5b are virtually identical, respectively, to 13.15, 10a* b, and 11a; v. 7b = 13.6b.

In fact, very little in 17.2-7 is not paralleled elsewhere in the laws of Deuteronomy. Seitz (1971: 154) has correctly pointed out contacts with the examples of 'case law' found in this book; to his list, one may add the injunction to bring out the culprit towards the gate (v. 5a, cf. 21.19; 22.15, 24), with (here only) 'gate' awkwardly in the plural.

The only ingredients which 17.2-7 does not share with ch. 13 nor with the casuistic laws of Deuteronomy are concentrated in vv. 2b-3. Phrases found in these verses tie 17.2-7 both to the latest parts of Deuteronomy and to historiographic and prophetical texts written under its influence:

'śh 't-hr' b'yny yhwh, 'to do what is evil in the sight of YHWH' (v. 2b): cf. Deut. 4.25; Deut. 9.18 (in a secondary stratum within the already deuteronomistic 9.1–10.11); Deut. 31.29 (in the external frame of the Song of Moses); Num. 32.13 (dtr influence); Judg. 2.11; 3.7, 12 (×2); 4.1; 6.1; 10.6; 13.1; 1 Sam. 15.19; 2 Sam. 12.9; 1 Kgs 11.6; 14.22; 15.26, 34; 16.19, 25, 30; 21.20, 25; 22.53; 2 Kgs 3.2; 8.18, 27; 11.6; 13.2, 11; 14.24; 15.9, 18, 24, 28; 17.2, 17; 21.2, 6, 15, 16, 20; 23.32, 37; 24.9, 19; Isa. 65.12; 66.4; Jer. 7.30; 18.10; 32.30; 52.2; Ps. 51.6; 2 Chron. 21.6; 22.4; 29.6; 33.2, 6, 22; 36.5, 9, 12.

This formula is frequent in the dtr writings and in later works influenced by them; in Deuteronomy itself it is manifestly characteristic of late strata. Oddly enough, it is missing from Joshua, and in 17.2b the infinitive of *k's* is not subjoined to the core of the formula as in the three other examples from Deuteronomy; but there is no solid reason for Richter's assertion (1964: 84) that the other examples of *'śh hr' b'ny yhwh* are derived from Deut. 17.2b. (Cf. Richter 1964: 58, 67, 79, 81-85; Dietrich 1972: 88-89.)

l'br brytw, 'to break his covenant' (v. 2b, end): cf. Josh. 23.16; Judg. 2.20; 2 Kgs 18.12.

wyšt̩ḥw... lšmš 'w lyrḥ 'w lkl-ṣb' hšmym, 'and they bowed down to the sun, the moon and all the heavenly host (v. 3a*-b): cf. 4.19; Jer. 8.2; cf. also (less close) 2 Kgs 17.16; 21.3.

'šr l' ṣwyty, 'that I had not enjoined' (v. 3b, end): cf. Jer. 7.22, 31; 19.5; 32.35. In all four places, *l' ṣwyty* is coupled with another negated verb, but these parallels are closer than Deut. 18.20 and Jer. 29.23, where the topic is prophetic inspiration rather than commands to the nation.

Hölscher (1922: 197 n. 3) thought v. 3b to be secondary because ideally it belongs before *wyštḥw lhm*; but the arrangement of the text should be explained otherwise. In v. 3, it is the whole of *wyštḥw... ṣwyty* that is to be distinguished from *wylk wy'bd 'lhym 'ḥrym*, taken directly from ch. 13. Unfortunately, it is unclear whether the latter part of v. 3 is to be regarded as an addition, or whether the original author first wrote what he was taking from his main model (Deut. 13) and then continued with phrases from his own time.

There is no such uncertainty about 2b. *'šr y'śh 't-hr' b'yny yhwh* is absolutely necessary to Deut. 17.2-7, and it seems gratuitous to cut off its continuation *l'br brytw*.

Therefore it appears that deuteronomistic phrases which entered late into the book of Deuteronomy are integral to the original draft of this instruction. As we shall see later, a different situation prevails in ch. 13, where such phrases are found in sections which can be neatly excised from the main body of the text.

This lack of distinctive vocabulary and these strong connections with the latest parts of Deuteronomy suggest that 17.2-7 was composed by a late redactor, who imitated ch. 13 and also inspired himself of the criminal laws already collected in the book. This writer's phraseology and his concern about astral cults bring him very close to the author of ch. 4.

In conclusion, Deut. 17.2-7 is not a broken-off piece of ch. 13, recycled and relocated. It is but a derivative of this chapter. As such it can help clarify particular problems of text and interpretation, such as the question about *hrg* or *hgd* at the beginning of 13.10 (see above), but it has no direct bearing on the background and original meaning of 13.2-18.

1.4. *The Form of Deuteronomy 13.2-18*[1]

Deut. 13.2-18 is written in a special legal form, common in Deuteronomy, which is conveniently dubbed 'If-you law'. In contrast to the impersonal style of case law ('If a man...'; Alt 1966: 88-103), the personal involvement of the addressee is stressed right from the outset: in the first and third laws, the crime is said to take place 'in thy midst'; in the second law the addressee himself is portrayed as the object of the attempted seduction. The form of these laws cannot be explained as a mere modification of case law nor of apodictic commands (Rose 1975: 23-25).

This chapter falls into three main divisions with essentially the same structure: law 1, vv. 2-6; law 2, vv. 7-12; law 3, 13-18. All three laws are written in the same conditional style, and include a protasis, an apodosis, and a set of motivating developments. My comments will show that the not inconsiderable differences separating law 2 from law 1, and especially law 3 from laws 1-2, are usually content-motivated.[2]

1. The following comments are meant to be read with constant reference to the Synopsis (see Appendix).

2. It is very doubtful that different origins should be predicated on these laws because of differences in their subject matters. Horst (1961: 48-49), for instance, thought law 1, which deals with the incitation to religious 'high treason', to be dependent on law 3, which deals with the *perpetrated* defection of a community; but the 'Ishmeriga-Vertrag' (quoted below, 2.2.2.1.) shows how these two topics can be original in the same document.

1.4.1. *The Protasis: the Eventuality of Alien Religious Propaganda (vv. 2-3, 7-8, 13-14)*

The protasis begins with *ky* and the imperfect. The presentation of the seducers (vv. 2-3a, 7a, 13-14a) is followed by an abstract of their propaganda pitch (vv. 3b, 7b-8, 14b).[1] It is surprising to hear them proselytizing for their new gods with a choice of expressions constantly used *in malam partem* in Deuteronomy, such as 'other deities', and 'that you do not know'.[2] However these phrases are not to be assigned to a later redaction; the lawgiver himself is passing judgment on the proselytizer's propaganda while pretending to sum it up.[3] This is made easier by the Hebrew tendency to use quotations where an Indo-European language would prefer indirect discourse.[4]

1.4.2. *The Apodosis: The Conduct Prescribed for such an Eventuality (vv. 4-6a, 9-11a, 15-18a)*

The backbone of the apodosis prescribing the appropriate conduct in such circumstances is made of second person singular *yiqtol* and *weqataltî* clauses.

The apodosis exhibits more variations than the protasis, but the reaction it enjoins on Israel can be divided into three sections: a

1. As confirmed to me by M. O'Connor, the speeches here put on the lips of prophets, family members, etc., belong to the 'displaced participant' type of quotation. This form of discourse, characterized by the insertion of *l'mr* between the quoted words and the verb which introduces them, is used, among others, when speech is quoted for its import rather than its exact wording (1 Kgs 1.13; 2.1-2). O'Connor's research on quotations is indebted to a forthcoming paper of Cynthia Miller, a graduate student of the University of Chicago.

2. Merendino (1969: 63) explains 'that you do not know' as a redactor's device to contrast the foreign deities with YHWH. Unfortunately, this solution would not do for *'lhym 'ḥrym*, which, because of its negative associations in the OT, is just as awkward as *'šr l' yd'tm* on the lips of the false prophet.

3. Horst (1961: 36 n. 30) rightly observes: 'Die Formulierung erweckt den Anschein, als wolle der Verfasser sein eigenen Urteil den Redenden in den Mund legen (vgl. Jes. 28.15; 29.15; 30.11)'. The third parallel quoted by Horst (Isa. 30.11) is quite apt; the citation form used by the prophet suggests that he is reporting actual demands of the Judaeans, while in fact he is putting in their mouths his own interpretation of their evil intentions. And yet, the prophet does not use the same construction with *l'mr* as the author of Deut. 13. In a private communication, M. O'Connor emphasizes the uniqueness of the quotations found in Deut. 13.

4. On the rarity of indirect discourse in Hebrew, see K.R. Crim (1973).

warning not to give in to the proselytizer (only laws 1-2: vv. 4-5, 9a); injunctions to report him or to ascertain his crime (only laws 2-3: vv. 9b-10a[a], 15), and finally, injunctions to execute the culprits (vv. 6a, 10a[b]-11, 16-18a).

Departures from this pattern are content-motivated and do not obscure the basic structure. The warning against alien propaganda is not represented in law 3, since this law is not addressed to people tempted by the proselytizers, but to those who might hear that others have been led astray. Neither report nor inquiry is prescribed in law 1, because prophets are assumed to speak out openly. Horst (1961: 37) aptly remarks that v. 15 is by no means superfluous in law 3, since the unfortunate city's defection is only known by hearsay; so much is at stake that this rumour must be verified scrupulously.

1.4.2.1. *Not to Give in to Proselytizers. l' tšm' 'l-* is clearly the nucleus of the warning section. In law 1, this prohibition is followed by two paragraphs in the second person plural: an explanatory sentence (*ky*, v. 4b), and a row of six prescriptive *yiqtols* with fronted objects, enjoining obedience to YHWH (v. 5). The affinity between 'loving Yawheh' (v. 4b) and the expressions of loyalty forming v. 5 ties these two paragraphs together.[1]

1.4.2.2. *Reporting or Ascertaining the Crime.* Due to the nature of the cases, the section on reporting the crime and examining the evidence is quite diversified.

In law 2, the positive injunction to report the proselytizer is preceded by three prohibitions against any form of pity toward the the brother turned tempter (v. 9b). Grammatically, these verbs form an unbroken row with those prohibiting assent to the seducer's plans (9a); but semantically this is a different stipulation, special to law 2 because of the secret nature of the offence.

As law 3 assumes that the mass apostasy of a particular town is already common knowledge (vv. 13-14), v. 15 concentrates on the evaluation of the evidence. Its emphasis on a careful investigation

1. The unity of vv. 4b-5 was correctly stressed by Lohfink (1963: 65). The internal arrangement of v. 5 has been discussed in the text-critical section. The loyalty phrases and their parallel occurrences will be discussed below, in the section on phraseology.

conforms to Deuteronomy's tendency to insert rules of procedure between protasis and apodosis, even in its few good examples of case law, e.g. 21.2, 19-20; 22.15-17; 25.7b-8.[1] Here, the three prescriptive *yiqtol*s enjoining an inquiry (v. 15a) are followed by two statements describing an eventual conviction (v. 15b); the roots *'mn* and *kwn* stress the need for certainty. In v. 15b as in v. 15a, parallel clauses are arranged by increasing lengths.

1.4.2.3. *Executing the Culprits.* In the section about executions (vv. 6a*, 10a^{b}-11, 16-18a), the common element is the capital punishment.

The identity of the convict is specified again in laws 1 and 3, but not in law 2, where an unbroken row of anaphoric pronouns makes this unnecessary. Law 3 aims its sanctions not only at the seducers of the apostate community, the *bny bly'l* of v. 13, but at the whole town fallen under their spell.

In contrast to its fervent plea for loyalty to YHWH (vv. 4b-5), law 1 is most impersonal in its formulation of the death penalty; it stands very close to case law.

Law 2 is more specific about the method of punishment, stoning (v. 11). In addition, it prescribes (v. 10) that the very friend or relative who reported the culprit start the execution personally, no doubt in order to give more weight and solemnity to his testimony. Verses 10-11 are linked by the repetition of the verb *mwt*. Verse 10 places this verb between two lines beginning by *yd* and ending by one of the two paired words *r'šwnh* and *'ḥrnh*.

Law 3, which deals with a whole community presumably capable of resistance, replaces the normal capital punishment vocabulary (the verb *mwt*, 'to die', used in laws 1-2) by war terminology ('smiting with the edge of the sword', v. 16).

This rather elaborate section of law 3 is articulated on the distinction between animate (v. 16) and inanimate (vv. 17-18a). The two segments are united by numerous references to the town and by the root *ḥrm*, which appears in the middle of the first part and at the end of the second.

1. Cf. also the law on not taking back one's divorced wife, Deut. 24.1-4, where the statement of the case (vv. 1-3) is overloaded with notes on how a divorce is enacted.

Verse 16 enjoins the death penalty twice; the second time, it intensifies its command by the use of *ḥrm* and by the explicit inclusion of animals. *lpy ḥrb*, as a refrain, concludes each clause.

Verses 17-18a deal with the town itself and its material goods. Measures regarding their disposal fall into four divisions, disposed chiastically: the first colon of 17a and 18a deal with the booty, the rest of 17a and 17b deal principally with the city, although the booty is mentioned again as something to be burnt along with the city.

1.4.3. *Motive Clauses (vv. 6, 11b-12, 18b)*
The laws of Deuteronomy 13 are concluded by two types of motive clauses, some more specific to the offence committed (vv. 6a, 11b), and the others of a more general scope (vv. 6b, 12, 18b).[1]

1.4.3.1. *Specific Motive Clauses.* Specific motive clauses are only represented in laws 1-2. Their nucleus is the phrase *hdyḥ mn-*, 'to thrust away from', with a modifier containing the name of 'YHWH thy God'. This phrase points out the essence of the crime: separating Israel from its God.

This element is found in its simplest form in law 2 (v. 11b). YHWH's name and title are followed by a participial clause recalling the Exodus, and showing the ungrateful character of the defection.

The same development appears in law 1, preceded by another encapsulation of the false prophet's crime, *dbr srh ʿl yhwh ʾlhykm.* Here, the name of the God of Israel is modified by two participial clauses elaborating slightly on that in law 2. In this piece of *Sondergut*, Israel is addressed basically in the second person plural, but the author does not hesitate to mix numbers (*hpdk*).

Law 3 has no peroration on the horror of the crime, but the protasis itself has already subtly contrasted it to YHWH's generous gift of the land (v. 13), described it as the initiative of 'worthless fellows', and defined it with the same verb **hdyḥ* as the motive clauses of laws 1-2 (v. 14).

1.4.3.2. *General Motive Clauses.* The formulaic motive clauses which conclude laws 1–2 (Dion 1980) are often appended to deuteronomic

1. Verse 19, the second part of the external frame which I have excluded from consideration, could be described as a continuation of the motive clauses of law 3.

laws sanctioned by the capital punishment; the first one (6b) emphasizes retribution and the other dissuasion (12). When these formulas are used concurrently (Deut. 17.12-13; 19.19-20; 21.21), they are always found in the same order as in Deuteronomy 13; their arrangement in this chapter is certainly meant to bind the first two laws together (cf. Merendino 1969: 80). Their firm insertion in Deut. 13.2-18 is evident from their final word **qrb*, which appears three other times in this chapter (vv. 2, 14, 15); the dissuasion motif (v. 12) is particularly appropriate at the end of law 2, which emphasizes the public character of the punishment (vv. 10-11a).

Once again, law 3 goes its own way. As the defection of a whole town has been represented from the very outset as a *fait accompli*, the reason for its annihilation is taken from the necessity of placating YHWH, whose wrath is already ablaze.

The internal cohesion of v. 18b is reinforced by the alliteration and root play in *ḥrwn...rḥmym wrḥmk whrbk*. These stylistic devices ease the transition from appeasing YHWH to winning back his favour.

1.4.4. *Conclusion*

This analysis has shown Deut. 13.2-18 to be composed of homogeneous instructions, using largely the same vocabulary, and applying essentially the same structure to the treatment of three related offences. Several departures from this common structure were explained by the requirements of the specific cases envisioned in vv. 2-6, 7-12 and 13-18. It remains to be seen whether the unity of this chapter is unassailable, and this will be achieved by testing more severely its grammatical and logical consistency, and by looking into the literary associations of its words and phrases.

1.5. *A Source-critical Analysis of Deuteronomy 13.2-18*

1.5.1. *The Criterion of Consistency*

1.5.1.1. *In Law 1*

*Verses 2b-3a**. In the protasis of law 1, the passage about 'sign and wonder' breaks the continuity of discourse. The word *l'mr*, which ends 3a, is not seriously prepared far within vv. 2b-3a, and we noted earlier (1.1.2) that both Vulgate and Peshitta had managed to avoid a direct subordination of v. 3b under vv. 2b-3a. The quotation introduced by *l'mr* does not sum up the giving of a sign (the object of 2b-3a), but the very message of the prophet. As such, *l'mr* and v. 3b are the direct continuation of v. 2a; logically, vv. 2b-3a*, which deal with a mere concomitant, should follow the prophet's speech, not precede it, and the text should run like this:

ky yqwm bqrbk	Should there arise among thee
nby' 'w ḥlm ḥlwm l'mr	a prophet or dreamer of dream, saying:
nlkh 'ḥry 'lhym 'ḥrym	'Let us go after other deities
'šr l' yd'tm	that thou hast not known
wn'bdm	and let us worship them';
wntn 'lyk 'wt 'w mwpt	and should he give thee a sign or wonder,
wb' h'wt whmwpt	and the sign and wonder
'šr dbr 'lyk	that he spoke to thee about be fulfilled,
l' tšm'. . .	do not listen. . .

The verb sequence *yqwm. . .l'mr* here postulated, and even the beginning of the quotation that follows, have a good analogy in Judg. 20.8: *wyqm kl-h'm k'yš 'ḥd l'mr l' nlk. . .*, 'And all the people rose as one man, saying "we shall not go. . ." '

The present arrangement of the text is not unintelligible (after all, biblical redactors were very clever), but it seems best explained by Löhr's suggestion (1925: 174) that vv. 2b-3a* only came in as an afterthought, along with vv. 4b-5. Perhaps in order to maintain a pattern common to all three laws of Deuteronomy 13, which place the proselytizer's speech at the very end of the protasis, the interpolator inserted the passage on sign and fulfillment immediately after introducing the prophet, thus breaking the continuity of 2a/3b. In v. 3a, he used the verb *dbr* instead of the more appropriate *ntn*, in order to give *l'mr* a semblance of immediate preparation.

Verses 4a-5*. The unity of vv. 4b-5 has been established above (1.4.2.1). This motivating development followed by a series of injunctions is oddly placed within the apodosis; it slows the progression of law 1 and has no formal counterpart in the other two laws. These verses stand out against the rest of law 1, and indeed against most of Deut. 13.2-18, by their massive use of the second person plural.

Verse 4b anticipates a legitimate objection, prepared by 2b-3a: how can we deny our following to a prophet supported by a miraculous sign? is not his word confirmed by YHWH himself? But this concern is out of touch with the spirit of Deuteronomy 13, which does not brook any discussion. The common presupposition of laws 2-3 is that action must be taken against the inroads of other religions, no matter how prestigious or dear the tempter, no matter how large the community involved. Without vv. 4b-5, law 1 would be an absolute, unreasoning condemnation, just as the other two laws.

The devaluation of fulfillment as a criterion for true prophecy voiced in vv. 2b-3a, 4b may presuppose and qualify Deut. 18.22, as some have suggested (Merendino 1969: 62; Seitz 1971: 152); but there is no certainty in this matter. With or without 18.22, fulfillment was popular enough as a criterion of true prophecy to elicit an explanation like 13.4b (see, e.g., 1 Kgs 22.28; Ezek. 33.33). Moreover, there is no direct clash between 13.4b and 18.22, since Deut. 18.22 only offers *non*-fulfillment as a proof of *pretended* inspiration. One might in fact suggest that it is the author of the law on prophecy (Deut. 18.9-22) who was aware of 13.2-6 in its finished state. 18.20a^{b}b could be a passing summary of 13.2-6, and 18.22 may deliberately limit its own statement because of the possibility of fulfilled false prophecy pointed out in 13.3a, 4b.

Verse 4b clearly presupposes vv. 2b-3a*; but 2b-3a* would make sense in law 1 even without the apologetic remark of 4b, as indicative of the extreme challenges a faithful Israelite must be prepared to face in the fight for YHWH alone (cf. the endearing epithets appended to the mention of brother, wife and friend in v. 7a).

The use of *'wt 'w mwpt* in the singular, instead of the plural formula *'wtwt wmwptym* common elsewhere, has been construed as a sign of relative antiquity (Seitz 1971: 151-52) or of relative lateness (Merendino 1969: 62), but this argument is not convincing; in Deuteronomy *'wtwt wmwptym* is only used about the Exodus, and the existence of this formula does not preclude a more flexible use of the same terms in other contexts. Parsimony recommends the ascription of vv. 2b-3a and 4b-5 to one redactor only, concerned about the impressive signs which could be produced even on behalf of deities other than YHWH. At 2b-3a, this redactor conformed his style to the rest of vv. 2-3, but he wrote his longer and more loosely attached contribution (vv. 4b-5) in his preferred form of address, the second person plural.

The repetitive exhortation to YHWH-istic loyalty in v. 5[1] makes no contribution other than rhetorical to the main thrust of Deuteronomy 13, the forcible elimination of alien propaganda. The relatively late origin of this verse emerges clearly from a comparison with four other rows of loyalty phrases found in Deuteronomy:[2]

13.3b
nlkh 'ḥry
'lhym 'ḥrym. . .

13.4b
. . . hyškm
'hbym 't-y.km
bkl-lbbkm
wbkl-npškm

13.5	10.20	6.13	10.12b	30.20
'ḥry y.km tlkw				
w'tw tyr'w	*'t-y.k tyr'*	*'t-y.k tyr'*	*lyr'h 't-y.k*	
w't mṣwtyw tšmrw				
			llkt bkl-drkyw	
			wl'hbh 'tw	*l'hbh 't-y.k*
bqlw tšm'w				*lšm' bqlw*
w'tw t'bdw	*'tw t'bd*	*w'tw t'bd*	*wl'bd 't-y.k*	
wbw tdbqwn	*wbw tdbq*			*wldbqh-bw*
	wbšmw tšb'	*wbšmw tšb'*		
			bkl-lbbk	
			wbkl-npšk	
			10.13	
			lšmr 't-mṣwt yhwh	
6.14		*l' tlkwn 'ḥry*		
		'lhym 'ḥrym		

The unity of this row of parallel passages is quite strong.[3] All the

1. All the phrases in v. 5 are general expressions of submission to YHWH (Lohfink 1963: 64-80; Helfmeyer 1968: 105-17; Floss 1975: 84-93).

2. In the following chart, *y.k* stands for *yhwh 'lhyk*, *y.km* stands for *yhwh 'lhykm*.

3. This is not true of the most closely related text outside Deuteronomy, Josh. 22.5. This is a late imitation in which five of the phrases used in Deut. 13.5 and its parallels are arranged in a completely different order, i.e., by decreasing sizes:

phrases of v. 5 that are also found in its parallels occur there in the same order, except for *lšmr 't-mṣwt-*.[1] All the examples name *yhwh 'lhyk/km* in full in the first member of the row. All the texts using the imperfect place the object before the verb, while the two passages using the infinitive naturally place the object after it. Affinities are particularly strong among the first four passages, which all have the *yr'* and the *‘bd* phrases in common;[2] but even the second passage with the infinitive, 30.20, is not really isolated; beside contacts visible from the synopsis above, it is linked with 10.20 by the form (if not the meaning) of the immediately subsequent context.

Deut. 13.5 stands out among its parallels by its use of the plural form of address and by its larger size. Its special length is due to its exclusive possession of the first formula, whose *raison d'être* in the final form of Deuteronomy 13 is not difficult to understand. Lohfink (1963: 65 n. 1) already stressed the rarity of the phrase ‘following YHWH’ (13.5) and the deliberate antithesis it forms with ‘following other deities’ (13.3b); but this is even more evident when the arrangement of v. 5 is compared to that of the other rows of loyalty phrases (Merendino 1969: 64). Verses 6.13; 10.12b-13, and 10.20[3] all begin by the *yr'* phrase, which is moved down to the second place in 13.5. Here, *'ḥry yhwh 'lhykm tlkw* has been put at the head of the whole row, before the *yr'* phrase, so as to turn it into a better foil to the proselytizer's speech in v. 3b. The same intended contrast with v. 3

l' hbh 't-yhwh 'lhykm
wllkt bkl-drkyw
wlšmr mṣwtyw
wldbqh bw
wl‘bdw *bkl-lbbkm wbkl-npškm.*

1. On the chart, examples of the phrases *'hb 't-yhwh* and *hlk 'ḥry* seem to appear out of their normal place (13.4b; 6.14), but these occurrences do not formally belong in the parallel rows under discussion. In 13.4b, *hyškm 'hbym 't-yhwh* is not a prescription using the indicative as the phrases in 13.5; and in 6.14, *l' tlkwn 'ḥry 'lhym 'ḥrym* differs from the injunctions of 6.13 by its negative character, its use of the plural, and its word order. As for *bkl-lbbk wbkl-npšk*, it is not joined to the same phrase in 13.4b and in 10.12b, but it is a mere modifier, not a ‘loyalty phrase’.

2. See also 1 Sam. 12.14, which contains four positive expressions of loyalty, plus a negative one. The first expression is the *yr'* phrase, and it is followed by the *‘bd* phrase.

3. Cf. also 1 Sam. 12.14.

also explains why v. 5 contains the rare injunction to 'follow YHWH', whereas all the other examples of *hlk 'ḥry* found in Deuteronomy are prohibitions concerning 'other deities' (6.14; 8.19; 11.28; 28.14; cf. 4.3).

The phrase *w't-mṣwtyw tšmrw* is interesting too. In the other examples, this phrase only appears in 6.13-14, in the last slot; here it is given a central position, no doubt because it points out that the loyalty due to YHWH extends to his commandments. This notion is implicitly contained elsewhere, and above all in *bqlw tšm'w*, but *'t-mṣwtyw tšmrw* makes it much clearer. This special thrust given to the general exhortation to loyalty, as well as the similar vocabulary used in vv. 1 and 19, suggest a common origin for vv. 4b-5 and the external frame of this chapter, whose secondary character has been demonstrated earlier.

In the present economy of law 1, vv. 4b-5 mediate between the two full namings of the prophet or dreamer in vv. 4a and 6a. In immediate succession these two verses seem exceedingly repetitious, and one may wonder if, before 4b-5 was inserted, v. 4a was not shorter, consisting only of something like *l' tšm' 'l dbryw* (cf. *l' tšm' 'lyw*, v. 9a).

*Verse 6a**. This verse is more developed than its counterpart in law 2 (v. 11b). At first sight, the imbalance might seem to be caused by the phrase *mn-hdrk* etc., which is not repeated in 11b. But the kind of parallelism prevailing elsewhere between the laws of ch. 13 does not require full repetition, and 'to thrust thee aside from the way in which YHWH thy god commanded thee to walk' (v. 6) is similar enough to 'to thrust thee aside from YHWH thy god' (v. 11).

The phrases evoking the Exodus, identically repeated in v. 11b, are more open to suspicion. In law 2, the reference to Exodus is formulated in the second person singular as most of this chapter, and it is subjoined to the verb *hdyḥ*, common to all three laws. But in law 1, the mention of Exodus stands in a separate clause, and is formulated basically in the second person plural, as vv. 4b-5. Moreover, it adds to its counterpart in v. 11b an unnecessary participle (*whpdk*), which may have been meant to ease out the return to the second person singular. It is probable that, the reference to Exodus was belatedly added to law 1, in order to achieve greater uniformity between laws 1 and 2.

1.5.1.2. *In Law* 2. In law 2, the proselytizer's speech begins (7b) like its counterparts in the other two laws (vv. 3b, 14b); but the mention of the 'other deities' is considerably expanded by v. 8, which oddly puts the would-be convert before a large choice of new deities, envisions a much wider horizon than deuteronomic laws usually do ('from one end of the earth to the other'), and, unlike the rest of law 2, seems to address the nation instead of an individual.

This matter of who is being addressed deserves special attention. Laws 1 and 3 address Israel as a whole, but law 2, as many cultic laws in chs. 12 and 14–16, addresses the head of a family, a paterfamilias with son, daughter and wife (v. 7a), able to hush at will the attempts made on his loyalty, or on the contrary, to initiate procedures and to throw the first stone (vv. 9b-11a).[1]

The reference to 'all Israel' in v. 12 is not inconsistent with this insight. This phrase is used in passages where a particular group is addressed, such as 17.8-13 (local judges) or 21.18-21 (the men of the local community), but it is avoided when the whole nation is being addressed. Only *bqrbk*, the last word of law 2, might suggest that all Israel is the addressee; but this word is merely used to stress continuity with v. 6b, in a rather external framework of correlated formulas (cf. 19.19b-20).[2]

Verse 8 deviates from the presuppositions of law 2 more seriously. It portrays the addressee as 'surrounded' by other peoples, 'near or far', 'from one end of the earth to the other'. Such language is more appropriate with reference to Israel than to the head of a family. This is particularly evident in the case of *'šr sbybt-*; see 17.14, where this phrase clearly applies to the whole nation. This discrepancy suggests a separate origin for v. 8.

At a pinch, this conclusion could be avoided by the removal of *'šr*

1. On the typical influential Israelite addressed in Deut. 12–26, see Cazelles 1985: 101-102. However, this writer unfortunately ignores the distinction between the typical Israelite and personified Israel. This distinction is not always easily applicable, but this fact does not undermine its validity; it is but natural that personified Isael should 'look' like a typical Israelite!

2. Karl Budde (1916: 192-93) and Friedrich Horst (1961: 46-47) argue that v. 11 would apply more naturally to Israel than to an individual, but this change of referent for the second person singular is not entirely obvious. In v. 10, 'thou' was still explicitly distinguished from 'the people', and the Jewish tradition attributes a prominent role to the blows administered by the witnesses (*m. Sanh.* 6.4).

sbybtykm; one might argue that this clause is written in the second person plural, unlike the rest of v. 8. However, this clause contributes positively to the rhetorical balance of the sentence; with it, v. 8 falls into three pairs of short phrases, as vv. 9-10a[a]. As with vv. 1 and 6a, v. 8 seems to go back to an author who moved freely between plural and singular. It must be regarded as a single entity, which clashes with the general presuppositions of law 2.

For the same reason, the end of v. 7, *'th w'btyk*, is probably secondary as well. This phrase might very well be addressed to the whole nation, as it certainly is in 28.36, 64. It may not be entirely irrelevant that *'th w'btyk* has no equivalent in vv. 3 and 14, which otherwise parallel 7b so narrowly.

The importance given to the example of surrounding nations and the universal horizon of this verse ('from one end of the earth to the other') suggest a date posterior to the national catastrophe of 587 (Rose 1975: 45).

1.5.1.3. *In Law 3*. Literary critics (e.g. Horst 1961: 38-40; Merendino 1969: 69-71, 74-75) often manage to bracket off considerable parts of vv. 13-18, but this operation is only based on phraseology (Merendino) or on the application of too subtle canons (Horst); it is not supported by the detection of serious inconsistencies.

Horst, for instance, would eliminate from the earliest form of the text both the explicit mentions of the *ḥrm* as well as the 'too theological' end of v. 17. In his opinion, the repetition of *lpy ḥrb* which concludes the first clause about the *ḥrm* (16b) brands it as a gloss, and the second one unduly shifts the focus from the convict to the executioner. Horst also takes offence at 16b-17a[a], which, in his opinion, jumps too suddenly into commands about the town, after a command relative to its inhabitants.

These shrewd remarks ignore too much the highly rhetorical and repetitive nature of the whole chapter and especially of law 3. Horst's radical surgery on v. 17 reduces it to a bare command to burn the town, from which not only the dramatic colouring supplied by *klyl lyhwh 'lhyk* is missing, but also the procedural indication about the gathering of all the booty to the central piazza. Horst's detection of a brief and sober stratum at the basis of law 3 is in keeping with his general assumption of an early nucleus for this chapter. It seems more cautious to retain the wordy but well-built structure I described earlier (1.4.2.3).

1.5.1.4. *Conclusion.* Testing the grammatical, stylistic and logical consistency of Deut. 13.2-18, we have been led to question seriously the original character of parts of laws 1-2. The heaviest editing took place in law 1; vv. 4b-5 are secondary, and their insertion may have entailed that of 2b-3a and of *hnb' hhw' 'w 'l-ḥwlm hḥlwm hhw'* in v. 4a. Verse 6a too, from *'l-yhwh* to *'bdym*, is secondary. Verse 8 (with the last two words of v. 7) is the only apparent interpolation in law 2. These insertions are characterized by a free mixture of singular and plural in the second person address. It remains to be seen whether these provisional results are matched by indications derived from the phraseology.

1.5.2. *The Criterion of Phraseology*

1.5.2.1. *Preliminaries: Literary–historical Presuppositions.* A separate origin has already been tentatively assigned to vv. 2b-3a, 4a*(from *dbry*)-5, $6a^{a}$*(*'l-yhwh... 'bdym*) and $7b^{g}$* (*'th w'btyk*) -8, on the basis of discrepancies between these verses and their context. Turning to the words and phrases used in Deut. 13.2-18, I will try to find out whether the other contexts in which these expressions occur confirm my preliminary conclusions and give any clue to the place of Deuteronomy 13 and its expansions in the progressive formation of Deuteronomy.

As in earlier essays (especially Dion 1985: 201-202), I will assume as a working hypothesis four main stages in the formation of Deuteronomy: (1) Pre-deuteronomic sources, mostly of a legal or ritual nature; (2) the composition of Deuteronomy proper, an extended process that took place some time between the destruction of Samaria (722) and the discovery of the Book of the Law in 622 (texts belonging in this period will be referred to as 'D'); (3)–(4) at least two 'deuteronomistic' editions (referred to as 'dtr'), respectively influenced by the militancy of Josiah and by the stunning divine rebuke of 587.

Dtr ingredients contributed by successive editors are often difficult to distinguish from each other, and cannot always be extricated easily from the earlier components of Deuteronomy. It is generally admitted that original ingredients of this book are found mainly in the laws of chs. 12–26, and that they usually address Israel or the typical Israelite paterfamilias in the second person singular, while dtr elements are found mainly in the surrounding, non-legal parts of Deuteronomy, and often use the second person plural form of address. The dtr parts of Deuteronomy find their best stylistic and ideological match in many sections of the books of Joshua, Judges, Samuel and Kings; the largest unquestionable examples are found in Josh. 1; 23; Judg. 2.6–3.6; 2 Kgs 17; 21.[1] Moreover, with increasing variation and sophistication, many modern scholars follow Sigmund Mowinckel (1914: 31) in recognizing dtr influence and phraseology in the prose sermons of the book of Jeremiah (e.g. Jer. 7.1–8.3; 11.1-5). Contacts with this book may suggest a dtr origin for various passages of Deuteronomy itself. Furthermore, contacts with texts of well-established post-exilic origin, such as Deuteronomy 4 and 29.21–30.10 (Lohfink 1964; Levenson 1975; Mayes 1981), and Josh. 23 (Smend 1971: 501-503), can be crucial in identifying contributions of the latest dtr writers.

The impossibility of assigning confidently a 'correct place' in this literary–historical framework to each parallel occurrence of the phrases of Deuteronomy 13 is a serious challenge, but it does not radically jeopardize the undertaking. My aim will be limited to pointing out the periods in the formation of Deuteronomy and the work of the deuteronomic school when this or that expression, used in Deuteronomy 13, seems to have been most popular. Such a method certainly cannot lead to firm conclusions all by itself, but its results should prove useful when combined with other approaches.

For this purpose, all but the most banal words and phrases of Deut. 13.2-18, such as *bn*, *bt*, have been examined. Special attention has been given to deuteronomic usage; Deuteronomy has been searched by computer, on the transliterated text produced by the University of Pennsylvania's Center for Computer Analysis of Texts. This facility was also consulted, occasionally, about the other books, but their evidence was mainly gathered with the help of the well-known Hebrew concordances, of Weinfeld's Appendix A (1972: 320-65), Driver's still useful lists (1901: lxxviii-lxxxii), and the more specialized lists

1. In spite of all the refinements introduced since Martin Noth, the current identification of typical dtr passages in the books Joshua–Judges–Samuel–Kings remains close enough to the positions of this scholar in his classical *Überlieferungsgeschichtliche Studien* (1943).

drawn up by such scholars as Helfmeyer (1968), Floss (1975) and Hoffmann (1980: 327-66).

1.5.2.2. *Classified List of the Expressions That Were Examined*

1.5.2.2.1. *Expressions of Unique Occurrence.* Two phrases from laws 1 and 3 are only documented in Deuteronomy 13:

1. *ḥlm ḥlwm* (vv. 2a, 4a, 6a, beginning):
In spite of the frequent use of *ḥlwm* with the verb *ḥlm*, this expression is remarkable; contrast *b'l hḥlmwt*, Gen. 37.19. *ḥōlēm ḥlwm* seems to be a technical term. Along with *nby'*, it could form part of a list of divination experts differing from that usually found in the Bible and best represented by Deut. 18.10-11.

2. *wl'-ydbq bydk m'wmh mn-hḥrm* (v. 18):
Not the same metaphor as at Job 31.8, *wbkpy dbq m'wm*. There, *m'wm* is a misspelling for *mwm*, '(moral) stain'.

1.5.2.2.2. *Non-deuteronomic Expressions.* Deut. 13.2-18 contains twenty-six expressions which are not demonstrably deuteronomic favourites. These phrases are mainly documented in texts from the late monarchial era and later:

3. *b'* = 'is fulfilled, comes to pass' (v. 3a):
Deut. 18.22;
Josh. 21.45; 23.14;
1 Sam. 9.6; NB 10.7, 9 (subject: *h'twt*);
Isa. 42.9; 66.18;
Jer. 28.9;
Ezek. 21.12; 24.14; 39.8;
Ps. 105.19;
cf. Job 3.25; 6.8; Prov. 13.12.

4. *ywmt/hwmt*, taken absolutely, and used in a law or decree as a technical term for the capital punishment (v. 6a, beginning):
Deut. 21.22;
Exod. 21.29; 35.2;
Lev. 19.20 (negative); 24.16 (short for *mwt ywmt*); 24.21;
Num. 1.51; 3.10, 38; 18.7 (all four against illegal cultic officiants);
Josh. 1.18; 2 Kgs 11.8 // 2 Chron. 23.7; 2 Chron. 15.13.

Contrast *wmt*, a standing technical term in Deuteronomy (see below, phrase 31).

5. *hsyt* only followed by a direct object, 'deceitfully incite someone' (v. 7):

1 Kgs 21.25 (closest; vv. inspired of Deut. 12.29–13.19?);
2 Kgs 18.32 // Isa. 36.18 // 2 Chron. 32.15;
Jer. 38.22; Job 36.18; 36.16 seems corrupt.

This expression cannot be separated from other constructions of *hsyt* apparently documented in earlier times, e.g. *hēsît* + object + *b*-, 2 Sam. 24.1; *hēsît* + object + *l*-, Josh. 15.18.

6. *'ḥyk bn-'mk* (v. 7):

Gen. 43.29;
cf. (without *'ḥ*) Gen. 27.29; Ps. 50.20.

7. *'št ḥyqk* (v. 7):

Deut. 28.54 (. . . *ḥyqw*), 56 (*'yš ḥyqh*).

8. *'šr knpšk* (v. 7):

1 Sam. 18.1, 3 (both *knpšw*).
(In Deut. 23.25 *knpšk* is not the same idiom.)

9. *bstr* (v. 7):

Deut. 27.15, 24; 28.57
(vv. 53-57 are further related to law 2 by family vocabulary: *bn, bt, 'yš/'št ḥyq*);
1 Sam. 19.2; 2 Sam. 12.12;
Isa. 45.16, 19;
Jer. 37.17; 38.16; 40.15;
Pss. 101.5; 139.15; Job 13.10; 31.27; Prov. 21.14.

10. *hqrbym. . .hrḥqym* (v. 8):

1 Kgs 8.46 (*'rṣ h'wyb hrḥwqh 'w hqrwbh*);
Isa. 33.13; 57.19;
Jer. 25.26 (*hqrbym whrḥqym*, after a long list of geographical expressions);
Ezek. 6.12; 22.5 (4. . .*kl-h'rṣwt 5 hqrbwt whrḥqwt mmk*);
Prov. 27.10;
Est. 9.20 (*'l-kl-yhwdym. . .hqrwbym whrḥwqym*);
Dan. 9.7 (*hqrwbym whrḥwqym bkl-h'rṣwt. . .*).
Cf. Deut. 20.15 (*h'rym hrḥqt mmk*, without *hqrbt*).

11. *ḥws* + *ḥml* with negative particles (v. 9):

Jer. 13.14; 21.7;
Ezek. 7.4, 9; 8.18; 9.5, 10.

12. *l'-t'bh lw* (v. 9):
    Ps. 81.2 (*wyśr'l l'-'bh ly*).

13. *l'-tksh 'lyw* (v. 9):
    Prov. 10.12; Neh. 3.37.

14. *hgyd* 'to report' (v. 10 as emended; 17.4):
    Lev. 5.1; Jer. 20.10 (*hgydw wngdnw*); Prov. 29.24; Qoh. 10.20;
    cf. Est. 2.22.

15. *br'šwnh...b'ḥrnh* (v. 10):
    1 Kgs 17.13.

16. *bqš l-* + infinitive (v. 11):
    Gen. 43.30;
    Exod. 2.15; 10.11;
    Lev. 19.31;
    1 Sam. 14.9; 19.2, 10; 23.10; 2 Sam. 20.19; 21.2;
    1 Kgs 11.22, 40;
    Zech. 6.7; 12.9;
    Ps. 37.22;
    Qoh. 12.10;
    Est. 2.21; 3.6; 6.2.

17. *'nšym bny-bly'l* (v. 13):
    Judg. 20.13; 1 Kgs 21.10, 13;
    cf. Judg. 19.22 (*'nšy...*).

18. *n'śth htw'bh hz't bqrbk* (v. 15; cf. 17.4):
There is no perfect match to the phrase of Deuteronomy 13 and 17, but *tw'bh* appears ten other times with the verb *'śh* in Leviticus, Jeremiah, Ezekiel (×5) and Malachi.

19. *hkh tkh 't-yšby h'yr* (v. 16):
Jer. 21.6 (*whkyty 't-yšby h'yr hz't*); but Jer. 21.2-10 shows several contacts with Deuteronomy 13, and may not be an independent witness.

20. *hkh lpy ḥrb* (v. 16):
    Deut. 20.13;
    Josh. 8.24; 10.28, 30, 32, 35, 37, 39; 11.11, 12, 14; 19.47;
    Judg. 1.8, 25; 18.27; 20.37, 48; 21.10;
    1 Sam. 22.19; 2 Sam. 15.14;

2 Kgs 10.25;
Jer. 21.7;
Job 1.15,17.

This expression is noticeably absent from the narrative parts of Deuteronomy and from clearly dtr sections in books dealing with the monarchial era. It is a moot question whether examples from Joshua (esp. from chs. 10–11) should be attributed to a dtr redactor or to an earlier 'collector'; other examples (e.g. Jer. 21.7) were influenced by the dtr school.

21. *hḥrm... w't-kl-'šr-bh ... lpy-ḥrb* (v. 16):
Josh. 6.21 (*wyḥrymw 't-kl-'šr b'yr... lpy ḥrb*).
Cf. *hḥrm 'th w't-kl-'šr-bh*:
Josh. 10.37 (*wyḥrm 'th w't-kl-hnpš 'šr bh*);
10.39 (*wyḥrymw 't-kl-hnpš 'šr bh*).

The last two examples coincide with examples of *hkh lpy ḥrb*, and the same remarks apply to both expressions.

22. *tqbṣ 'l-twk* (v. 17):
Ezek. 22.19 (*hnny qbṣ 'tkm 'l-twk yršlm*).

23. *wśrpt b'š* (v. 17):
b'š is associated with *śrp* in 69 out of the 117 occurrences of this verb. These occurrences are widely distributed, and they are particularly frequent in Leviticus and Ezekiel, as in the deuteronomistic historical books.

24. *klyl lyhwh 'lhyk* (v. 17):
1 Sam. 7.9 (without *'lhyk*).

25. *tl 'wlm* (v. 17):
Josh. 8.28.

26. *l' tbnh 'wd* (v. 17):
Ezek. 26.14.

27. *yšwb yhwh mḥrwn 'pw* (v. 18):
Exod. 34.12 (*šwb mḥrwn 'pk*);
Num. 25.4 (*wyšb ḥrwn-'p yhwh myśr'l*);
Josh. 7.26 (*wyšb yhwh mḥrwn 'pw*);
2 Kgs 23.26 (*l' šb yhwh mḥrwn 'pw hgdwl*);
Jon. 3.9 (*yšb mḥrwn 'pw*).

28. *wntn-lk rḥmym wrḥmk* (v. 18):

Jer. 42.12a (*w'tn lkm rḥmym wrḥm 'tkm*);
cf. 1 Kgs 8.50 (*wntnm lrḥmym lpny šbyhm wrḥmwm*).
wntn-lk rḥmym without the verb *rḥm*:
Gen. 43.14 (*w'l šdy ytn lkm rḥmym lpny h'yš*; P?);
Isa. 47.6 (*l' śmt lhm rḥmym*).
The phrase with the verb *śym* is also found in 407 BC in the Aramaic papyri of the Jews from Elephantine (Porten 1986: 69, 73), who were notoriously not ruled by Deuteronomy.

1.5.2.2.3. *Deuteronomic Expressions*. Another ingredient of Deuteronomy 13 (and 17.2-7) consists of seven formulaic expressions well documented in the laws of Deuteronomy but rare or non-extant in the rest of this book and other dtr writings:

29. *wb'rt hr' mqrbk* (v. 6b; cf. 17.7):
Pre-D origin: 2 Sam. 4.11, with background in the older civilizations (Dion 1980: 336-47; Weinfeld 1982: 243-44); Deut. 17.12; 19.19; 21.21; 22.21, 22, 24; 24.7; the only probably late example: Judg. 20.13.

30. *wl'-tḥws 'ynk 'lyw* (v. 9):

Deut. 7.16; 19.13, 21; 25.12;
Ezek. 5.11 (with the next phrase!); 7.4 (*idem*), 9 (*idem*); 8.18 (*idem*); 9.5 (*idem*);
Isa. 13.18 (*l' tḥws 'ynm*);
Jer. 21.7 (Nebuchadrezzar *l' yḥws 'lyhm wl' yḥml*);
Judt. 2.11 (*ou pheisetai ho ophthalmos sou*);

Gen. 45.20 could be earlier than Deuteronomy, but there the object of the verb is belongings left behind; this is not an example of the formula applying to unrelenting punishment. There is no firm indication of an early, pre-D origin for this formulaic usage.

31. *wsqltw b'bnym wmt* (v. 11; cf. 17.5):

Deut. 22.21 (*wsqlwh 'nšy 'yrh b'bnym wmth*);
22.24 (*wsqltm 'tm b'bnym wmtw*);
With *rgm* for 'stoning', instead of *sql*:
21.21.
Laws with *wmt* for the death penalty, no explicit *sql*:
17.12; 18.20; 19.12; 22.22;
22.25 (connection with 22.24 clearly implies *sql*);
24.7.

Cf. related expressions used elsewhere in the Pentateuch:
with *rgm* and *mwt ywmt* for the death penalty:
Lev. 20.2, 27; 24.16;
cf. Num. 15.35-36 (a normative story, not a law).
with *sql* alone for the death penalty of an animal:
Exod. 21.28, 29, 32.
A decree with *sql* and *mwt ywmt*:
Exod. 19.12-13.

This expression will be discussed below (1.6.1).

32. *wkl-yśr'l yšm'w wyr'wn wl'-ywspw l'śwt kdbr hr' hzh bqrbk* (v. 12):
Exclusive to the laws of Deuteronomy: 17.13; 19.20; 21.21. Deut. 13.12 contains the most complete formulation.

33. *b'ḥt 'ryk 'šr yhwh 'lhyk ntn lk lšbt šm* (v. 13; cf. 17.2):
Cf. Deut. 16.5 (*b'ḥd š'ryk 'šr-yhwh 'lhyk ntn lk* (no *lšbt sm*);
cf. Deut. 16.18 (*bkl-š'ryk...*, as 16.5);
cf. Deut. 23.17 (*b'ḥd š'ryk* without further modifiers).
Cf.*b'rṣk 'šr-yhwh 'lhyk ntn lk*:
Deut. 15.7; 19.2, 10; 28.52.
Cf. *m'rṣk 'šr-yhwh 'lhyk ntn lk...*: Deut. 26.2.

This form found in Deut. 13.13 seems to be a mere adaptation of phrases with *š'ryk*. The use of *'ryk* instead of *š'ryk* or *'rṣk* as in other laws was necessary because law 3 was focused on a town, not on the land, and because the town had to be mentioned again in contexts where *š'r* would have been odd: vv. 14a (end), 16a, 17a.

34. *wdršt wḥqrt wš'lt hyṭb whnh* + declarative verbless clause + asyndetic *qatal* clause (v. 15):
Parallels to this expression and the next one will be quoted when they are discussed below, 1.6.2.

35. *'mt nkwn hdbr* + an asyndetic *qatal* statement (v. 15):
See below, 1.6.2.

1.5.2.2.4. *D/dtr Expressions*. Deut. 13.2-18 contains ten phrases appearing sometimes in texts of Deuteronomy which may be prejosianic, but occurring mainly in dtr parts of Deuteronomy and in literature influenced by it:

36. *'wt wmwpt* (vv. 2b, 3a):
Deut. 28.46a (*whyw bk l'wt wlmwpt*);

Isa. 20.3 (a predicative modifying *'bdy yš'yhw*);
cf. *'wtwt wmwptym*:
Exod. 7.3; Deut. 4.34; 6.22; 7.19; 26.8; 29.2; 34.11; Isa. 8.18; Jer. 32.20, 21; Ps. 105.27; Neh. 9.10.

'wt wmwpt is certainly related to the D/dtr stereotype *'wtwt wmwptym*. The coupling of these terms is more significant than the number difference; the plural subset was simply thought more appropriate to celebrate the mighty deeds of YHWH.

37. *wntn 'lyk 'wt 'w mwpt* (v. 2b):
cf. *ntn 'wtwt wmwptym*:
Deut. 6.22 (*wytn yhwh 'wtwt wmwptym*);
Neh 9.10 (*wttn 'wtwt wmwptym*).

See remarks on *'wt wmwpt*, above.

38. *'šr l'-yd'tm* (vv. 3b, 7, 14):
Deut. 8.13, 16; 11.28; 28.33, 36, 64; 29.25; 32.17;
Jer. 7.9; 9.15; 15.14 (= 17.4); 16.13; 17.4 (not in LXX); 19.4; 22.28; 44.3.

Among these occurrences, only Deut. 8.3, 16 and 28.33 might be pre-josianic, and Jer. 15.14/17.4 (hardly two separate witnesses) and 22.28 not of dtr origin.

39. *ky mnsh yhwh 'lhykm 'tkm ld't* + interrogative *h-* (v. 4b):
Cf. Deut. 8.2 (*lnstk ld't 't-'šr blbbk htšmr mṣwtw*), and a less complete example in v. 16. Pre-josianic?
Judg. 3.4 (*lm'n nswt bm 't-yśr'l ld't hyšm'w*) (and a less pure form in v. 1);
Judg. 2.22 (*lm'n nswt bm 't-yśr'l...hšmrym hm...*);
Exod. 16.4 (*lm'n 'nsnw...hylk btwrty*) (Priestly);
2 Chron. 32.31 (*lnswtw ld't kl-blbbw*).

40. *'hb 't-yhwh 'lhyk/km bkl-lbbk/km wbkl-npšk/km* (v. 4b):
6.5 (*w'hbt 't-yhwh 'lhyk bkl-lbbk wbkl-npšk*);
10.12 (*l'hbh 'tw wl'bd 't-yhwh 'lhyk bkl-lbbk wbkl-npšk*);
11.13 (*l'hbh 't-yhwh 'lhykm wl'bdw bkl-lbbkm wbkl-npškm*);
30.6 (*l'hbh 't-yhwh 'lhyk bkl-lbbk wbkl-npšk*).
'hb 't-yhwh without the *bkl-...* modifier:
Deut. 5.10 // Exod. 20.6; Deut. 7.9; 11.1, 22; 19.9 (in a dtr addition, containing *mṣwh*);

30.16; 30.20; Josh. 22.5; 23.11;
1 Kgs 3.3.

For even less accurate parallels, see the 'Cf.' paragraph in Weinfeld (1972: 333).

This expression has a rich background in the political literature of the ancient Near East; 6.5 may be pre-josianic and the ending of Exod. 20.6 even earlier, but occurrences are overwhelmingly found in later texts.

41. *šmr* + *mṣwh* (as the only word for 'commandment') (v. 5):
With only *šmr* and *mṣwh*:
Deut. 5.10; 5.29; 7.9; 8.2 (with related phrases in the context);
Exod. 20.6 (like Deut. 5.10);
Lev. 22.31; 26.3b;
1 Sam. 13.13; 1 Kgs 8.61; 13.21b; 14.8; 2 Kgs 17.19; 18.6;
Pss. 89.32b; 119.60b; Qoh. 12.13; Neh. 1.9.
Examples adding *kl*:
Deut. 13.19; 26.18; 28.1 (*lšmr l'śwt 't-kl-mṣwtyw*);
1 Kgs 6.12; Neh. 10.30 (*lšmwr wl'śwt...*).

42. *hmwṣy' 'tkm*/*hmwṣy'k m'rṣ mṣrym* (vv. 6a, 11):
Deut. 8.14 (*hmwṣy'k*; continued by *mbyt 'bdym*, as in 13.11);
Lev. 22.33 (*'tkm*);
Judg. 2.12 (*'wtm*).

43. *hwṣy'...m'rṣ mṣrym mbyt 'bdym* (v. 11):
Deut. 5.6; 6.12; 8.14;
Exod. 13.14; 20.2 (as at Deut. 5.6);
Jer. 34.13.
Cf., with the verb in the qal, Exod. 13.3.

44. *hpdk mbyt 'bdym* (v. 6a):
Nowhere else is this formulated as a hymnic participle;
pdh and *mbyt 'bdym*:
Deut. 7.8 (*wypdk mbyt 'bdym*);
Mic. 6.4 (*wmbyt 'bdym pdytyk*).

In itself, *pdh mbyt 'bdym* is probably not of deuteronomic origin (Floss 1975: 56-63); but as for the present example, the relative frequency of *hwṣy'...m'rṣ mṣrym mbyt 'bdym*, the parallelism with v. 11, and the closer conformity of v. 11 to 8.14, all seem to support the hypothesis formulated above, that v. 6 was overloaded secondarily by an insertion based on v. 11.

45. *k'šr nšb' l'btyk* (v. 18):

Deut. 19.8 (in a secondary insertion); 29.12.
k'šr nšb' lk wl'btyk: Exod. 13.11;
k'šr nšb' lk: Deut. 28.9;
k'šr nšb'...lhm: 2.14;
kkl 'šr nšb' l'btm: Josh. 21.44.
Other occurrences of *nšb'/nšb'ty* in Deuteronomy:
1.8, 35; 4.31; 6.10, 18, 23; 7.8, 12, 13; 8.1, 18; 9.5; 10.11; 11.9, 21; 26.3, 15; 28.11; 30.20; 31.7, 20, 21, 23; 34.4.

For a list of occurrences of YHWH's oath outside Deuteronomy, see Driver (1901: lxxix 13).

1.5.2.2.5. *Deuteronomistic Expressions*. Finally, eleven phrases used in Deut. 13.2-18 are not to be found in presumably pre-josianic parts of Deuteronomy, but only in late strata of this book and in other dtr writings.

Because of their location, phrases 46, 47, 51, 52, 53, 55, 56 are particularly crucial; their occurrences will be listed when they are brought into the discussion (below, 1.5.2.4).

46. *hlk 'ḥry* + a word for 'deity' (vv. 3b, 5).

47. *hlk* + *'bd 'lhym 'ḥrym* (vv. 7, 14; cf. 17.3).

48. *yr'* as a global description of religion (v. 5):
The following list omits passages like Ps. 128.1 where *yr'* is used as a noun in the bound form before *yhwh*.

Deut. 4.10; 5.26; 6.2; 6.13; 6.24; 8.6; 10.12; 10.20; 14.23; 17.19; 28.58; 31.12; 31.13;
Josh. 4.24; 22.25; 24.14;
1 Sam. 12.14, 24; 1 Kgs 8.40, 43;
2 Kgs 4.1; 17.32, 33, 34, 39, 41; Jer. 32.39;
Isa. 29.13;
Jer. 5.22, 24; 10.7; 26.19;
Jon. 1.9;
Pss. 34.10; 67.8; 112.1; 130.4;
Prov. 3.7; 24.21;
2 Chron. 6.31, 33.

This expression is deeply rooted in the semantics of the Semitic languages, and some examples, such as Isa. 29.13 and Prov. 24.21, are probably exempt of dtr influence. However, in Deuteronomy itself, all examples seem to be dtr. A pre-josianic origin could be envisioned for 14.23b, but the weak link between this phrase and its context, and its equivalence to the phrase found in 17.19 (the law on kingship, certainly exilic; cf. also 4.10; 31.12, 13) suggest that it is dtr as all the other examples.

49. *šm‘ bql* for submission to the deity (v. 5):

Deut. 4.30; 8.20, 23; 13.19; 15.5; 26.17; 27.10; 28.1, 2, 15, 45, 62; 30.2, 8, 10, 20;

Josh. 5.6; Judg. 6.10; 1 Sam. 12.14, 15; 15.19; 28.18; 2 Kgs 18.12;

Jeremiah's sermons: 7.23, 28; 9.12; 11.4, 7; 18.10; 32.23.

Jeremiah's biography: 40.3; 42.6 (×2),13, 21; 43.4, 7; 44.23.

The OT contains 63 examples of *šm‘ bql yhwh* in addition to Deut. 13.15. Sixteen of them are in Deuteronomy, apparently all in dtr passages. At least 7 are found in dtr sections of Joshua–Judges–Samuel–Kings. Seven more are found in prose sermons of Jeremiah; 8 (listed below) in the Jeremiah biography; 4 in other parts of Jeremiah. Among the 21 remaining examples, several (from Exod. 19; 23; Zechariah; Daniel) were probably influenced by the dtr tradition.

50. *‘bd* as a global description of religion (vv. 3b, 5, 7b, 14b):
Floss (1975: 10-11) counted 142 examples of the verb *‘bd* + a word designating a deity. In 63 of them, the God of Israel (called YHWH almost everywhere) is the object; in 79, another god or group of deities. According to my rather conservative estimate, dtr passages of Deuteronomy (outside ch. 13 and 17.2-7), of Joshua–Judges–Samuel–Kings, and of Jeremiah account for 78 (more than half) of the total, and for 51, i.e. 64 per cent, of the texts mentioning the worship of another deity:

Deuteronomy: object = YHWH:
(5.9: decalogue); 6.13; 7.4; 10.12, 20; 11.13.

Deuteronomy: object = other deities:
4.19, 28; 7.16; 8.19; 11.16; 12.2, 30; 28.14, 36, 64; 29.17, 25; 30.17; 31.20.

Joshua: object = YHWH:
22.5; 24.14 (×2), 15(×3), 18, 19, 21, 22, 24, 31.

Joshua: object = other deities:
23.7, 16; 24.2, 14, 15, 16, 20.

Judges: object = YHWH: 2.7; 3.16; 10.6, 16.
Judges: object = other deities: 2.11, 13, 19; 3.6, 7; 10.6, 10, 13.
1 Samuel: object = YHWH: 7.3, 4; 12.14, 20, 24.
1 Samuel: object = other deities: 8.8; 12.10.
1 Kings: object = other deities: 9.6, 9; 16.31; 22.54.
2 Kings: object = other deities: 17.12, 16, 33, 35, 41; 21.3, 21(×2).
Jeremiah, dtr sections: object = other deities: 5.19; 11.10; 13.10; 16.11, 13; 22.9; 25.6; 35.15.

51. *dbq b-* with a deity as modifier (v. 5).

52. *dbr-srh ʻl-yhwh* (v. 6a).

53. *hdyḥ* as a metaphor of religious subversion (vv. 6a, 11, 14).

54. *hdrk 'šr ṣwk yhwh* (v. 6a):
Deut. 5.33 (*bkl-hdrk 'šr ṣwh yhwh 'lhykm 'tkm tlkw*);
9.12 (*mn-hdrk 'šr ṣwytm*) (= Exod. 32.8, down to the very *scriptio defectiva*);
9.16 (*mn-hdrk 'šr-ṣwh yhwh 'tkm*; depends on preceding);
11.28 (*mn-hdrk 'šr 'nky mṣwh 'tkm hywm*);
31.29 (*mn-hdrk 'šr ṣwyty 'tkm*);
Exod. 32.8 (*mn-hdrk 'šr ṣwytm*).

55. *m'lhy hʻmym 'šr sbybtykm* (v. 8).

56. *mqṣh h'rṣ wʻd-qṣh h'rṣ* (v. 8).

1.5.2.3. *Distribution of the Types of Expressions Across Deut. 13.2-18*

Verse	*Unique*	*Non-D*	*D*	*D/dtr*	*dtr*
2a	1				
2b-3a		3		36, 37	
3b				38	46, 50
4a	1				
4b				39, 40	
5				41	46, 48, 49, 50, 51
6 down to *ywmt*	1	4			
6a *ky . . . 'lhykm*					52
6a from *hmwṣy'*				42, 44	53, 54

Verse	*Unique*	*Non-D*	*D*	*D/dtr*	*dtr*
6b			29		
7		5, 6, 7, 8, 9		38	47
8		10			55, 56
9		11, 12, 13	30		
10		14, 15			
11		16	31	42, 43	53
12			32		
13		17	33		
14				38	47, 53
15		18	34, 35.		
16		19, 20, 21			
17		22, 23, 24, 25, 26			
18	2	27, 28		45	

1.5.2.4. *Discussion and Conclusion.* The distribution of the various categories of phrases found in Deuteronomy 13 generally confirms the conclusions of the consistency test. There is a definite concentration of deuteronomic and deuteronomistic expressions in vv. 2b-3a, 4b, 5, 6a (beginning with the epithets of YHWH), and 8. Most impressive is the case of v. 5, which is entirely made of favourite expressions of the D and dtr writers. This is also true of v. 4b; it is made of two long and remarkable expressions, which may have been coined and adopted by the deuteronomic school in pre-josianic times, but continued in use later on. The typically D/dtr character of vv. 2b-3a is less strongly established by phraseology; the case for the secondary origin of these verses still leans predominantly on the less than ideal arrangement of vv. 2-3, an argument which is admittedly not compelling. Stronger is the case for v. 8 as a secondary expansion, especially because of the *sbybt* phrase (55), as we shall see later.

In v. 6a the situation is less straightforward. On the one hand, there is no reason for questioning the beginning of this verse, down to *ywmt*, 'he shall be put to death'. But all the rest consists of D and dtr expressions. These include *ky dbr-srh*, 'because he spoke mendaciously',[1] on which everything else is grammatically dependent, and

1. Rose (1975: 42 n. 1) states too categorically that '*srh* (*srr*) hat keine Heimat in der dtr Formelsprache gefunden'. The phrase *dbr srh* matters more than *srh* taken in isolation (this word was discussed above, in the text-critical and philological notes). For *srh* before *dbr*, see Jer. 28.16; 29.32; in both places, the phrase is

hdyḥk mn-, 'to thrust thee aside from',[1] an ingredient likely to be original since v. 6a shares it with v. 11, its counterpart in law 2. The dtr character of phrase 53, 'to thrust thee aside', is important. Admittedly, v. 11 as well as v. 6 is just a motivating development, and one might insist that these verses are not really essential to the integrity of laws 1 and 2 (Merendino 1969: 65); but 'to thrust aside from' is also found at the heart of v. 14, the main part of the protasis of law 3. A dtr phrase thus appears to play an essential role in the original version of Deuteronomy 13.

Even more significant is the dtr character of another phrase, 'Let us go and worship other deities' (vv. 7, 14, cf. 3b), which, in two slightly different forms (46, 47), is the pivot of all three laws:

hlk 'ḥry 'lhym 'ḥrym, 'to go after other deities', (v. 3b):

Deut. 6.14 is a dtr passage (Merendino 1969: 67; Mayes 1979: 175-76) closely related to ch. 13: everything in 6.12b-14 has a direct counterpart in ch. 13, and much of 6.15-18 is also related to this chapter;

Deut. 8.19 in the dtr layer (Mayes 1979: 189) of ch. 8;
Deut. 11.28 a dtr text (Mayes 1979: 207-208) related to ch. 13;
Deut. 28.14 a dtr expansion, related to ch. 13;
Judg. 2.12, 19; 1 Kgs 11.10;
Jer. 7.6, 9; 11.10; 13.10; 16.11; 25.6; 35.15.
Cf. *hlk 'ḥry* + word for 'idol', name of a foreign deity:
Deut. 4.3; 1 Kgs 18.18, 21; 21.26; 2 Kgs 17.15;
Jer. 2.5, 23; 8.2.
Cf. *hlk 'ḥry yhwh*: Deut. 13.5; 1 Kgs 14.8; 18.21; 2 Kgs 23.3;
Jer. 2.2.

hlk + *'bd 'lhym 'ḥrym*, 'to go and serve other deities', (vv. 7, 14; cf. 17.3):

Deut. 29.25 (*wylkw w'bdw 'lhym 'ḥrym*);
Josh. 23.16 (*whlktm w'bdtm...*);

omitted by LXX and is probably a dtr addition (Tov 1985: 233; Carroll 1986: 540). The relevance of Isa. 59.13 is not so clear; on this passage see van der Ploeg (1948: 142-45).

1. *hdyḥ* as a religious metaphor (vv. 6a, 11, 14): 2 Kgs 17.21 (Qrê); 2 Chron. 21.11. The two examples with the *nip'al* (Deut. 4.19; 30.17) are certainly relevant, and cast doubt on Rose's statement (1975: 42 n. 2), 'so ist auch für Hifil *ndḥ*—verleiten eine Zuordnung zur dtr Schicht nicht zu Vertreten'.

1 Sam. 26.19 (*lk ʿbd...*);
1 Kgs 9.6 and // 2 Chron. 7.19 (*whlktm wʿbdtm...*);
cf. Jer. 44.3 (*llkt lqṭr lʿbd...*).
The following examples have *ʿbd* after *'lhym 'ḥrym*:
Deut. 8.19 (*whlkt 'ḥry...wʿbdtm*);
Deut. 28.14 (*llkt 'ḥry 'lhym 'ḥrym lʿbdm*);
Judg. 2.19 (*llkt 'ḥry 'lhym 'ḥrym lʿbdm*);
Jer. 11.10 (*hlkw...lʿbdm*);
Jer. 13.10 (*wylkw...lʿbdm*);
Jer. 16.11 (*wylkw...wʿbdwm*);
Jer. 25.6 (*w'l-tlkw...lʿbdm*);
Jer. 35.15 (*'l-tlkw...lʿbdm*).

The dtr associations of these phrases are strengthened by those of *'lhym 'ḥrym 'šr l'-ydʿtm*, 'other deities that you have not known' (vv. 3, 7, 14):

Deut. 11.28; Jer. 7.9;
cf. Deut. 28.64 (*...l'-ydʿt 'th w'btyk*);
Jer. 19.4; 44.3 (*...l'-ydʿwm*);
Deut. 29.25 (*...'lhym 'šr l'-ydʿwm*);
Deut. 32.17 (*...'lhym l'-ydʿwm*).

Finally, as Perlitt (1969: 36-37) pointed out, in Deut. 29.24-25; Josh. 23.16; and Jer. 11.10, *hlk 'ḥry 'lhym 'ḥrym* is associated with the typically dtr concept of covenant-breaking.

Therefore, *hlk 'ḥry 'lhym 'ḥrym* is clearly a dtr phrase. Richter (1964: 84) tried to avoid this conclusion by positing that in chapter 13 of Deuteronomy this phrase 'still' referred to processions honouring idols; but this is gratuitous; the secular image, common in the Bible and the ancient Near East, on which the dtr theological expression is based, is that of the servant or vassal following the master, particularly in war contexts (Helfmeyer 1968). Rose (1975: 21-22) also envisions and rejects the dtr character of *hlk 'ḥry 'lhym 'ḥrym* and therefore also of Deuteronomy 13, but his discussion is irrelevant, because it revolves entirely on the shorter phrase *'lhym 'ḥrym*.

In view of the dtr character of the all-important phrases 46, 47 and 53, it seems logical to conclude that Deut. 13.2-18 in its entirety is a dtr composition. This thesis is not incompatible with the indications pointing to a secondary origin for vv. 4b-5, 8, *et al.*, because some of the phraseology contained in these verses links them particularly or perhaps even exclusively to post-587 literature; such is the case with the *dbq* phrase of v. 5, and the *sbybt-* and *mqṣh h'rṣ* phrases of v. 8:

wbw tdbqwn, 'and it is to him that you shall cleave' (v. 5):
Deut. 4.4; 10.20; 11.22; 30.20;
Josh. 22.5; 23.8; 2 Kgs 18.6.

Deut. 30.16-20 has other privileged links with ch. 4, above all *h'ydty bkm*...(v. 19, cf. 4.26), and, like it, was probably written after the final collapse of Judah. The same may be true of Deut. 10.20. This verse forms part of a long section (10.12–11.21) containing a later version of the speeches in chs. 6.1–9.6; more immediately, it is related to vv. 21-22 as exhortation to motivation, and v. 22 reflects the priestly notion of the seventy ancestors who went down to Egypt (Gen. 46.27; Exod. 1.5). On the other hand, 11.22 forms part of a promise of extensive conquests reminiscent of David's empire (11.22-25), which would make perfect sense in the days of Josiah.

m'lhy h'mym 'šr sbybtykm, 'from the deities of the peoples around you' (v. 8):
Deut. 6.14;
Judg. 2.12 (...*sbybtyhm*).
Cf. (without *m'lhy*): *hgwym 'šr sbybt-*:
Deut. 17.14;
Lev. 25.44;
2 Kgs 17.15;
Ezek. 5.7 (×2), 14, 15; cf. v. 6 (*h'rṣwt*);
Neh. 5.17; 6.16.

It is hard to put a date on Deut. 6.14, but this phrase is one of the links tying it to relatively late literature. The law on kingship, including 17.14, is definitely postexilic.

mqṣh h'rṣ w'd-qṣh h'rṣ, 'from one end of the earth to the other end of the earth' (v. 8):
Deut. 28.64 (*bkl-h'mym mqṣh h'rṣ w'd-qṣh h'rṣ*);
Jer. 12.12 (*'rṣ* = country); 25.33 (*'rṣ* = earth).
Cf. Deut. 4.32 (*wlmqṣh hšmym w'd-qṣh hšmym*).

Deut. 28.64 is important; this verse has many links with ch. 13, and Merendino (1969: 67) is certainly right to maintain that *mqṣh h'rṣ w'd-qṣh h'rṣ* is more at home there than in 13.8.

The identification of Deut. 13.2-18 as a dtr composition with later expansions, instead of a D composition based on earlier material, flies in the face of what could be called the current consensus; but this source-critical conclusion makes perfect sense in the light of observations made above. We noticed that these three parallel laws had little in common with the surrounding cultic laws (the core of chs. 12 and 14–16). We also observed that Deuteronomy 13 was tied to 12.29-31 by a loosely attached external frame (12.28; 13.1, 19), which cut into the structure of ch. 12, already complete with its dtr parts. Since v. 5 is related to this external frame by the common emphasis on keeping YHWH's commands (root *ṣwh*), the whole process can be hypothetically reconstructed like this:

Deuteronomy 13 is the work of a deuteronomistic writer, who placed it after 12.29-31. This chapter was expanded in a theological direction (vv. 2b-3a, 4b-5, 6a*) by a later dtr redactor with a widened horizon (v. 8), who also tried to build a special unit covering 12.28–13.19. This redactor may have written 17.2-7 also, but for our purposes this question may rest.

It would be premature at this point to put a date on Deuteronomy 13. These laws can hardly predate the reform of Josiah, but the deuteronomistic school was long-lived, and one might legitimately consider a later period for their origin as well as for their theological expansion. We can only hope to reach a more definite conclusion by inquiring into their life-setting and determining what historical period offers the most likely background for their composition and the best potential for their application.

1.6. *A* Sitz im Leben *for Deuteronomy 13.2-18*

1.6.1. *Verse 11a and Case Laws Involving Town Elders*

The method of execution (*wsqltw b'bnym wmt*, 'and thou shalt stone him with stones and he shall die') prescribed by v. 11a, at the end of the apodosis of law 2, links Deuteronomy 13 to a compact group of other laws of Deuteronomy:

> 22.21 (*wsqlwh 'nšy 'yrh b'bnym wmth*);
> 22.24 (*wsqltm 'tm b'bnym wmtw*).
> With *rgm* for 'stoning', instead of *sql*: 21.21.
> With *wmt* for the death penalty, no explicit *sql*:
>> 17.12; 18.20; 19.12; 22.22; 22.25 (connection with 22.24 clearly implies *sql*); 24.7.

Only the laws of Deuteronomy use *wmt*, 'and he shall die', as a technical term for the death penalty; and, for 'stoning', they prefer *sql* over *rgm* more than the other pentateuchal laws.

This phraseology seems to go back to an early stage in D's background.

Among passages using the same expressions as Deut. 13.11, Deut. 19.12 and 22.21 belong to laws explicitly involving the town elders (*zqnym*); Deut. 21.21, which uses *rgm* instead of *sql*, belongs to another law involving the elders; and in ch. 22 the context suggests that the elders were also involved in the laws represented by vv. 22, 24, 25.

Sociologically, tribunals of elders form the backbone of the judicial apparatus in societies usually less developed than those where judges are professionals appointed by higher authorities (Newman 1983: 50-103). The judicial authority of elders is documented among relatively egalitarian pastoralists as well as among people practising the simplest forms of dry agriculture (Newman 1983: 160, 186-87), and these are the two types of societies most commonly believed to have characterized early, pre-monarchial, Israel. The appointment of specialized law-courts, on the other hand, is an accomplishment of the monarchy; in Judah, it may go back to King Jehoshapat in the ninth century (2 Chron. 19.5-11).[1] In Deut. 21.1-9, one can observe quite well the belated extension to judges of functions previously discharged by town elders. Both elders and judges are mentioned in this law; but the role assigned to the elders is clearly essential to its stipulations, whereas the judges were introduced secondarily, as a result of the reorganization of the judiciary (Dion 1982: 16, 19, 21).[2]

It is but tenuously that v. 11 binds Deuteronomy 13 to these old

1. The most detailed discussions in recent years have been those of Rofé (1982: 10-13) and Whitelam (1979: 185-91). Rofé builds a strong case for the purely midrashic character of the Chronicles narrative, but Whitelam maintains that it rests on a historical nucleus. In the absence of any full-scale and truly critical history of the Israelite judiciary (Niehr 1987), all that I can say is that some of the eighth-century prophets' references to judges seem to be authentic (e.g. Isa. 3.2), and that 2 Chron. 19 provides a plausible setting for the emergence of this institution.

2. Of course, elders continued to play a part in the life of Israelite communities even after the loss of statehood (see Ezek. 8.1 etc.); as shown by Eph'al (1978), the situation was much the same among Tyrian, Egyptian, Neirabaean (etc.) exiles. If the main affinities of Deut. 13 were to laws associated with the powers of elders, it might have been worthwhile to examine this possible setting more at length.

laws. The elders normally responsible for their implementation are never mentioned in Deuteronomy 13. In prescribing the capital punishment, v. 11 does use *wmt*, but law 1 is satisfied with the non-technical *ywmt*, the only strong traditional association of which is to a small group of priestly laws against encroachment by unauthorized officiants (Num. 1.51; 3.10, 38; 18.7).[1]

The laws concluded by *wmt* (whether death by stoning is specified or not) are mainly examples of more or less pure case law; the impersonal evocation of a case is followed by an equally impersonal sentence. But as we saw, Deuteronomy 13 belongs to another category ('if–you' law), that introduces second person address into the substantive parts of the law, and not only by way of concluding remarks.

1.6.2. *Verses 10 and 15 and the Laws Involving Professional Judges*

The jurisdiction accountable for the enforcement of Deuteronomy 13 is not explicitly designated in the text, but vv. 10 and 15 certainly imply the intervention of a judicial process. Indications given by these verses relate laws 2-3 to other laws of Deuteronomy involving regularly appointed judges (*špṭym*).

In light of the more explicit 17.7, it can be seen that 13.10 reflects a procedure requiring witnesses to demonstrate the firmness of their testimony by playing a leading role in the execution itself; and the only other deuteronomic laws to regulate the function of witnesses are found in 19.15-21, with reference to tribunals of judges rather than town elders (19.17-18).

We are brought back again to the same context by 13.15, which prescribes a careful scrutiny of the evidence against a city suspect of idolatry; aside from 17.4, its only good parallel is in Deut. 19.18:

wdršt	*wḥqrt wš'lt*	*hyṭb*	*whnh*	*'mt nkwn hdbr*	*n'śth htw'bh hz't bqrbk*	13.15
wdršt		*hyṭb*	*whnh*	*'mt nkwn hdbr*	*n'śth htw'bh hz't byśr'l*	17.4
wdršw hšpṭym		*hyṭb*	*whnh*	*'d šqr h'd*	*šqr 'nh b'ḥyw*	19.18

Unfortunately it is not possible to determine with certainty what authorities were responsible for the implementation of Deuteronomy 13 on the basis of these affinities for laws committed to the *špṭym*, because the deuteronomic pair elders/judges does not reflect

1. Other uses of *ywmt* for the death penalty in biblical laws and decrees: Exod. 21.29; 35.2; Lev. 19.20 (negative); 24.16 (short for *mwt ywmt*); 24.21; Deut. 21.22; Josh. 1.18; 2 Kgs 11.8 // 2 Chron. 23.7; 2 Chron. 15.13.

adequately the organization of the judiciary in ancient Israel.

In spite of establishing local tribunals, the kings had plainly not renounced their own judicial powers, and Isa. 11.3 tells of the ideal objectivity and accuracy expected of them (cf. Deut. 13.15; 17.4; 19.18). Especially during the last decades of the kingdom of Judah, another category of officials, the *śrym*, were competent in matters as diverse as the confiscation of a labourer's cloak (cf. the Yabneh Yam ostracon; see Lemaire 1977: 261-62) and the life and death of a dissenting prophet (Jer. 26.10-16; 37.14–38.27).

It stands to reason that, if the third law of Deuteronomy 13 was ever meant to be applied, the king himself was to be the judge. A sentence entailing the wiping out of a whole town was more than an ordinary judgment; it was a major political decision, and its implementation presupposed full control over the army. During the First Temple period, only a king could have marched against a city fallen into idolatry; after the collapse of Judah, there is no evidence that the Judaean community ever was able and willing to undertake any action comparable to the *ḥērem* of Deut. 13.13-18 until the time of the Maccabees.

1.6.3. *The if-you Form and the Royal Court*

The if-you form in which Deut. 13.2-18 is styled also points, more weakly, to a royal background for these laws.

This form of legislation is particularly germane to the rhetorical and personalizing tendencies of Deuteronomy, and it is used abundantly in this book (list in Seitz 1971: 143-44). It is found in domains as diverse as cultic regulations (e.g. 12.20-27), the conduct of war (e.g. 20.10-14), the administration of justice (e.g. 17.8-13), and especially social and caritative dispositions (e.g. 15.7-11); but H.W. Gilmer's study (1975) of its biblical and Near Eastern connections led him to ascribe the if-you formulations in Deuteronomy to a royal court milieu. This opinion will be tested in my historical discussion, when Deuteronomy 13 is compared to similarly formulated documents issued by kings of the ancient Near East.

1.6.4. *Provisional Conclusion*

Source-critical analysis revealed that deuteronomistic expressions were inseparable from the basic layer of Deut. 13.2-18 and that its the text once again in search of pointers to a possible institutional setting, we noticed that its provisions for the execution of individual proselytizers and for the careful scrutiny of rumors of mass apostasy linked Deuteronomy 13 with laws administered by professional judges, an institution which appeared under the monarchy, and that law 3 could only be enforced by the king himself. Even the if-you style of this chapter suggested some connection to the royal court.

It should be clear from these indications that the reigns of Josiah and his sons, at the end of the seventh century BC, are the only time when any literal implementation of Deuteronomy 13 could ever be envisioned; after 587 these laws would be reduced to a grim ethical paradigm, illustrating the boundless stringency of the undivided allegiance demanded by YHWH. As we shall see in the second part of this study, the repression laws of Deuteronomy bear the hallmark of a type of document well represented in the Near East during the seventh century and meant to be rigorously applied.

2. Historical Interpretation

2.1. *The Laws in Deut. 13.2-18 are Imitated from Political Models*

Before bringing out the contacts between Deuteronomy 13 and its Assyrian and (ultimately?) Hittite models, it is important to emphasize that these laws are anything but a mechanical calque of some foreign archetype. My study of phraseology made it clear that Deuteronomy 13 is written in the language of the late Judaean monarchy. From the legal standpoint, some of its most crucial formulations are typical of Deuteronomy and its later editors and imitators. This is true above all of the seditious speech in favour of 'other deities', which specifies the guilt of the culprits in all three parts of this chapter (vv. 3b, 7b, 14b); of death by stoning (*sql*, *wmt*), the verdict laid down against relatives and friends disloyal to YHWH (v. 11a); and of the use of *ḥrm* in the verdict pronounced against the apostate city (vv. 16b, 18a). With regard to content, it was noted at the very beginning of this essay that Deuteronomy 13 had been prepared for by the often violent efforts of the YHWH-alone party. It was also pointed out that these laws were foreshadowed not only by the first commandment of the decalogue, but more specifically by Exod. 22.19, condemning to the *ḥrm*those who sacrificed to other gods.[1]

However, if expansions such as vv. 4b-5 are disregarded and the three laws are clipped down to their original shape, Deuteronomy 13 loses much of its theological content and vocabulary.[2] This chapter remains a religious document by its topic, the suppression of propaganda for alien deities, and by the YHWH-istic formulas found in vv. 6 (*hdrk 'šr ṣwk yhwh 'lhyk llkt bh*, 'the way in which YHWH thy god commanded thee to walk'), 11 (*yhwh 'lhyk hmwṣy'k m'rṣ mṣrym mbyt 'bdym*, 'YHWH thy god, who took you out of Egypt, from the house of bondage'), 13 (*'šr yhwh 'lhyk ntn lk lšbt šm*, 'that YHWH thy god is about to give thee to to dwell there'), and the whole of v. 18b. But it becomes apparent that religion may not be the only factor at work in Deuteronomy 13.

All the explicit mentions of YHWH, his kindnesses and his demands are located in the margins of the law. Verses 6b, 11b and 18b are mere motivating developments, and v. 13 is only a backdrop to law 3; in v. 13 Israel hears about an incident which happened on its territory, but the crime itself is not described until v. 14.

As regards the content of Deut. 13.2-18, Horst (1961: 35 and *passim*) rightly compares this chapter to secular laws against high treason, quoting passages of the Prussian Code with reference to law 2 (1961: 52 n. 77). And indeed, the command to eliminate three categories of people who might incite Israel to switch its allegiance to other gods is the very core of Deuteronomy 13. In this command, just replace 'other gods' by 'other kings', and you obtain a piece of

1. As N. Lohfink suggested to me, it would be worth inquiring if Exod. 22.19 is not in effect the basis of Deut. 13. These laws extend the condemnation of Exodus to the very propaganda for alien deities, and not only to actual sacrifice; on the other hand, Lohfink notes that the *ḥrm* is now reserved for cases of mass apostasy, whereas in the Book of the Covenant, this punishment seems to apply to private Israelites, no doubt with dire consequences for the rest of their households. As Lohfink further remarks, it would be interesting to know whether similar developments (from the actual revolt to a mere incitation to rebel; from the punishment of whole families to that of the culprits alone) are also visible in the Mesopotamian documents relative to the repression of political defection.

2. This lack of YHWH-istic flavour in the core of Deut. 13 has been stressed by Rose (1975: 21), who incorrectly ascribes it to an early, pre-deuteronomic form of this chapter.

legislation against *political* subversion, which would make perfect sense in the authoritarian monarchies of the ancient Near East.

In the Hebrew kingdoms themselves, there is good evidence for political subversion and its ruthless suppression. Prophets were often involved in revolutionary activities (Ahijah, 1 Kgs 11.29-39; Elisha, 2 Kgs 9.1-10; etc.), and could get turned out of the country (Amos 7.10-13), imprisoned (Jer. 38.1-6) or even put to death for treason (Jer. 26.20-23). A town suspected of supporting a would-be usurper could have the same fate as the apostate city condemned in Deut. 13.13-18 (Nob, 1 Sam. 22.9-19; cf. 2 Sam. 20.14-22, Abel of Beth-Maacah).[1]

This analogy between the laws of Deuteronomy 13 and political repression in the biblical world raises the possibility that political models had an impact on their formulation, or even contributed to the atmosphere which led to their promulgation.

2.2. *The Impact of Assyrian Statecraft*

2.2.1. *The Likelihood of Mesopotamian Models in the Josianic Age*

As far as the Hebrew kingdoms are concerned, legal documents ensuring the safety of the king and the firmness of his control have not been preserved; but the older oriental monarchies have left us a rich legacy of treaties (Korošec 1931), instructions (Rose 1975: 27-30) and oaths of allegiance (Weinfeld 1976) protecting rulers against all manner of conspiracies. It is in Mesopotamian garb that this literature is most likely to have been known to the Judaean court, even late in the

1. Examples from the 'secular' sphere do not come to mind so readily with respect to the suppression of alien proselytism in private circles (cf. Deut. 13.7-12). For the Israelite's obligation to adhere to YHWH even at the cost of his friends and near kin, the YHWH-alone-party had an exemplary model on the religious level itself. Here, the archetype was the murderous reaction of the Levites against the worshippers of the golden calf narrated in Exod. 32.26-29. In Deuteronomy this story is reflected in the praise of Levi, 33.9. As suggested by Seitz (1971: 151 n. 184) the use of *hārag* ('to kill') in this context may have influenced the secondary substitution of this verb for **hgyd* at Deut. 13.10a. Philo's praise of Phinehas in conclusion of his treatment of Deut. 13 (*Spec. Leg.* 1.56-57) suggests an early association between texts like these, since Phinehas was another levitical hero famous for his reaction against the corruption of Israel by foreign women (Num. 25).

seventh century, the time suggested for Deuteronomy 13 by the dtr formulas it contains.

The reign of Josiah (639–609 BCE), a period of militant reassertion of Judah's national ethos and religion after a century of foreign domination (Josiah's reform, 622), coincided with the prolonged and spectacular death throes of the Neo-Assyrian empire and the rise of 'new' imperial powers. Among these new contenders for hegemony, the pharaohs of the XXVIth Dynasty were nearest to the Judaean hills, and their ambitious schemes could not be ignored (cf. Miller and Hayes 1986: 383-85); and yet, at the peak of the world pyramid, Babylonia was obviously the most direct rival of Assyria. The Mesopotamian cultural supremacy impressed upon the people of Jerusalem by a century of military, diplomatic, administrative and commercial contacts was not seriously imperiled by this challenge, since Babylonia, in all essentials, shared the language, religion and political structure of Judah's former masters. The military decline of Assyria gave Judaean nationalism its long awaited opportunity; but, at the level of expression, the imitation of long-familiar Assyrian models remained as natural an option as under the empire, and fiercely YHWH-istic imperatives could be laid down in forms inspired of Mesopotamian statecraft.

2.2.2. *Positive Analogies between Deuteronomy 13 and Near Eastern Texts*

The relevant comparative material was diligently exploited by Moshe Weinfeld (1972: 91-100; 1976), and his demonstration of an actual Assyrian influence on Deuteronomy 13 has been received favourably by most. McCarthy (1978: 171 n. 27) and Nicholson (1987: 66), who rejected it, had not even tried to come to terms with the evidence that supports it. Since this point is very important to my argument, I will give a few examples not quoted by Weinfeld,[1] and elaborate on some of those which he quoted.

1. Grayson (1987) and Parpola (1987) published several Neo-Assyrian treaties of the eighth–seventh centuries which were not available to Weinfeld; and Parpola (Treaty No. 1) gives a much improved edition of the loyalty oath to Ashurbanipal prescribed by Zakutu in 669 BC (*ABL* 1239, now completed by the British Museum fragment 83-1-18, 45). Note also (Parpola 184-85) a list of forty-seven treaties referred to in Assyrian sources of the eighth–seventh centuries.

2.2.2.1. *Specific Contacts.* The stipulation against prophets and 'dreamers of dream' inciting Israel to turn to other deities than YHWH (Deut. 13.2-6) is narrowly paralleled by one of the obligations laid by Esarhaddon (king of Assyria, 680–669) on his Iranian vassals in 672 to ensure the smooth accession to power of his designated successor Ashurbanipal (*VTE* ll. 116-17, as restored by Borger 1961: 178). Esarhaddon's subjects are to report all treasonable utterances against the crown prince emanating from ecstatic prophets (*raggīmu* and *maḫḫû*)[1] or from dream interpreters (*šā'ilu*; see Oppenheim 1956: 221-22).[2]

Weinfeld (1972: 98) correctly noted that this short list of interpreters of the deity boils down to a dichotomy, similar to the unique pair *nby' 'w ḥlm ḥlwm* found in Deut. 13.2-6. Its presence in the josianic law is all the more indicative of foreign cultural influence since we do not know of the existence of specialized dream interpreters in ancient Israel; all that our sources indicate is the importance of dreams in the professional activity of the *nby'* (Jer. 23.25-32; cf. Num. 12.6; Jer. 27.9; 29.8; Joel 3.1).

In the treaty quoted above, Esarhaddon urges his vassals from Media to report any plots of their 'brothers, sons or daughters' (*VTE* 115-16) as well as the subversive words of prophets and dream interpreters. In the oath of allegiance to Ashurbanipal urged on the Assyrians by Queen Zakutu in 669, the whole reverse of the tablet deals with conspiracies, and the obligation to report 'brothers and friends' is explicitly mentioned (line 22; Parpola 1987: 166-67). In a

1. These two categories are closely related together, and they are the nearest Mesopotamian equivalents of the biblical *nby'*. See Huffmon (1976: 173-76)—Esarhaddon's suspicion of ecstatics was not groundless. Spontaneous messages from the deity could interfere with his royal designs in quite troublesome ways. In 669, he sent the statue of Bêl (Marduk) back to newly rebuilt Babylon; but this long journey had to be called off near its end because of an obscure oracle in the name of Bêl and his consort Zarpanitum, uttered by a member of the god's escort who was not even a professional *maḫḫû* (Parpola 1970: 18-19; 1983: 32-33).

2. The monitoring of divination by Assyrian *contre-espionnage* was serious business, as one can see by another document of the seventh century, a letter to Esarhaddon from Shamash-shumu-ukin, the crown prince of Babylon (BM 135586; Parpola 1972). Government spies have reported on the treasonable activities of a specialist of liver omens (*bārû*) and of two astrologers ('scribes of the omen series Enuma Anu Enlil'), and their message is forwarded to the high king in Nineveh.

treaty (tablet BM 82-5-22, 130; Grayson 1987: 139-47) that he imposed on the Babylonians in 652, Ashurbanipal caused them to swear, in more general terms:

> A conspirator (*mušadbibu*) who speaks unfriendly words against [Ashurbanipal, king of Assyria, our lord], or against an official of [Ashurbanipal, king of Assyria, our lord]; when we have heard and seen this we swear to throw him in irons and [take him] to Ashurbanipal [king of Assyria, our lord]. (Recto, ll. 13'-16'; Grayson 1987: 141 [Akkadian], 144 [English]).

Long before Esarhaddon and Ashurbanipal, Late Bronze Age treaties and related documents (listed by Kestemont 1974: 404, Tableau 30) made it an obligation for vassals to denounce all conspiracies against their lords. An interesting example is found in the so-called 'Ishmeriga-Vertrag', the fifteenth-century protocol of a loyalty oath imposed by the Hittite king Arnuwanda I on warriors from Ishmeriga, a land of northern Syria (*Keilschrifturkunden aus Boghazköi*, XXIII, 68+, recto, ll. x + 21-24; Kempinski and Košak (eds.) 1970: 194-95). These troops were responsible for protecting the Great King's interests in the subject country of Kizzuwatna (Beal 1986: 437); in his instructions to this effect, Arnuwanda even includes father and mother among potential agitators to be brought to trial.

The 'Ishmeriga-Vertrag' continues its precautions against conspiracies with a good parallel to the third part of Deuteronomy 13:

> If, in the midst of my country, a city si[ns], you, [people] of Ishmeriga, shall intervene, and you shall destroy [this city] and its men. However you shall bring the rest of the 'transplantees' to His Majesty; and, as for the cattle and sheep, [take them for your]selves (ll. x + 25-26; Kempinski and Košak 1970: 194-95; Beal 1986: 437).

As in the previous quotation, the 'sin' threatened with this punishment is disloyalty to the king of Hatti. Arnuwanda's instructions about booty disposal suggest that comparable specifications may have been original in Deuteronomy 13, thus casting doubt on the secondary character attributed to v. 17 by Merendino (1969: 69-71) and other critics (e.g. Rose 1975: 21).

The deuteronomic prescription of a careful inquiry into the rumour about a whole town's defection (v. 15) is very close to Mesopotamian formulations. In neo-Assyrian texts, similar phrases are used to demand an investigation into an informer's allegations. The tablet K

211, verso, line 49 // K 2729, verso, line 49 (Postgate 1969: 29, 31, 37) has to do with a report about a royal favour's beneficiary suspected of 'sinning' against God or king; it prescribes:

> *ša'al kîn šumma abûtu šalimtu šî*
> Investigate, and establish whether the statement is true.

ša'âlu, the first verb in this example, is the Akkadian cognate of the third verb in Deut. 13.15. This use of *ša'âlu* is common in neo-Assyrian letters; to Weinfeld's examples (1972: 92 n. 1) add *ABL* 557, lines 21-24 (where it is coupled with *kîn* as in K 211), and *ABL* 524, line 8.

As for the phrase *abûtu šalimtu šî*, it corresponds to Hebrew *nkwn hdbr*. An earlier analogy for this Hebrew phrase, noted by Horst (1961: 37 n. 33), is the coupling of the verbs *bâru* and *kânu* in the Dt stem ('to examine and to establish') in the Middle Assyrian Laws, e.g., tablet A, col. II, ll. 49-50, 100-101; col. V, ll. 98-99; col. VII, ll. 4-5 (Borger 1979: 55, 57).

The accumulation of three synonyms for 'inquiring' in v. 15a is more than matched by the five synonyms in a hymn in Standard Babylonian to Gilgamesh, Judge in the Netherworld (Haupt 1891: 93, No. 53, l. 7; trans. *CAD* 3. 101; Seux 1976: 428-29):

> *tašâl taḫâti tadanni tabarri u tuštêšir*
> You interrogate, you investigate, you render judgment, you examine and you settle correctly.

These Akkadian affinities of Deut. 13.15a are all the more significant since this Hebrew formula is only found in Deuteronomy (13.15; 17.4; 19.18), a book widely considered as written during the Assyrian domination of Judah and its aftermath.

The stipulations relative to the destruction of an apostate city and the massacre of its inhabitants (Deut. 13.16-18a) very obviously share the language of biblical stories of annihilation (*ḥrm*) of the non-YHWH-istic population of Canaan, especially frequent in the first half of the book of Joshua; and the word *ḥrm* is applied to Hebrew idolators in Exod. 22.19. However, even here affinities can be found with phrases used in the Assyrian world.

With Weinfeld (1972: 99), the phrase for 'smiting' used in Deut. 13.16a can be compared to that of an eighth-century treaty of Assyrian inspiration (Lemaire and Durand 1984: 23-36) found at

Sefire in northern Syria. The Aramaic document (Stele III, ll. 12-13; Lemaire and Durand 1984: 119, 145) enjoins the junior treaty partner to avenge his overlord upon a rebellious city by 'smiting' it (verb *nkh* in both texts) 'by the sword' (*ḥrb* in both texts):

Deut:		*hkh tkh 't-yšby h'yr hhw' lpy-ḥrb*[1]	
Sefîre:	*whn qryh h' nkh tkwh*		*bḥrb*[2]

Even the description of the punished city as an 'eternal mound of ruins' (*tl 'wlm*, v. 17b) has an interesting Assyrian counterpart. This phrase is very rare in Hebrew, the only other example being Josh. 8.28; but it corresponds functionally to the Akkadian expression *til abû-bi*, 'mound of ruins (left by a/the) flood', common in war narratives where it evokes the irreparable devastation of enemy or rebellious cities (see *CAD* 1. 78).

It should be evident from these examples that the suppression of political subversion is richly documented in the political literature of the ancient Near East, and this in terms often identical to those of Deuteronomy 13; *VTE*, a text of the seventh century, even provided an explanation for the unique pair prophet/'dreamer of dream' of vv. 2-6.

2.2.2.2. *The If-You Style, from the Hittite Treaties to Esarhaddon.* The style of Hittite treaty stipulations is far from uniform (McCarthy 1978: 59-63), but if–you formulations comparable to those of Deuteronomy are common enough in these documents and in other Near Eastern treaties, royal instructions and loyalty oaths. Paragraphs of this type are used, among others, to prescribe the reporting of plots or seditious speech against the king and drastic action in quenching political defection. Among the examples above, the *VTE* stipulations are clad in an entirely conditional form, only sanctioned at the end by a long series of curses; but Arnuwanda's demands on the men of Ishmeriga combine a conditional protasis with second person address, just as in Deuteronomy 13. For more examples like this, see, for example, the treaties between Murshili II of Hatti (c. 1335–1300) and Duppi-Teshub of Amurru (*ANET* 204); the same Murshili II and

1. 'Thou shalt definitely smite the inhabitants of this town with the edge of the sword.'

2. 'If it is a town, you shall definitely smite it by the sword.'

Niqmepa' of Ugarit (Nougayrol 1956: 97); Tudhaliya IV of Hatti (1250–1220) and Kaushkamuwa of Amurru (Malamat 1970: 204). In his otherwise useful discussion of the instructions of Hittite kings, Rose (1975: 27-33) stresses much too exclusively the affinity between Deuteronomy 13 and this type of document which apparently did not survive the Hittite empire; form and content are just as close to Deuteronomy in the treaty stipulations quoted above as in Rose's own examples (1975: 28-29).

The if-you form is not confined to treaties and instructions of the second millennium, long forgotten when Deuteronomy was written. It dominates the third Sefîre stele, a vassal treaty of Assyrian inspiration which may go back to the early eighth century (Lemaire and Durand 1984: 58). Even closer to Deuteronomy 13, it is still visible in the poorly preserved treaty of Esarhaddon with Baal, king of Tyre, in a passage (col. iii l. 14; Weidner 1932–33: 31) whose topic is admittedly different from the suppression of subversive activities.

2.3. *The Author Likely to Belong to Josiah's Entourage*

The author of Deut. 13.2-18 was familiar with traditional Hebrew phraseology, and could handle masterfully the native religious rhetoric; and yet he consciously borrowed the instruments of domination developed by the old monarchies. In order to prevent his nation from drifting back to the attitudes that prevailed before Josiah's reform, he designed laws heavily indebted to a thousand-year-old statecraft still practiced in Mesopotamia. Conversant with a literature borne in royal chanceries, and bent on ensuring the permanence of Josiah's reform, this writer is probably to be sought in close proximity to the reformer king himself.

No doubt the political information and the educational background revealed by the parallels that we have sampled could still be found among the remnant of Judah in the decades that followed the fall of the kingdom. We know through allusions like Ezek. 17.13 and through surviving documents such as the treaty between Hannibal and Philip V (Polybius 7.9) that the Near Eastern treaty form long survived the Neo-Assyrian era; and students of Deuteronomy agree that this book is most heavily indebted to political treaties in some of its latest ingredients (especially in chs. 4; 29–30).

Nonetheless, the closer to 672 BC one places the composition of

Deuteronomy 13, the easier to understand are its precise contacts with the vassal treaties of Esarhaddon. Furthermore, we noted that law 3 could only have been implemented under a king devoted to YHWH, a situation that would disappear for several centuries after the fall of Jerusalem to the Babylonians. As a result, the only alternative to a Josianic date is Hölscher's assignment of the deuteronomic laws to post-exilic utopian thinking.

2.4. *Deuteronomy 13 does not Issue from Postexilic Utopian Thinking*

In dealing with preceptive literature, and preceptive literature inspired of models such as the oaths and treaties protecting the ancient monarchies, the burden of proof is on those who dispute the law-maker's intention to be taken literally. But Hölscher's case against the plausibility of the harsh stipulations of Deuteronomy 13 in pre-exilic times (Hölscher 1922: 192-93) is not compelling.

It is true that no historical example has been preserved of the horrors of law 3 being brought down on any Israelite city, but the zealous enforcement of Deuteronomy probably ended with Josiah's life in 609, thirteen years after his first radical measures. Until then the reformer king's authority is not known to have been challenged, but this ruthless desecrator of Bethel and other shrines of the North (2 Kgs 23.15-20) would hardly have hesitated to smash any community attempting to return to the old ways. Deuteronomy 13 did not particularly threaten Jerusalem, since this law was most likely promulgated in the wake of the reform, when the capital of Judah was already purified and firmly under control.

In spite of the difficulty of interpreting Jer. 23.25-32 and other texts quoted by Gressmann (1924: 333) against Hölscher, the raucous phalanx of meddling prophets with conflicting dreams revealed by the book of Jeremiah and Lachish ostracon 3 (Pardee 1982: 84) accounts sufficiently for law 1. As for law 2, the pagan practices which rose again under Josiah's successors (Jer. 44; Ezek. 8; etc.) clearly imply that if during his reign the older, less-than-monotheistic religious tendency had been forced to seek cover, they had not really been extirpated. Meanwhile, anyone who felt impelled to promote other deities than YHWH had very good reasons to act secretly (*bstr*), as does the tempter evoked in Deut. 13.7.

General Conclusion

The first edition of Deut. 13.2-18 was neither sheer rhetoric, nor the manifesto of a circle of dissidents not yet confronted with the responsibility of practical applications, nor again the ineffective daydreaming of fanatics of later times. It reflected the will of an idealistic ruler who wanted his covenant with YHWH alone to be taken in dead earnest, and whose inclination to draconian initiatives is evident from his eradication of the clergy of the local shrines of YHWH (2 Kgs 23.8-9), his massacres of priests in the *quondam* kingdom of Israel (2 Kgs 23.19-20), and his reckless and fatal clash with the full power of Egypt at Megiddo (2 Kgs 23.29).[1]

1. The spirit of Deut. 13 is in keeping with a Jewish legend about Josiah, preserved by Josephus and various rabbinical writings. After these things, Josiah searched the houses, the villages, and the cities, out of a suspicion that somebody might have idols in private (Josephus, *Ant.* 10.4.5.69). See Marcus (1937: 195 n. c), for a reference to the rabbinical material. Contrast *Sifre* 92, which prescribes not to search actively for contravenors of Deut. 13.13-19. Another legend, found in *2 Baruch* (66.4), narrates that Josiah had the false prophets burned and their followers crushed under heaps of stones in Kidron valley.

APPENDIX

A Synopsis of Deuteronomy 13.2-18

I. *Protasis: The Eventuality of Alien Religious Propaganda*

1. *The Proselytizer*

	Prophet		*Brother*		*City Clique*
				13	*ky tšm‘*
					b’ḥt ‘ryk
					’šr yhwh ’lhyk
					ntn lk
					lšbt šm
					l’mr
2a	*ky yqwm bqrbk*	7a*	*ky ysytk*	14a*	*yṣ’w*
	nby’		*’ḥyk bn-’mk*		*’nšym bny bly‘l*
	w ḥlm ḥlwm		*’w bnk*		*mqrbk*
			’w btk		
			’w ’št ḥyqk		
			’w r‘k ’šr knpšk		
			bstr		
2b	*wntn ‘lyk*				
	’wt ’w mwpt				
3a*	*wb’*				*wydyḥw*
	h’wt whmwpt				*’t-yšby ‘yrm*
	’šr-dbr ‘lyk				

2. *His Speech*

	l’mr		*l’mr*		*l’mr*
3b	*nlkh*	7b	*nlkh*	14b	*nlkh*
	’ḥry				
			wn‘bdh		*wn‘bdh*
	’lhym ’ḥrym		*’lhym ’ḥrym*		*’lhym ’ḥrym*
	’šr l’ yd‘tm		*’šr l’ yd‘t*		*’šr l’ yd‘tm*
			’th w’btyk		
		‘8a	*m’lhy h‘mym*		
			’šr sbybtykm		
			hqrbym ’lyk		
			’w hrḥqym mmk		

		8b	*mqṣh h'rṣ*		
			w'd-qṣh h'rṣ		
	wn'bdm				

II. *Apodosis: The Conduct Prescribed*

1. *Not to Give in to the Proselytizer*

		9a	*l'-t'bh lw*		
4a	*l' tšm'*		*wl' tšm'*		
	'l dbry hnb' hhw'		*'lyw*		
	'w 'l-ḥwlm hḥlwm hhw'				
4b	*ky mnsh yhwh 'lhykm 'tkm*				
	ld't hyškm 'hbym				
	't-yhwh 'lhykm				
	bkl-lbbkm wbkl-npškm				
5	*'ḥry yhwh 'lhykm tlkw*				
	w'tw tyr'w				
	w't-mṣwtyw tšmrw				
	wbqlw tšm'w				
	w'tw t'bdw				
	wbw tdbqwn				

2. *To Report on Him / To Ascertain His Crime*

		9b	*wl'-tḥws 'ynk 'lyw*		
			wl'-tḥml		
			wl'-tksh 'lyw		
		10a[a]	*ky hgd tgdnw*		
				15a	*wdršt*
					wḥqrt wš'lt hyṭb
				15b	*whnh 'mt nkwn hdbr*
					n'šth htw'bh hz't bqrbk

3. *To Execute Him*

				16	*hkh tkh*
6a	*whnby' hhw'*				*'t-yšby h‘yr hhw'*
	'w				*lpy xrb*
	ḥlm hḥlwm hhw'				
		10a[b]	*ydk thyh-bw br'šwnh*		
			lhmytw		
		10b	*wyd kl-h‘m b'ḥrnh*		
		11a	*wsqltw b'bnym*		*hḥrm 'th*
	ywmt		*wmt*		*w't-kl-'šr-bh*
					w't-bhmth
					lpy ḥrb
				17a	*w't-kl-šllh*
					tqbṣ 'l-twk rḥbh
					wśrpt b'š
					't-h‘yr
					w't-kl-šllh
					klyl lyhwh 'lhyk
				17b	*whyth tl ‘wlm*
					l' tbnh ‘wd
				18a	*wl' ydbq bydk*
					m'wmh mn-hḥrm

III. *Motive Clauses*

1. *Specific: The Heinous Character of Incitement to Defection*

6a	*ky*	11b	*ky*
	dbr srh		*bqš*
	‘l-yhwh 'lhykm		
	hmwṣy' 'tkm m'rṣ mṣrym		
	hpdk mbyt ‘bdym		
	lhdyḥk mn-		*lhdyḥk m‘l*
	hdrk 'šr ṣwk		
	yhwh 'lhyk		*yhwh 'lhyk*
	llkt bh		
			hmwṣy'k m'rṣ mṣrym
			mbyt ‘bdym

2. *General*

	To Destroy Evil		*As a Deterrent*		*To Placate YHWH*
6b	*wb'rt hr'*	12	*wkl-yśr'l yšm'w*	18b	*lm'n yšwb yhwh*
			wyr'wn		*mḥrwn 'pw*
			wl'-ywspw		*wntn-lk rḥmym*
			l'śwt kdbr hr' hzh		*wrḥmk*
	mqrbk		*bqrbk*		*whrbk*
					k'šr nšb' l'btyk

ABBREVIATIONS

ABL	R.F. Harper, *Assyrian and Babylonian Letters*
ANET	Pritchard (ed.), *Ancient Near Eastern Texts.*
CAD	Oppenheim and Reiner, *et al.*, *Chicago Assyrian Dictionary.*
D	A deuteronomic writer or deuteronomic material apparently earlier than Josiah's reform.
dtr	A deuteronomistic writer or deuteronomistic material from the time of Josiah or later.
KAI	Donner and Röllig, *Kanaanäische und Aramäische Inschriften.*
VTE	Wiseman, *The Vassal Treaties of Esarhaddon.*

BIBLIOGRAPHY

Alt, A.

1966 The Origins of Israelite Law. In *Essays on Old Testament History and Religion*, 79-132. Oxford Basil: Blackwell.

Barthélemy, D., OP, and J.T. Milik.

1955 *Qumran Cave I*. DJD, 1. Oxford: Clarendon Press.

Beal, R. H.

1986 The History of Kizzuwatna and the Date of the Šunaššura Treaty. *Or* ns 55: 424-45.

Borger, R.

1961 Zu den Asarhaddon Verträgen aus Nimrud. *ZA* ns 20: 173-96.

1979 *Babylonisch-Assyrische Lesestücke*. 2nd edn. Rome: Biblical Institute Press.

Budde, K.

1916 Dtn 13.10, und was daran hängt. *ZAW* 36 (1916): 187-97.

1926 Das Deuteronomium und die Reform König Josias. *ZAW* 44: 177-224.

Carmichael, C. M.

1974 *The Laws of Deuteronomy*. Ithaca: Cornell University Press.

Carroll, R.P.

1986 *Jeremiah*. OTL. Philadelphia: Westminster Press.

Cazelles, H.

1985 Droit public dans le Deutéronome. In *Das Deuteronomium: Entstehung, Gestalt und Botschaft*, 99-106. Ed. N. Lohfink. BETL, 68. Leuven: Leuven University Press.

Crim, K.R.

1973 Hebrew Direct Discourse as a Translation Problem. *BT* 24: 311-16.

Dietrich, W.

1972 *Profetie und Geschichte: Eine Redaktionsgeschichtliche Untersuchung zum deuteronomistischen Geschichtwerk*. FRLANT, 108. Göttingen: Vandenhoeck & Ruprecht.

Dion, P.E.

1980 'Tu feras disparaître le mal du milieu de toi'. *RB* 78: 321-49.

1982 Deutéronome 21,1-9: Miroir du développement légal et religieux d'Israël. *Studies in Religion/Sciences Religieuses* 11: 13-22.

1984 The Greek Version of Deut. 21.1-9 and Its Variants: a Record of Early Exegesis. In *De Septuaginta, Studies in Honour of J.W. Wevers on his Sixty-fifth Birthday*, 151-60. Ed. A. Pietersma and C. Cox. Toronto: Benben.

1985 Deuteronomy and the Gentile World: A Study in Biblical Theology. *Toronto Journal of Theology* 1: 200-21.

Donner, H., and W. Röllig.

1966 *Kanaanäische und Aramäische Inschriften*. 3 vols. Wiesbaden: Harrassowitz.

Driver, S.R.
1901 *A Critical and Exegetical Commentary on Deuteronomy*. ICC. 3rd edn. Edinburgh: T. & T. Clark.

Dussaud, R.
1921 *Les origines cananéennes du sacrifice israélite*. Paris: Presses Universitaires de France.

Eph'al, I.
1978 The Western Minorities in Babylonia in the 6th–5th Centuries BC: Maintenance and Cohesion. *Or* ns 47: 74-90.

Floss, J. P.
1975 *Jahwe dienen, Götter dienen*. BBB, 45. Bonn: Hanstein.

Gilmer, H.W.
1975 *The If–You Form in Israelite Law*. Missoula, MT: Scholars Press.

Grayson, A.K.
1987 Akkadian Treaties of the Seventh Century BC. *JCS* 39: 127-60.

Gressmann, H.
1924 Josia und das Deuteronomium. Ein kritisches Referat vom Herausgeber. *ZAW*, 42: 313-37.

Halbe, J.
1975 *Das Privilegrecht Jahwes, Ex 34, 10-26*. FRLANT, 114. Göttingen: Vandenhoeck & Ruprecht.

Harper, R.F.
1892-1914 *Assyrian and Babylonian Letters*. 14 vols. Chicago: University of Chicago.

Haupt, P.
1891 *Das babylonische Nimrodepos, Keilschrifttext der Bruchstücke der sogenannten Izdubarlegenden mit dem keilschriftlichen Sintflutberichte nach den Originalen im Britischem Museum copiert und herausgegeben.* Assyriologische Bibliothek, 3. Leipzig: Hinrichs.

Helfmeyer, F.J.
1968 *Die Nachfolge Gottes im Alten Testament*. BBB, 29. Bonn: Hanstein.

Hoffmann, H.-D.
1980 *Reform und Reformen, Untersuchungen zu einem Grundthema der deuteronomistischen Geschichtsschreibung*. ATANT, 66. Zurich: Theologischer Verlag Zürich.

Hölscher, G.
1922 Komposition und Ursprung des Deuteronomiums. *ZAW*, 40: 161-255.

Horst, F.
1961 *Gottes Recht, Gesammelte Studien zum Recht im Alten Testament*. TBü, Altes Testament, 12. Munich: Kaiser.

Houwink Ten Cate, P.H.J.
1983–84 'The History of Warfare According to Hittite Sources: The Annals of Hattusilis I'. *Anatolica* 10: 91-109; 11: 47-83.

Huffmon, H.B.
1976 The Origins of Prophecy. In *Magnalia Dei, The Mighty Acts of God, Essays on the Bible and Archaeology in Memory of G. Ernest Wright*,

176-86. Ed. F.M. Cross, W.E. Lemke, and P.D. Miller, Jr. Garden City, NY: Doubleday.

Jenni, E.
1981 Dtn 19,16: sarā 'Falschheit'. In *Mélanges bibliques et orientaux en l'honneur de M. Henri Cazelles.* AOAT, 212: 201-11. Kevelaer: Butzon & Bercker.

Kempinski, A., and S. Kosak.
1970 Der Išmeriga-Vertrag. *WO* 5: 191-217.

Kestemont, G.
1974 *Diplomatique et droit international en Asie Occidentale 1600–1200 av. J. C.* Publications de l'Institut Orientaliste de Louvain, 9. Louvain-la-Neuve: Institut Orientaliste.

König, E.
1917 *Das Deuteronomium.* KAT, 3. Leipzig: Scholl.

Korošec, V.
1931 *Hethitische Staatsverträge, Ein Beitrag zu ihrer juristischen Wertung.* Leipziger rechtswissenschaftliche Studien, 60. Leipzig: Weicher.

Lang, B.
1984 George Orwell im gelobten Land. Das Buch Deuteronomium und der Geist kirchlicher Kontrolle. In *Kirche und Visitation: Beiträge zur Erforschung des frühneuzeitlichen Visitationswesen in Europa*, 21-35. Ed. E.W. Zeeden and P.T. Lang. Spätmittelalter und Frühe Neuzeit, 14. Stuttgart: KlettCotta.

Lemaire, A.
1977 *Inscriptions hébraïques I. Les Ostraca.* Littératures Anciennes du Proche-Orient. Paris: Cerf.

Lemaire, A., and J.-M.Durand.
1984 *Les Inscriptions araméennes de Sefiré et l'Assyrie de Shamshi-ilu.* Hautes-Etudes Orientales, 20. Geneva: Droz.

Lemaire, A., and P. Vernus.
1983 L'Ostracon paléo-hébreu no 6 de Tell Qudeirât (Qadesh-Barnéa). In *Fontes atque Pontes, Festschrift für H. Brunner*, 302-26 and Pl. 6. Ed. M. Görg. Ägypten und Altes Testament, 5. Wiesbaden: Harrassowitz.

Levenson, J.
1975 Who Inserted the Book of the Torah? *HTR* 68: 203-33.

Lohfink, N.
1963 *Das Hauptgebot, Eine Untersuchung literarischer Einleitugsfragen zu Dtn 5–11.* Anbib, 65. Rome: Biblical Institute Press.
1964 Auslegung deuteronomischer Texte, IV. Verkündigung des Hauptgebots in der jüngsten Schicht des Deuteronomiums (Dt 4, 1-10). *BibLeb* 5: 247-56.

Löhr, M.
1925 *Das Deuteronomium (Untersuchungen zum Hexateuchproblem II).* Schriften der Königsberger Gelehrten Gesellschaft, Geisteswissenschaftliche Klasse, 1.6. Berlin: Deutsche Verlagsgesellschaft für Politik und Geschichte.

Loretz, O.
1975 Der hebräische Opferterminus KLJL 'Ganzopfer'. *UF* 7: 569-70.

McCarthy, D.J.
1978 *Treaty and Covenant*. AnBib 21A. 2nd edn. Rome: Biblical Institute Press.

Malamat, A.
1970 *Sources for Early Biblical History: The Second Millennium BC, in Hebrew Translation*. 2nd edn. Jerusalem: Akademon.

Marcus, R., trans.
1937 *Josephus with an English Translation*. VI. *Josephus, Jewish Antiquities, Books IX–XI*. LCL. London, Heinemann.

Mayes, A.D.H.
1979 *Deuteronomy*. NCB. Greenwood, SC: Attic Press.
1981 Deuteronomy 4 and the Literary Criticism of Deuteronomy. *JBL* 100: 23-51.

Merendino, R.P., OSB
1969 *Das deuteronomische Gesetz*. BBB, 31. Bonn: Peter Hanstein.

Miller, J.M., and J.H. Hayes.
1986 *A History of Ancient Israel and Judah*. Philadelphia: Westminster Press.

Mowinckel, S.
1914 *Zur Komposition des Buches Jeremia*. Kristiania: Jacob Dybwad.

Newman, K.S.
1983 *Law and Economic Organization*. Cambridge: Cambridge University Press.

Nicholson, E.W.
1987 *God and His People: Covenant and Theology in the Old Testament*. Oxford: Clarendon Press.

Niehr, H.
1987 Zur Gerichtsorganisation Israels. *BZ* ns 31: 206-27.

Noth, M.
1943 *Überlieferungsgeschichtliche Studien. Die sammelnden und bearbeitenden Geschichtswerke im Alten Testament*. Tübingen: Mohr.

Nougayrol, J.
1956 *Textes accadiens des archives sud (archives internationales)*. Le Palais Royal d'Ugarit, 4 = Mission de Ras Shamra, 9. Paris: Geuthner.

Pardee, D.
1982 *Handbook of Ancient Hebrew Letters*. Chico, CA: Scholars Press.

Oppenheim, A.L., and E. Reiner eds.
1956–1984 *The Chicago Assyrian Dictionary*. Chicago: The Oriental Institute.
1956 *The Interpretation of Dreams in the Ancient Near East*. Transactions of the American Philosophical Society n.s., 46. 3. Philadelphia: American Philosophical Society.

Parpola, S.
1970 *Letters from Assyrian Scholars to the Kings Esarhaddon and Assurbanipal, Part I: Texts*. AOAT 5.1 Kevelaer: Butzon & Bercker.
1972 A Letter from Shamash-shumu-ukin to Esarhaddon. *Iraq* 34: 21-34.
1983 *Letters from Assyrian Scholars to the Kings Esarhaddon and Assurbanipal, Part II: Commentary and Appendices*. AOAT 5.2. Kevelaer: Butzon & Bercker.

1987 Neo-Assyrian Treaties from the Royal Archives of Nineveh. *JCS* 39: 161-89.

Patrick, D.
1985 *Old Testament Law*. Atlanta: John Knox.

Perlitt, L.
1969 *Bundestheologie im Alten Testament*. WMANT, 36. Neukirchen–Vluyn: Neukirchener Verlag.

Ploeg, J. van der
1948 Notes lexicographiques. *OTS* 5: 142-50.

Porten, B., and A. Yardeni.
1986 *Textbook of Aramaic Documents from Ancient Egypt*. I. *Letters*. The Hebrew University, Department of the History of the Jewish People, Texts and Studies for Students. Winona Lake IN: Eisenbrauns.

Postgate, J.N.
1969 *Neo-Assyrian Royal Grants and Decrees*. Studia Pohl, Series Major, 1. Rome: Biblical Institute.

Pritchard, J.B., ed.
1969 *Ancient Near Eastern Texts Relating to the Old Testament*. 3rd Edition with Supplement. Princeton, NJ: Princeton University Press.

Rad, G. von
1963 *Das fünfte Buch Mose: Deuteronomium*. ATD, 8. Göttingen: Vandenhoeck & Ruprecht.

Reiner, E.
1969 Translation of The Vassal Treaties of Esarhaddon: In *ANET*: 534-41.

Renan, E.
1891 *Histoire du peuple d'Israël*. III. Paris: Calmann–Lévy.

Richter, W.
1964 *Die Bearbeitungen des 'Retterbuches' in der deuteronomischen Epoche*. BBB, 21. Bonn: Hanstein.

Rofé, A.
1982 *Introduction to Deuteronomy: Further Chapters*. (Hebrew). Jerusalem: Akademon.
1987 The Arrangement of the Laws in Deuteronomy. In *Studies on the Bible. M.D. Cassuto Centennial Volume* (Hebrew), 217-35. Jerusalem: Magnes.

Rose, M.
1975 *Der Ausschliesslichkeitsanspruch Jahwes. Deuteronomische Schultheologie und die Volksfrömmigkeit in der späten Königszeit*. BWANT, 6.6. Stuttgart: Kohlhammer.

Sala-Molins, L.
1973 *Le manuel des inquisiteurs*. Le Savoir historique, 8. Paris: Mouton.

Schorr, M.
1909 Einige hebräisch-babylonische Redensarten. *MGWJ* 53: 428-42.

Seitz, G.
1971 *Redaktionsgeschichtliche Studien zum Deuteronomium*. BWANT, 93. Stuttgart: Kohlhammer.

Seux, M.-J.

1976 *Hymnes et prières aux dieux de Babylonie et d'Assyrie.* Littératures Anciennes du Proche-Orient, 8. Paris: Cerf.

Smend, R.

1971 Das Gesetz und die Völker, Ein Beitrag zur deuteronomistischen Redaktionsgeschichte. In *Probleme biblischer Theologie, G. von Rad zum 70. Geburtstag*, 494-509. Ed. H.W. Wolff. Munich: Kaiser.

Streck, M.

1916 *Assurbanipal und die letzten assyrischen Könige bis zum Untergang Nineveh's.* 3 vols. Vorderasiatische Bibliothek, 7. Leipzig: Hinrichs.

Tov, E.

1985 The Literary History of the Book of Jeremiah in the Light of Its Textual History. In *Empirical Models for Biblical Criticism*, 211-37. Ed. J. H. Tigay. Philadelphia: University of Pennsylvania Press.

Weidner, E.F.

1932–33 Der Staatsvertrag Aššurniraris VI. von Assyrien mit Mati'ilu von Bît-Agusi. *Archiv für Orientforschung* 8: 17-34.

Weinfeld, M.

1972 *Deuteronomy and the Deuteronomic School.* Oxford: Clarendon Press.

1976 The Loyalty Oath in the Ancient Near East. *UF* 8: 379-414.

1982 Instructions for Temple Visitors in the Bible and in Ancient Egypt. In *Egyptological Studies*, 224-50. Ed. S. Israelit-Groll. Scripta Hierosolymitana, 28. Jerusalem: Magnes.

Wevers, J.W.

1978 *Text History of Deuteronomy.* Abhandlungen der Akademie der Wissenschaften in Göttingen, Mitteilungen des Septuaginta-Unternehmens (MSU), 13. Göttingen: Vandenhoeck & Ruprecht.

Whitelam, K.W.

1979 *The Just King.* JSOTSup, 12. Sheffield: JSOT Press.

Wiseman, D.J.

1958 The Vassal Treaties of Esarhaddon. *Iraq* 20: 1-99; pls. 1-53.

Yadin, Y.

1977 *The Temple Scroll* (Hebrew Edition). 3 vols. Jerusalem: The Israel Exploration Society, The Archaeological Institute of the Hebrew University, The Shrine of the Book.

INDEXES

INDEX OF REFERENCES

HEBREW SCRIPTURES

OTHER JEWISH REFERENCES

CLASSICAL AUTHORS

INDEX OF AUTHORS

JOURNAL FOR THE STUDY OF THE OLD TESTAMENT

Supplement Series

53 THE MAKING OF THE PENTATEUCH:
A METHODOLOGICAL STUDY
R.N. Whybray
54 FROM REPENTANCE TO REDEMPTION:
JEREMIAH'S THOUGHT IN TRANSITION
J. Unterman
55 THE ORIGIN TRADITION OF ANCIENT ISRAEL:
THE LITERARY FORMATION OF GENESIS AND EXODUS 1–23
T.L. Thompson
56 THE PURIFICATION OFFERING IN THE PRIESTLY LITERATURE:
ITS MEANING AND FUNCTION
N. Kiuchi
57 MOSES: HEROIC MAN, MAN OF GOD
G.W. Coats
58 THE LISTENING HEART: ESSAYS IN WISDOM AND THE PSALMS
IN HONOR OF ROLAND E. MURPHY, O. CARM.
Edited by K.G. Hoglund
59 CREATIVE BIBLICAL EXEGESIS:
CHRISTIAN AND JEWISH HERMENEUTICS THROUGH THE CENTURIES
B. Uffenheimer & H.G. Reventlow
60 HER PRICE IS BEYOND RUBIES:
THE JEWISH WOMAN IN GRAECO-ROMAN PALESTINE
L.J. Archer
61 FROM CHAOS TO RESTORATION:
AN INTEGRATIVE READING OF ISAIAH 24–27
D.G. Johnson
62 THE OLD TESTAMENT AND FOLKLORE STUDY
P.G. Kirkpatrick
63 SHILOH: A BIBLICAL CITY IN TRADITION AND HISTORY
D.G. Schley
64 TO SEE AND NOT PERCEIVE:
ISAIAH 6.9-10 IN EARLY JEWISH AND CHRISTIAN INTERPRETATION
C.A. Evans
65 THERE IS HOPE FOR A TREE:
THE TREE AS METAPHOR IN ISAIAH
K. Nielsen
66 SECRETS OF THE TIMES:
MYTH AND HISTORY IN BIBLICAL CHRONOLOGY
J. Hughes

67 ASCRIBE TO THE LORD:
BIBLICAL AND OTHER ESSAYS IN MEMORY OF PETER C. CRAIGIE
Edited by L. Eslinger & G. Taylor
68 THE TRIUMPH OF IRONY IN THE BOOK OF JUDGES
L.R. Klein
69 ZEPHANIAH, A PROPHETIC DRAMA
P.R. HOUSE
70 NARRATIVE ART IN THE BIBLE
S. Bar-Efrat
71 QOHELET AND HIS CONTRADICTIONS
M.V. Fox
73 DAVID'S SOCIAL DRAMA:
A HOLOGRAM OF THE EARLY IRON AGE
J.W. Flanagan
74 THE STRUCTURAL ANALYSIS OF BIBLICAL AND CANAANITE POETRY
Edited by W. van der Meer & J.C. de Moor
75 DAVID IN LOVE AND WAR:
THE PURSUIT OF POWER IN 2 SAMUEL 10–12
R.C. Bailey
76 GOD IS KING:
UNDERSTANDING AN ISRAELITE METAPHOR
M. Brettler
77 EDOM AND THE EDOMITES
J.R. Bartlett
78 SWALLOWING THE SCROLL:
TEXTUALITY AND THE DYNAMICS OF DISCOURSE IN EZEKIEL'S PROPHECY
E.F. Davies
79 GIBEAH: THE SEARCH FOR A BIBLICAL CITY
P.M. Arnold
80 THE NATHAN NARRATIVES
G.H. Jones
81 ANTI-COVENANT:
COUNTER-READING WOMEN'S LIVES IN THE HEBREW BIBLE
Edited by M. Bal
82 RHETORIC AND BIBLICAL INTERPRETATION
D. Patrick & A. Scult
83 THE EARTH AND THE WATERS IN GENESIS 1 AND 2
D.T. Tsumura
84 INTO THE HANDS OF THE LIVING GOD
L. Eslinger
85 FROM CARMEL TO HOREB: ELIJAH IN CRISIS
A.J. Hauser & R. Gregory
86 THE SYNTAX OF THE VERB IN CLASSICAL HEBREW PROSE

A. Niccacci

87 THE BIBLE IN THREE DIMENSIONS
Edited by D.J.A. Clines, S.E. Fowl & S.E. Porter

88 THE PERSUASIVE APPEAL OF THE CHRONICLER: A RHETORICAL ANALYSIS
R.K. Duke

89 THE PROBLEM OF THE PROCESS OF TRANSMISSION IN THE PENTATEUCH
R. Rendtorff

90 BIBLICAL HEBREW IN TRANSITION: THE LANGUAGE OF THE BOOK OF EZEKIEL
M.F. Rooker

91 THE IDEOLOGY OF RITUAL: SPACE, TIME, AND STATUS IN THE PRIESTLY THEOLOGY
F.H. Gorman

92 ON HUMOUR AND THE COMIC IN THE HEBREW BIBLE
Edited by Y.T. Radday & A. Brenner

93 JOSHUA 24 AS POETIC NARRATIVE
W.T. Koopmans

94 WHAT DOES EVE DO TO HELP? AND OTHER READERLY QUESTIONS TO THE OLD TESTAMENT
D.J.A. Clines

95 GOD SAVES: LESSONS FROM THE ELISHA STORIES
R.D. Moore

96 ANNOUNCEMENTS OF PLOT IN GENESIS
L.A. Turner

97 THE UNITY OF THE TWELVE
P.R. House

98 ANCIENT CONQUEST ACCOUNTS: A STUDY IN ANCIENT NEAR EASTERN AND BIBLICAL HISTORY WRITING
K. Lawson Younger, Jr

99 WEALTH AND POVERTY IN THE BOOK OF PROVERBS
R.N. Whybray

100 A TRIBUTE TO GEZA VERMES. ESSAYS ON JEWISH AND CHRISTIAN LITERATURE AND HISTORY
Edited by P.R. Davies & R.T. White

101 THE CHRONICLER IN HIS AGE
P.R. Ackroyd

102 THE PRAYERS OF DAVID (PSALMS 51–72)
M.D. Goulder

103 THE SOCIOLOGY OF POTTERY IN ANCIENT PALESTINE: THE CERAMIC INDUSTRY AND THE DIFFUSION OF CERAMIC STYLE IN THE BRONZE AND IRON AGES
Bryant G. Wood

104 PSALM-STRUCTURES:

122 IMAGES OF EMPIRE
Edited by Loveday Alexander

123 THE FABRIC OF HISTORY:
TEXT, ARTIFACT AND ISRAEL'S PAST
Edited by Diana Vikander Edelman

124 LAW AND IDEOLOGY IN MONARCHIC ISRAEL
Edited by Baruch Halpern and Deborah W. Hobson